Natural Resources, Conflict, and Sustainable Development

Routledge African Studies

1 **Facts, Fiction, and African Creative Imaginations**
Edited by Toyin Falola and Fallou Ngom

2 **The Darfur Conflict**
Geography or Institutions?
Osman Suliman

3 **Music, Performance and African Identities**
Edited by Toyin Falola and Tyler Fleming

4 **Environment and Economics in Nigeria**
Edited by Toyin Falola and Adam Paddock

5 **Close to the Sources**
Essays on Contemporary African Culture, Politics and Academy
Abebe Zegeye and Maurice Vambe

6 **Landscape and Environment in Colonial and Postcolonial Africa**
Edited by Toyin Falola and Emily Brownell

7 **Development, Modernism and Modernity in Africa**
Edited by Augustine Agwuele

8 **Natural Resources, Conflict, and Sustainable Development**
Lessons from the Niger Delta
Edited by Okechukwu Ukaga, Ukoha O. Ukiwo and Ibaba Samuel Ibaba

Natural Resources, Conflict, and Sustainable Development

Lessons from the Niger Delta

Edited by Okechukwu Ukaga, Ukoha O. Ukiwo and Ibaba Samuel Ibaba

Routledge
Taylor & Francis Group
NEW YORK LONDON

First published 2012
by Routledge
711 Third Avenue, New York, NY 10017

Simultaneously published in the UK
by Routledge
2 Park Square, Milton Park, Abingdon, Oxfordshire OX14 4RN

First issued in paperback 2014

Routledge is an imprint of the Taylor and Francis Group, an informa company

Library of Congress Cataloging-in-Publication Data

Natural resources, conflict, and sustainable development : lessons from the Niger Delta / edited by Okechukwu Ukaga, Ukoha O. Ukiwo, and Ibaba Samuel Ibaba.
p. cm. — (Routledge African studies ; 8)
Includes bibliographical references and index.
1. Natural resources—Nigeria—Niger River Delta—Management.
2. Sustainable development—Nigeria—Niger River Delta. I. Ukaga, Okechukwu, 1961– II. Ukiwo, Ukoha. III. Ibaba, Ibaba S. (Ibaba Samuel)
HC1055.Z7N636 2012
338.9669'4—dc23
2011045015

ISBN13: 978-0-415-80691-6 (hbk)
ISBN13: 978-0-415-75450-7 (pbk)

Typeset in Sabon by IBT Global.

Dedicated to the long-suffering people of the Niger Delta.

Contents

Figures

Tables

Foreword

Much has been written about the resource curse and the costs of resource dependency. *Natural Resources, Conflict, and Sustainable Development* explores the case of Nigeria and the Niger Delta oil-producing region—both typically seen as exemplary cases of failed oil development—in new and compelling ways, and provides a provocative and complex analysis of the complex historical and political forces that have shaped the descent into an oil insurgency. This book contains some of the leading Nigerian commentators and analysts on the Niger Delta crisis and offers a magnificent *tour d'horizon* of the relations between natural resources, violence, and human development. An important and pathbreaking book.

Michael Watts
Class of '63 Professor
University of California
Berkeley

Acknowledgments

First, we want to acknowledge Diane Seefeldt's role in helping review and format the entire manuscript and thank her for her contributions. We also want to thank the Department of Political Science, Niger Delta University, Nigeria, and the Centre for Applied Environmental Research, Department of Geosciences, University of Missouri Kansas City, United States, for organizing the March 2010 international conference on Niger Delta titled "Natural Resource, Security, and Development in the Niger Delta," at Yenagoa, Bayelsa State, Nigeria. The core chapters in this volume were selected from the over fifty papers presented at that conference. Finally, we want to thank our respective families for their wonderful support.

1 Introduction

Natural Resource, Conflict, and Sustainable Development in the Niger Delta

Ibaba Samuel Ibaba, Okechukwu Ukaga, and Ukoha O. Ukiwo

Sustainable development of the Niger Delta Region of Nigeria is vital not only to the stability and prosperity of Nigeria, but also to global energy security. However, the Niger Delta has in the past two decades experienced protracted violent conflicts. At the roots of these violent conflicts are the genuine quest of the people for sustainable development that is based on social justice, equity, fairness, and environmental protection. Although richly endowed, the region is hopelessly poor. This paradox of poverty in the midst of plenty has been attributed to a myriad of fractors ranging from Nigeria's centralized federalism, to ethno-regional domination, corruption, poor governance, and oil-related environmental degradation.

Natural resources can (and often do) play cataclysmic roles in the development of countries. In Nigeria, the discovery of oil in commercial quantity in 1958 marked a turning point in the nation's economy. The country moved away from agriculture, which hitherto provided the revenue base, and to dependency mainly on oil for revenue and foreign exchange (Usman 2008). Notably, oil and gas contribute 40 percent of the Gross Domestic Product (GDP), 90 percent of total earnings, and 87 percent of gross national income (Akinola 2010). The country earned \$500 billion from oil between 1960 and 2006 (Nafziger 2008). Other estimates indicate that the country also generates \$4 billion annually from the export of natural gas (Obi 2009). Since 2000, with the increase from three percent to 13 percent of the share of oil revenue that goes to the relevant state, the Niger Delta region has witnessed huge revenue inflows. In 2008, for instance, six Niger states (Akwa-Ibom, Bayelsa, Cross River, Delta, Edo, and Rivers States) received the sum of \$7.1 billion out of \$16.5 billion allocated to the thirty-six states of the federation[1]). Despite these huge revenues generated by oil and gas, for the entire country in general and state governments in the region, the Niger Delta, which hosts the oil and gas industry, remains one of the least developed parts in the country (Obi 2010).

The concern for the poor state of development in the region dates back to the colonial period when Niger Deltans, along with other ethnic minorities in the country, expressed fear of domination and development neglect. The colonial government responded by setting up the Willinks Commission in 1957 to determine the veracity of these fears and to proffer solutions. Although the commission acknowledged the validity of the concerns, it failed to agree that state creation, a major demand of the people, was the solution. Instead, it recommended the declaration of the region as an area for special development attention, and recommended the establishment of a special agency to facilitate its development. The commission recognized democratic governance as the only guarantee of the rights of minorities, and predicated its recommendations on the practice of democratic governance in postcolonial Nigeria (Willinks Commission Report 1958).

In 1966, late Major Isaac Adaka Boro, an Ijaw, led the Niger Delta Volunteer Service (NDVS) to declare a Niger Delta Republic. While the goal of becoming a separate country was not achieved, this effort once again highlighted the regions concerns. Development neglect, despite the region's vast resource potentials, was cited as the justification for the rebellion (Tebekaemi 1982). Later in the early 1970s, oil-producing communities (OPCs) in the region began agitations against the transnational oil companies (TOCs) engaged in oil production in the Niger Delta. The Nigerian oil industry is dominated by TOCs. The most notable is the Shell Petroleum Development Company (SPDC), which operates a joint venture with the state-owned Nigerian National Petroleum Corporation (NNPC), and produces about half of the country's oil. The dominance of TOCs in the Nigerian oil industry, and the fact that Nigerian oil is a significant source of oil for the United States and other countries in Europe and Africa, explains the globalization of the Niger Delta question and the complex dynamics associated with it.

The concerns that resulted in agitations by OPCs pertained mainly to the payment of inadequate compensation for properties destroyed by oil production activities, the destruction of livelihoods without the provision of viable alternatives, and the environmental destruction caused by oil spills and gas flare. The OPCs demanded the payment of adequate compensation for their destroyed properties, basic social amenities such as water and health facilities, environmental protection, employment opportunities, and the award of contracts to indigenes (Okoko 1998). The TOCs responded with community-development support by providing boreholes to supply potable water, school buildings, health centers/cottage hospitals, scholarships, among other things. But the conflicts did not abate, as these provisions made very little impact on the quality of life. OPCs linked protests to the provision of such development support and thus continued to agitate for more, while the TOCs could not respond adequately to the demands for adequate compensation, citing state legislations that had fixed the compensation rates without negotiation or recourse to existing realities (Ibaba 2008). The engagement tactics of the OPCs, which included blockade of oil production facilities such as roads, rig sites, and flow stations, soon became a major concern to the TOCs who lost man hours and missed production targets. The TOCs thus called in security operatives to either quell community protests or protect their facilities.

The repressive tactics of the security operatives—who attacked, injured, and killed people and destroyed property—turned the hitherto peaceful protests violent. A classic example is the case of Umuechem community, where a peaceful protest against the SPDC was met with force by the anti-riot police who killed twenty persons and destroyed 495 houses with hand grenades. Significantly, the protesters' main complaint was the pollution of their river and source of water, destruction of farmlands, and disruption of normal economic activities by the SPDC oil production (Alapiki 2001). State repression set the stage for the emergence of pan-ethnic and civil society organizations that mobilized the people against the TOCs and the Nigerian government. Organizations such as the Movement for the Survival of the Ogoni People (MOSOP), Movement for the Survival of the Izon Ethnic Nationality in the Delta (MOSIEND), Ijaw National Congress (INC), among others, embarked on mobilization and peaceful protests, demanding development attention as well as an end to oil-induced environmental degradation. MOSOP, the forbearer of these organizations, proclaimed the Ogoni Bill of Rights, a charter of demands on the TOCs and the Nigerian government in 1990, and pursued it vigorously. But the Nigerian government responded with violence, which culminated in the hanging of MOSOP leader Ken Saro-Wiwa and eight of his compatriots following a widely condemned trial and conviction in 1995.

The repression of the Ogoni struggle and the militarization of the region set the stage for violent mobilization against the Nigerian State and the TOCs. Groups such as the Niger Delta People Volunteer Force (NDVF), Niger Delta Vigilante (NDV), and others began to engage security operatives in armed confrontation. The Ijaw Youths Council (IYC), the umbrella body of Ijaw youth, met in Kaima, Bayelsa State, in December 1998 and proclaimed the Kaima Declaration. Among others, the Kaima Declaration demanded the withdrawal of the Nigerian military from the Niger Delta, and the cessation of oil production activities by TOCs, whom they gave an ultimatum to leave the region. The resolution also claimed ownership of all lands and resources in Ijaw land, ceased to recognize all state legislations on the oil industry, and called for the convoking of a sovereign national conference to renegotiate the existence of the Nigerian State (Kaima Declaration 1998). The Kaima Declaration, which closely followed the resolutions of the First Urhobo Economic Summit held in November 1998, was copied by other ethnic groups, which proclaimed their own chatter of demands such as the Warri Accord (1999), the Aklaka Declaration (1999), and the Bill of Rights of the Oron People (1999). The common elements found in all of these demands are self-determination, resource ownership/control, and the convoking of a sovereign national conference.

However, it was youth from the Ijaw ethnic group that led the armed struggle that later turned into insurgency in 2005 (Watts 2007). Ijaw resistance in the Niger Delta is historic, and this latest phase can be located in that historic context. King William Koko of Nembe led a rebellion against the British from 1894 to 1895, over attempts by the latter, represented by the

Royal Niger Company, to preclude the Nembe from the palm oil trade that was very lucrative then (UNDP 2006). Ijaw youth were also inspired by Major Adaka Boro, who led the 1966 rebellion to declare the Niger Delta Republic. It is noteworthy that his hometown was chosen for the all Ijaw youth conference that resulted in the Kaima Declaration. The Ijaw role in the counterattacks on security operatives resulted in reprisal attacks on Ijaw communities by Nigerian security forces. Examples include Odi in 1999, Okerenkoko in 2006, Gbaramatu in 2009, and Ayakoromo in 2010. These attacks also led to the proliferation of militia groups, which later formed the Movement for the Emancipation of the Niger Delta (MEND), which coordinated activities of the militia movement and engaged the military directly in armed combats.

MEND's engagement tactics were mainly attacks on oil infrastructure and kidnapping (hostage taking) of TOCs' foreign workers. Between 2006 and 2008, it carried out 66 attacks, leading to 317 deaths, 30 injured persons, and 113 victims of kidnapping (NDTCR 2008: 116–119). These attacks disrupted oil production and reduced oil production and exports (Obi 2010; Joab-Peterside 2010), forcing the Nigerian government to proclaim amnesty for militia combatants. The Amnesty Program offered forgiveness to combatants in return for the renunciation of militancy, arms surrender, reintegration, and provision of alternative source of livelihood (Adeyemi-Suenu and Inokoba 2010). The program ended violence as envisaged by the Nigerian government; attacks on oil infrastructure and oil workers are almost non-existent, and oil production has risen to 2.3 million barrels per day (Joab-Peterside 2010). However, there is the possibility of violence recurring if the Amnesty Program fails to address the fundamental issues that caused the violence.

NIGER DELTA: CHALLENGES TO SUSTAINABLE DEVELOPMENT

The Niger Delta is rich in numerous natural resources that endow it with great potentials for sustainable development. But this has been strained by factors that include governance deficits, resource-extraction-induced environmental degradation, and violence.

GOVERNANCE DEFICITS

The Niger Delta is a strange paradox. Despite its vast natural resources, including oil and gas, the region ranks low in several indicators of development. This strange paradox of poverty and suffering in a region endowed with so much wealth in form of natural resources illustrates both the symptom and effect of governance deficit. For example, Table 1.1 provides information on quality of life indicators and shows how huge oil and gas revenues have barely touched the lives of majority of the citizens.

Table 1.1 Quality of Life Indicators in the Niger Delta: 2006 Only

	Niger Delta	*Niger Delta Low*	*Niger Delta High*
Access to pipe borne water (%)	6.4	2.4 (Cross River State)	12.4 (Rivers State)
Access to electricity (%)	34.3	3.5 (Bayelsa State)	70.7 (Edo State)
Access to flush toilet (%)	8.1	1.0 (Akwa-Ibom State)	NA
Probability at birth of not surviving to age forty (%)	25.5	20 (Delta State)	30 (Bayelsa State)
Adult literacy rate	25.9	18 (Delta and Edo States)	31 (Bayelsa State)
Human development index (scale of 0–1)	0.564	0.499 (Bayelsa State)	0.591 (Rivers State)
Life expectancy index (scale of 0–1)	0.527	0.455 (Bayelsa State)	0.587 (Delta State)
Education index (scale of 0–1)	0.596	0.52 (Bayelsa State)	0.638 (Akwa-Ibom State)

Source: Adapted from Ibeanu (2008: 214).

Although current data on basic amenities is not readily available, the figures provided by the 2006 UNDP Niger Delta Human Development Report are instructive. The report shows, for instance, that one primary school served a population of 3,700 or an area of 14 square kilometers, while a secondary serviced a population of 14,679 or an area of 55 square kilometers. For primary health care, the facility population ratio was discovered to be one facility for every 9,805 people, and one secondary health facility for a population of 131,174. The same report indicated that the pipe-borne water provided an infinitesimal source of water, representing only 7.37 percent in Akwa-Ibom State, 7.49 percent in Bayelsa State, 2.43 percent in Cross River State, 2.89 percent in Delta State, 9.70 percent in Edo State, and 12.42 percent in Rivers State.

The dominant view blames governance deficits on the ethnicized character of politics in Nigeria, the abnormal federal system, and the politics of oil wealth distribution. The point is that politics in Nigeria is used to pursue individual and ethnic group interest, and thus, when a particular ethnic group is in power, it allocates state resources to benefit its people and denies other groups a fair share of such resources. In the case of the Niger Delta, the argument is that because it is inhabited by minority ethnic groups, the Nigerian State, which until 2010 was headed by persons from the majority Hausa-Fulani, Igbo, and Yoruba ethnic groups, neglected and deprived the area of development funds and attention, despite its huge contributions to the national treasury. The changes in the revenue allocation formula, which coincided with the emergence of oil as the mainstay of the national economy, is usually cited to vindicate this point. At independence in 1960 and until 1970, derivation[2] was a major component of revenue allocation in Nigeria. Within this period, which saw the country depend on agricultural products produced in the home lands of the majority groups, the share of derivation in revenue allocation was 50 percent. But beginning from 1970, when oil displaced agriculture as the basis of the national economy, derivation was reduced first to 45 percent, and later to as low as 1.5 percent in 1981 (Mbanefoh and Egwaikhide 1998; Jega 2007; Idemudia 2009). This is seen as a deliberate ploy to deny the region of development funds. The country's federal system, characterized by centralization of powers and resources, intersegmental imbalance, and the privatization/personalization of the Nigerian State, is blamed for creating the conditions that supports ethnicity-based political domination[3] (Naanen 1995; Okoko, Nna, and Ibaba 2006).

The second-most prominent explanation of the lack of development in the Niger Delta is the nonchalant attitude of TOCs toward corporate social responsibility, exacerbated by the state legislations on the oil industry that has alienated the people from the oil wealth and their environment. Oil industry laws such as the Petroleum Act of 1969, the Land Use act of 1978, and the Oil Pipelines Act of 1956 are highlighted as instruments of disempowerment that have created conditions for underdevelopment (Nna 2001; Idemudia 2010).

But Ikelegbe (2011) has noted correctly that these explanations locate the causal factors of the Niger Delta crisis in externalities by blaming the federal government and the TOCs, and neglects the governance deficits in the region that is part of the fundamentals that underlie its underdevelopment. This view links governance deficits to the political elite and ruling class at the communal, ethnic, state, and regional levels in the Niger Delta, characterized by selfishness, decadence, corruption, ineptitude, and arrogance, which has resulted in the lack of accountability, transparency, and openness in resource use and management. The high-profile corruption cases involving some past governors of the region, who were prosecuted by the Nigerian anti-graft agency, the Economic and Financial Crimes Commission (EFCC), vindicates this point. There are two classic examples. First was the arrest and conviction of Chief D. S. P. Alamieyeseigha, former governor of Bayelsa State, for corrupt practices involving the diversion of public funds to personal use. This was followed by the conviction of Mr. Lucky Igbinedion, former governor of Edo State, for similar reasons. Presently, the former governor of Delta State, Chief James Ibori, is also standing trial in London for allegedly stealing public funds. These three cases alone involve monies running into multi-millions of U.S. dollars. Such diversion of public resources to private accounts explains the poor service delivery and inadequate infrastructure development by governments in the region despite the huge oil revenue noted earlier.

RESOURCE EXTRACTION AND ENVIRONMENTAL/ SOCIOECONOMIC CHALLENGES IN THE NIGER DELTA

The recent United Nations Environment Program (UNEP) Report on the Ogoni environment has vindicated the Niger Delta regarding concerns about the impact of oil production on the Niger Delta environment. The report noted how the SPDC breached regulations and safety procedures, leading to the pollution of the environment, and creating public health and safety hazards (*Business Day* 2011; *Ebiri* 2011). Oil production in the Niger Delta is reported to have resulted in several oil spill incidents that have impacted negatively on the environment. But this has been associated with controversies in different dimensions. One of such is variations in oil spill incidents data, blamed on the lack of transparency and full disclosures by TOCs. For example, Okodudu (2008) reported that 4,000 oil spill incidents have been recorded since 1960, while Nwilo and Badejo, (2008) indicates that the country recorded a total of 9,107 oil spills between 1976 and 2005 alone. SPDC records also show that the company alone recorded 1,243 oil spills between 2003 and 2007 (SPDC 2008). Another area of disagreement is the cause of oil spills. Oil spills are caused by a combination of factors such as equipment failure, corrosion, sabotage, and human error. But OPCs and the TOCs have always differed on the causes of oils spill incidents. While the TOCs blame sabotage for many cases of oil spills, the communities disagree and accuse the TOCs of wrongly attributing cases of oil spill caused by their operational activities to sabotage in order to avoid the payment of compensation.[4]

However, it is unarguable that oil spills have devastated the affected environments in the region, due partly to the large volume of oil that is spilled and the insignificant quantity that is recovered. Okodudu (2008) has noted that about 2 million barrels of crude oil has been spilled into the Niger Delta environment since 1960. Another account indicates that a total of 3,121,909.80 barrels of oil was spilled into the environment between 1976 and 2005 (Nwilo and Badejo 2008). Table 1.2 provides data on oil spill incidents and the volume recovered to show the negligible quantity of spilled crude that is recovered. For instance, out of 3,121,909.80 barrels of crude oil that was spilled between 1976 and 2005, only 550,232.90 were recovered (Emuedo 2011), indicating that only 1.76 percent was recovered, leaving 98.24 percent to either seep into the soil or flow through the creeks, streams, rivers, and the mangrove swamps, impacting negatively on the environment. The UNEP report on oil and the Ogoni environment noted, for instance, that the depth of oil in some areas covered by the study was as deep as five meters (*Ebiri* 2011). This destroys soil nutrients and makes farmlands useless for agricultural activities, in addition to destroying, crops, and trees (Adeyemo 2002). Similarly, oil spills pollute water (rivers, creeks, and streams) and destroy marine life such as fish. As a result, farmers and fishermen are displaced from their activities for as long it takes for the polluted land or river/creek to be remedied and restored to its original state, which in most cases is forever. This is compounded by gas flares, which are a major part of oil production in the Niger Delta. The World Bank reported that as of 1991, Nigeria flared 76 percent of its gross production of gas (Singh, Moffat, & Linden 1995: 59). Despite the fact that this was reduced to 38.8 percent in 2005 (Adeyemo 2008), the country still flared about 17.2 billion cubic feet of gas in 2008 (Onyekonwu 2008; Uzoma 2008). In addition to representing enormous loss in potential revenue, gas flares destroy the vegetation, inhibit plant growth, and diminish crop yield (Emuedo 2011). Studies have shown that gas flares diminish crop yield by 100 percent for farmlands within 200 meters of flare area, 45 percent for crops planted within 600 meters distance, and 10 percent for crops located within 1 kilometer (Salau 1993: 19–22).

These effects directly touch on the local economies, largely based on fishing and farming, and the compensation rates for damages to properties are meager. The oil laws in Nigeria—the constitutional provisions (section 44(3) of the 1999 Constitution) the Petroleum Act (1969), the Land Use Act (1978), and the Oil Pipelines Act (1966)—deny the people ownership of land and natural resources, and more importantly, the right to negotiate the rates of compensation for their damaged properties. Thus, the government and the oil multinationals (TOCs) either ignore communal rights to resource or pay inadequate compensation for land take or damages to resources (Singh, Moffat, & Linden1995). Oil industry activities such as pollution and taking land for exploration and production have also reduced available land for cultivation, which has encouraged over-cropping and unsustainable exploitation of land resources. Worse, neither the TOCs nor the government at all levels (federal, state, or local[5]) have provided alternative means of livelihood. Consequently, people are displaced occupationally, resulting in the exacerbation of poverty, forced migration, and social disintegration. The negative impact of oil production on the environment, economy, and society of the Niger Delta has undermined the potentials for sustainable development and created conditions for violence. The highlight of oil-related resource extraction and its impact on the environment is not to suggest that non-oil-related resource exploitation has not contributed to the degradation of the environment. The point to note, however, is that non-oil-related environmental problems are not linked to the violence in the region.

OIL-RELATED CONFLICTS AND IMPLICATIONS FOR SUSTAINABLE DEVELOPMENT IN THE NIGER DELTA

Conflicts in the Niger Delta have taken dimensions that have impacted on the sustainable development of the region. The engagement tactics that result in violence have taken a toll on the natural and human environment, as well as on the production capabilities of the people. Table 1.2 illustrates this point.

Table 1.2 The Impact of Conflicts on the Environment

Type of Conflict	*Engagement Tactics*	*Outcome/Impact on the Environment*
Intra-community conflict	Violent attacks on opposing factions by armed youths	Destruction of properties (buildings and personal effects), deaths/ injuries, population displacement, and exacerbation of poverty
Inter-community conflicts	(a) Violent attacks on opposing communities by armed youths (b) Attacks on rivers, streams, and creeks with dangerous chemicals such as Gamalin 20 and dynamites	(a) Destruction of properties (buildings and personal effects), deaths/ injuries, population displacement, and exacerbation of poverty (b) Pollution of water and destruction of marine life
Community–oil company conflict	(a) Occupation of oil-production facilities such as flow stations, blockade of access roads to oil production sites, seizure of equipment such as boats and vehicles (b) Sabotage of oil infrastructure such as oil pipelines and well heads	(a) Oil companies invited the police and military to protect their equipment and facilities. These interventions led to violent clashes, causing deaths, injuries, destruction of homes and other properties (b) Results in oil spills that devastate the environment
Community–state conflict	(a) Militant strategy of forceful seizure of, and attacks on, oil production infrastructure, kidnapping /hostage taking of oil workers, attacks and counterattacks between militants and the military (b) Oil theft (oil bunkering) to raise funds for recruitment and mobilization of militants, and as economic enterprise	(a) Destruction of communities and properties, deaths and injuries, internal population displacement, exacerbation of poverty, and pressure on natural resources caused by life-coping measures of displaced persons (b) Results in oil spills that devastate the environment
Inter-ethnic	(a) Violent attacks on opposing ethnic groups by armed youths	Destruction of properties (buildings and personal effects), deaths/injuries, population displacement, and exacerbation of poverty

(continued)

Table 1.2 The Impact of Conflicts on the Environment

Type of Conflict	*Engagement Tactics*	*Outcome/Impact on the Environment*
Intra-militia/cult/ confraternity groups conflict	(a) Violent attacks on opposing groups	Deaths and injuries
Inter-militia/cult/ confraternity groups conflict	(a) Violent attacks on opposing groups	Deaths and injuries

Source: Owugah (1999), Ibaba and Ikelegbe (2009), Ibaba (2009).

Thus, conflicts undermine the central goals of sustainable development, which include environmental protection, sustainable exploitation of natural resources, enhancement of production capabilities, and creation of wealth and poverty reduction. Oil spills and attacks on creeks, rivers, and streams with dangerous chemicals and dynamites undermine environmental protection and sustainable use of resources. The constraints on sustainable exploitation of resources is further compounded by violence-induced population displacement, which puts pressure on natural resources on account of the life coping measures of displaced persons. Furthermore, population displacement, deaths, injuries, and destruction of settlements and homes inhibit production capabilities, wealth creation, and poverty reduction (Ibaba 2009).

THE FAILURE OF CONFLICT RESOLUTION: FROM COMMUNITY PROTESTS TO INSURGENCY

The Niger Delta conflict has passed through several transformations that have been characterized by failed attempts to resolve each phase of the conflict. The mapping of the conflict has varied from one author to another, but the criteria for mapping—changes in the character of conflict, the nature of demands made by the people, and engagement tactics of the people, the Nigerian government, and TOCs—have remained the same. For example, Owugah (1999) has divided the conflict into four phases: (1) the mid-1980s, which had legal action as the strategy of engagement, (2) early 1990s characterized by peaceful demonstrations that later turned violent, (3) mid-1990s noted for the emergence of militant strategy, and (4) from 1998, characterized by political demands such as resource control. Similarly, Ibaba and Ikelegbe (2009) have divided the conflict into six phases, beginning from 1950, while Idemudia (2009) has categorized it into three periods, also commencing from 1950. However, looking at the phases of the conflict from the perspective of the kinds of regime in power in Nigeria (i.e., civilian or military) and the pattern of responses or intervention can provide some insight into the transformation and phases of the conflict. Based on these criteria, the conflict is divided into six periods (phases) for discussion.

October 1960–July 1966

Agitations for development attention and political autonomy by chiefs and political leaders of the Niger Delta that began in the pre-independence era continued after independence. In response to the 1958 Willink Commission Report, which rejected the demand for state creation and recommended the designation of the area for special development intervention, the Nigerian government (under the Abubakar Tafawa Balewa regime) created the Niger Delta Development Board (NDDB) in 1961. However, the NDDB made insignificant impact on the region's development, a situation largely attributed to NDDB's lack of executive powers and poor funding. In 1976, the NDDB was renamed Niger Delta Basin Development Authority (NDBDA), and nine other River Basin Development Authorities were created across the country for a total of ten. Consequently, the NDDB lost its special status as a development intervention agency in the Niger Delta (Ibaba 2005). The nonresolution of the concerns of the people triggered the Adaka Boro–led rebellion, under the Niger Delta Volunteer Service (NDVS). The NDVS declared the Niger Delta Republic and took steps to achieve it, but was crushed by Nigerian military forces twelve days after the declaration. The "rebels" were jailed for treason and sentenced to death. While the revolt was short lived due partly to the lack of total support from the people (Tebekaemi 1982), it planted the seed of political consciousness that was later mobilized to achieve the latest insurgency.

July 1966–1970

The year 1966 marked the emergence of military rule in Nigeria, and this also defined the context of the Niger Delta situation. First, was the release of Adaka Boro and his men from jail. The second was the return of the country to unitary rule by the Aguiyi Ironsi regime—a situation that did not change with the Yakubu Gowon government, even though the decision of the previous government to make the country unitary was reversed. Because the military is a unitary command system, it brought this to bear on the country's federal system, leading to a federal system in form, but unitary in content. Political powers were concentrated in the federal government, and revenues, including tax revenue, were nationalized (Naanen 1995). This added to the intersegment imbalance created by the colonial government, setting the stage for the strengthening of ethnicity-based political domination and deprivation of minority ethnic groups, including those in the Niger Delta. This period did not witness any agitations from the Niger Delta, but saw the country at war. The thirty-month civil war triggered by the secessionist bid of Biafra raged on within this period. Incidentally, one major demand of the Niger Delta people, state creation, was granted by the federal government. Although it was seen as a war strategy to weaken Biafra, the creation of Rivers State in 1967 fulfilled the desire of political autonomy championed by leaders of the region. But the 1969 Petroleum Decree (now an Act of Parliament), enacted by the Yakubu Gowon regime, is crucial to the conflict in the region. This law precluded the people from the oil industry, including the right to grant access to their lands to TOCs, and to negotiate for their properties destroyed by oil production activities. TOCs were given the right to explore and produce oil wherever it is found, just as the law failed to make adequate provisions for the protection of the environment. Extant provisions are either vague, difficult to enforce, or weak. Penalties for violation are not stringent enough, and thus fail to deter the TOCs from abusing the environment and engaging in unsustainable exploitation of oil. As a result, their activities devastated the environment. This law has been linked to the impoverishment of the people, and its repeal is seen as a requirement for the resolution of the conflict. The Kaima Declaration (1998) made reference to this when it listed the Petroleum Act as one of the laws responsible for the deprivation of Ijaws and the degradation of the environment by the TOCs, and resolved to reject it. Thus, the gain that came with the creation of Rivers State was eroded by the promulgation of the Petroleum Act.

1970–October 1979

This period, which includes part of the Yakubu Gowon military regime and the emergence of the Murtala/Obasanjo military governments, is significant to the Niger Delta conflict for a number of reasons. First, oil took over from non-oil products as the main engine of the Nigerian economy. Available data show that in 1960, the percentage of oil in total exports was 2.7. This rose to 32.4 percent in 1968, and later dropped to 17.5 percent in 1968. But by 1970, it became 57.6 percent, and rose to 97.6 percent in 1997 (Usman 2008). The second point is that the reduction in the derivation component of revenue allocation began this period. It was reduced from 50 percent to 45 percent in 1970, and further reduced to 20 percent in 1975 (Egwaikhide and Mbanefoh 1998; Jega 2007). This era also marked the emergence of oil-related conflicts in the Niger Delta. OPCs took TOCs to court, largely over damages and compensatory payments. The rates for the payment of compensation were inadequate, as they did not reflect market realities—a situation attributed to the fact that the rates were fixed by the government and not reviewed regularly. Unfortunately, the oil laws do not allow claimants to negotiate the value of claims with the TOCs. However, the cost of litigation and the delays associated with the Nigerian legal system resulted in frustrations that later made protests a preferred option. The communities also demanded for development support and environmental protection. The TOCs responded with community-assistance projects, such as providing potable water, school buildings, and scholarships. They could not address the issues related to inadequate pricing of properties destroyed by oil-production activities, as the oil laws reserved that for the government. Issues related to the impact of oil production on the environment were overlooked. The protests/agitations in this period were peaceful. This period also marked the promulgation of the Land Use Decree of 1978, seen as one of the obnoxious oil laws that disempowered the Niger Delta people and created conditions for violence.

October 1979—December 1983

This period, the reign of the Shehu Shagari government, after the military returned power to civilians, was not different from the military era. The regime further reduced the derivation share of revenue from 20 percent to 2 percent, and set aside 1.5 percent for development intervention in the OPCs. A presidential committee was set up to manage the fund. Although data are not available on projects executed by the committee, projects inherited from it by the Oil Minerals Producing Areas Development Commission (OMPADEC), which succeeded it later, show that it embarked on the execution of quick impact projects, such as roads, school buildings, potable water schemes, health facilities, electricity, market stalls, landing jetties, and residential buildings for doctors and nurses. OMPADEC records indicate that a total of 1,207 uncompleted projects were inherited from the committee, and completed by the OMPADEC (1993). The projects made meager impact on the people, a situation attributed to factors such as disconnect with the needs of the people, poor execution, and lack of alignment of projects provided by the government and TOCs. Indeed, the TOCs continued with their community-assistance projects, which complimented faint efforts by the government at all levels. Significantly however, the presidential committee on the management of the 1.5 percent oil derivation fund overlooked the environmental damage caused by oil production. This meant that the destructions caused to the local economies by oil spills and gas flares were not mitigated, nor was the devastated environment remedied. Sustainable development was not part of the focus, and the outcome was the exacerbation of environmental degradation, poverty, and grievance.

December 1983–May 1999

This period was the era of the Buhari/Idiagbon, Ibrahim Babangida, and Sanni Abacha military governments. It was remarkable for a number of reasons. First, was the reduction of the derivation principle from 2 percent to 1.5 percent by the Buhari/Idiagbon regime, and later its increase to 3 percent by the Babangida government. The present 13 percent derivation also derive its root in this era, as it was recommended by the constitutional conference set up by the Abacha regime. The Babangida government, which increased the derivation principle to 3 percent, also set up the OMPADEC to intervene in the development of the region. But OMPADEC replicated all the wrong things that were done by the 1.5 percent presidential committee, and thus made very little impact. Unlike the presidential committee, it had a mandate to intervene in the devastated environment, but it abandoned it, leaving the people to live with the negative environmental consequences of oil production. The programs of OMPADEC barely touched the lives of the people and therefore could not steer them away from conflict. Community agitations continued, just as the TOCs also provided minimal development support. But the invitation of the police and the military by the TOCs, to protect their facilities and personnel from protesting communities marked a turning point in community protests. The hitherto peaceful protests turned violent as security forces employed repressive tactics. One of the most celebrated cases in this period is that of Umuechem in Rivers State, where police invasion led to the death of twenty persons. The Ogoni invasion and killing of MOSOP leader Ken Saro-Wiwa and eight others of his kinsmen, and the killing and maiming of Ijaw youth in Bayelsa on account of the Kaima Declaration, are some other graphic examples. The violent tactics of the Nigerian state encouraged the emergence and proliferation of pan-ethnic, and youth groups that mobilized the people against the state.

May 1999–2011

This period marked the rebirth of democratic governance in Nigeria and is also noted as the high point of the conflict. Incidentally, the country earned most of its oil revenue within this period (Nafziger 2008). This period, which also saw the creation of the Niger Delta Development Commission (NDDC) and the Ministry of Niger Delta Affairs for development intervention in the region, experienced the rebirth of insurgency. Armed confrontation between militia groups and the military resulted in loss of lives, property, and in some instances the total destruction of communities. The Odi community in Bayelsa State is a classic example. This period witnessed drastic cut in oil production, kidnappings and hostage taking of mainly oil company personnel, implementation of 13 percent oil derivation principle, the establishment of NDDC, and the federal government amnesty for militia combatants. Thus far, the Amnesty Program has focused on the individual needs of former militia combatants, neglecting the fundamental issues that threw up the violence.

It is clear here that whether military or civilian, the Nigerian government has intervened in the conflict in similar patterns that fail to address the fundamental issues that have created the conditions for violence. Thus, the unwillingness or inability to effectively address the fundamental issues important to the Niger Deltans set the stage for the transformation of the conflict from one phase to another. This seemingly intractable violence has attracted the concern of scholars who have gathered in several conferences and workshops to analyze and proffer solutions to the conflict. It was in this context that the Department of Political Science, Niger Delta University, Nigeria, in Collaboration with the Centre for Applied Environmental Research, Department of Geosciences, University of Missouri Kansas City, United States, organized its second international conference with the theme, "Natural Resource, Security, and Development in the Niger Delta," in March 2010, at Yenagoa, Bayelsa State, Nigeria. The chapters in this volume were selected from the over fifty papers presented at the conference.

SCOPE OF THE BOOK

This edited volume explores complex interactions among natural resources, conflict, and development in the Niger Delta. Beyond contributing specifically to the debate about the challenges to sustainable development in Niger Delta, the book offers some insights that are useful in understanding other resource-rich but poverty-stricken, conflict-prone regions of the world in general.

The interplay of natural resources, wealth, poverty, and conflicts is best understood within some historical context. In Chapter 2, Obi adopts a historical perspective in examining how the commodification of the oil resources (palm oil, crude oil) of the Niger Delta has over the centuries transformed it into an outpost of global commerce with far-reaching implications for the socioeconomic life in the Niger Delta. This includes a critical examination of the ramifications of the transition from the palm oil trade to the production and export of crude oil from the Niger Delta. Further, the chapter analyzes the ways in which this transition has led to the integration and transformation of the region into an outpost of global commerce, its conquest and integration into the British colony of Nigeria, and subsequently the definition of its place in postcolonial Nigeria. At the core of the chapter lies a critical analysis of the implications of the most recent phase of the globalization of the Niger Delta represented by oil and gas production by oil multinationals operating in partnership with the Nigerian state. It includes a discussion of the high stakes and intense local and global struggles over oil, resulting in violent conflict and the marginalization and impoverishment of the people of this highly strategic oil-rich region. It also shows that far from being a local region of Nigeria, events in the Niger Delta on account of its globally strategic place in global oil supplies has much wider international consequences. Suggestions are made for an alternative agenda for conflict resolution, peace, and development in the Niger Delta based on aligning oil production and the distribution of its benefits more with local demands, welfare, and priorities as a basis for more sustainable global production of oil from the region.

Working toward sustainable development requires appropriate development, engagement, and utilization of local human resources. In Chapter 3, Akinola traces the protracted governance crisis and elusive development in the Niger Delta to the centralized system of governance characterized by despotism, tyranny, and politics of exclusions that neglect the development of human resources. Using the Institutional Analysis and Development (IAD) framework, the chapter explores the missing links in the operations of developers and users of human resources. Further, the author makes the following observations. First, that most socioeconomic, technical, and political decisions in the region do not reflect the wishes and aspirations of the people. Second, that neglect of human resources is largely responsible for lack of sustainable development in the Niger delta. Third, a Eurocentric approach to human resources tend to exclude the informal sector where the majority of Deltans belong while "Africentric" perspective emphasizes the convergence of formal and informal activities at community level, thus enabling citizens to be trained and have their skills and entrepreneurial capability enhanced so that they can be productively engaged in socioeconomic and techno-political activities and then get out of poverty. Fourth, appropriate development and utilization of local human resources is imperative for peace, security, and sustainable development in the Niger Delta. Hence, the chapter suggests Africentric human resources development and utilization process to enable the Niger Delta citizens to effectively check and control their leaders as change agents.

Human resource development is usually not effective without an appropriately planned, adequately financed, culturally sensitive, and effectively implemented mechanism to achieve that goal. In Chapter 4, Dokpesi and Ibiezugbe discuss the efforts of the NDDC in addressing critical areas of human development needs in selected communities in Delta State. Data revealed that the NDDC has not made appreciable efforts in meeting the crucial needs of vulnerable groups. It therefore suggests that for any intervention instrument to make quick and decisive impacts in developing human capital in the Niger Delta, it must design three quick intervention programs that will operate simultaneously. First, a program that addresses the problems affecting traditional occupations by determining needs of vulnerable groups, and then providing funds to help them revitalize their failing occupations. Second, there is a critical need for a youth-empowerment program that begins with massive injection of funds for education and skill acquisition, but also provides access to capital and supports the establishment of non-oil industries. This is necessary because sustainable livelihood rests not only on knowledge and skills, but also on the opportunities created to earn a living. Third, infrastructure development program is imperative if the gains recorded in other areas must be meaningful. The chapter recommends an approach to development in which the "specific needs" of communities and groups are considered first before the "general needs," and the "oil-bearing communities" are considered first before the "non-oil-bearing communities."

Experience and theory both suggest how important entrepreneurial individuals, communities, and even governments can be for sustainable development. In Chapter 5, Bubou and Egai offer a strategic framework for the development of entrepreneurship as a means of poverty alleviation in the Niger Delta region. Noting the paradox of poverty in the mist of the surplus oil wealth that exists in the region, the authors suggest that the current situation of the people of the Niger Delta can somewhat be likened to that of the American Blacks during their struggle to free themselves from poverty after the abolishment of the slave trade. The theme of the struggle then centered on redistributing wealth, through affirmative action and other welfare programs. But these measures were at best palliative and therefore could not completely address the issues of poverty and unemployment among the population due partly to the lack of "entrepreneurship," an essential ingredient, necessary for their economic development. Similarly, findings suggest a near death of entrepreneurship in the Niger Delta. Against this backdrop, this chapter examines the position of Niger Delta entrepreneurs, the barriers they face, and the kind of support available.

Without peace, sustainable development is impossible. In Chapter 6, Etekpe discusses the Yakubu Gowon Centre's Peace Process in Ogoni. Crude oil was discovered in Bomu in Ogoni Kingdom in 1958. By 1995, when the Ogoni crisis reached its crescendo, the number of oil wells and flow stations had risen to forty-five, with a daily production of about 100,000 barrels. The Ogoni people complained that whereas that level of production provided Nigeria with total revenue of US$40 billion, they had received nothing in return. They also prepared the Ogoni Bill of Rights and formed MOSOP to pursue the realization of the tenets of OBR. In the process, there were ideological disagreements within MOSOP. This climaxed in the death of a total of thirteen prominent leaders and threw the Kingdom into "darkness" for three years. The Yakubu Gowon Centre, a nongovernmental organization, applied a multidimensional peace process between 1997 and 2002 to bring about peace in the kingdom. The author played a key role in the peace process, and shares in this chapter the strategies used, lessons learned and implications for the future.

A conducive legal environment is critical to sustainable development. In Chapter 7, Binuomoye, Ogbewo, Okoro, and Ukaga examine the design of Nigeria's Land Use Act, within the provision of the Human Rights Law with its implications on land transactional and development challenges. To understand the problem within the land law, the authors juxtapose these challenges with the country's constitutional provision and political setup. This allowed them to shed light on the weaknesses inherent in both the Land Use Act and the country's political institution. They further analyzed the effects of these weaknesses on the country's development, particularly within the Niger Delta. While recent arguments on the development of the Niger Delta have called for a high federal involvement (through massive project funding), this chapter proposes a thoughtful look at some of the salient issues raised in the buildup to the National Political Reform Conference (NPRC) in 2005 (and thereafter) wherein the question of identity was underlined as imperative for the continued existence of the entity called Nigeria. This chapter concludes that respecting the rights of both the individuals and groups in the Niger Delta region within constitutional provision, with emphasis on land rights, is critically important in addressing oil-related environmental and development challenges faced by the region.

Working toward sustainable development requires equal protection regardless of gender. In Chapter 8, Adaora Osondu discusses the security dimension of the Niger Delta crisis with particular attention to women's rights. The chapter notes many international instruments like 1979 Convention on the Elimination of All Forms Discriminations Against Women (CEDAW) are frequently violated in the region. Further, it argues that women and men have significantly different relationships with the environments, and on that basis examines environmental security in Niger Delta in the context of its challenges to fundamental rights of women.

Finally, the conclusion distills some lessons embodied in the various chapters, highlights practical strategies for meeting the challenges of sustainable development of resource-rich but poverty/conflict-prone regions of the world, and discusses global ramifications, implications and responsibilities.

NOTES

1. See www.fmf.gov.ng
2. As a criterion for revenue allocation, derivation retains a percentage of revenue generated from a particular region, and returns some to it.
3. The federal system in Nigeria subordinates the federating units (the states) to the central government by placing sixty-eight powers/functions in the exclusive list reserved for the federal government, and only thirty-three in the concurrent list, which is not only allows the federal government to share power with the states, but also gives the federal government overriding powers when conflict emerges. Further, the control of natural resources such as oil and gas and tax revenues are concentrated in the federal government. One consequence of this is the dependence of states on the federal government for revenues. Although the Federation Account, into which national revenues are paid, is owned by the federal government and the states, the federal government controls it by virtue of its enormous powers.
4. Nigerian oil laws stipulate that compensation should not be paid for properties destroyed by oil spills caused by sabotage.
5. Nigeria runs a three-tier system of government.

REFERENCES

Adeyemi-Suenu, W. and Inokoba, P. (2010). "Armed rebellion and the future of self-determination in the Niger Delta," Paper presented at the International Conference on Natural Resource, Security and Development in the Niger Delta, Organized by the Department of Political Science, Niger Delta University, in

Collaboration with the Centre for Applied Environmental Research, Department of Geosciences, University of Missouri Kansas City, U.S., March 8–11, 2010, Yenagoa, Bayelsa State, Nigeria.

Adeyemo, A. M. (2002). "The oil industry, extra-ministerial institutions and sustainable agricultural development: A case study of Okrika LGA in Rivers State," *Nigerian Journal of Oil and Politics*, Vol. 2, No. 1, pp. 60–78.

Adeyemo, A. M. (2008). "Environmental policy failure in Nigeria and the tragedy of underdevelopment of Niger Delta Region," Inaugural Lecture No. 63, University of Port Harcourt.

Akinola, S. R. (2010). "Restructuring the public sphere for social order in the Niger Delta through polycentric planning: What lessons for Arica," *Asian and African Studies*, No. 9, pp. 55–82.

Aklaka Declaration. (1999). Resolutions of the Egi Ethnic Nationality at the end of a conference on January 10, at Aklaka, Rivers State.

Alapiki, H. E (2001). "The environment and sustainable development: Global and national concerns," in H. E. Alapiki (ed.), *The Nigerian political process*, Port Harcourt, Nigeria: Emhai Printing and Publishing Company, pp.171–197

The Eagle. (2011). "Economic and Financial Crimes Commission (EFCC)," Channels Television, Nigeria, August 20.

Emuedo, C. G. O. (2011). "Oil and environmental despoliation: Implication for food and health security in the Niger Delta." paper presented at International Development Research Council (IDRC), Think Tank Initiative (TTI) & Center for Population and Environmental Development (CPED) Workshop on Confronting the Challenges of Development, Environmental Management and Peace Building in the Niger Delta: Beyond the Amnesty, July 28–29, Benin, Edo State, Nigeria.

Ebiri, K. (2011). "Justice comes for Ogoni, devastated by oil pollution," *The Guardian,* (Lagos, Nigeria) August, 12: pp. 21–23

Eze, I. (2011). "Ogoni May take 30 Years to Recover from Oil spill," *Business Day*, (Lagos, Nigeria) August, 9: p.40

The Kaima Declaration. (1998). Resolutions of the All Ijaw Youths Conference, held at Kaima, Bayelsa State, December.

Ibaba, S. I. (2005). *Understanding the Niger conflict*, Port Harcourt: Amethyst and Colleagues Publishers.

Ibaba, S. I. (2008). "Understanding oil company: Community conflicts in the Niger Delta (Nigeria)," *Peace and Conflict Studies*, Vol. 14, No. 1, pp. 1–18.

Ibaba, S. I. (2009). "Violent conflicts and sustainable development in Bayelsa State," *Review of African Political Economy*, Vol. 36, No. 122, pp. 555–573.

Ibaba, S. I. and Ikelebge, A. (2009). "Militias and pirates in the Niger Delta," Paper presented at Institute of Security Studies (ISS) South African, Workshop on Militia and Rebel Movements—Human Insecurity and State Crisis in Africa, April 20–21, Pretoria, South Africa.

Ibeanu, O. (2008). "Doves, hawks and vultures: Oil politics in the Niger Delta," in S. Oyovbaire (ed.), *Governance and politics in Nigeria: The IBB and OBJ years*, Ibadan, Nigeria: Spectrum Books Limited, pp.176–233.

Idemudia, U. (2009). "The changing phases of the Niger Delta conflict: Implications for conflict escalation and the return of peace," *Conflict, Security & Development*, Vol. 3, No. 9, pp. 307–331.

Idemudia, U. (2010). "Corporate social responsibility and the rentier state: Rethinking the role of government and the possibility of corporate social development in the Niger Delta," *Canadian Journal of Development Studies*, Vol. 30, Nos. 1–2, pp. 131–152.

Ikelegbe, A. (2011). "Governance deficits and subsisting underdevelopment: Rethinking the Niger problematic," Paper presented at International Development

Research Council (IDRC), Think Tank Initiative (TTI) & Center for Population and Environmental Development (CPED) Workshop on Confronting the Challenges of Development, Environmental Management and Peace Building in the Niger Delta: Beyond the Amnesty, July 28–29, Benin, Edo State, Nigeria.

Jega, A. M. (2007). *Democracy, good governance and development in Nigeria.* Ibadan: Spectrum Books Limited.

Joab-Peterside, S. (2010). "State and fallacy of rehabilitation of 'repentant militants' in the Nigeria's Niger Delta: Analysis of first phase of the federal government's Amnesty Program," *Pan-African Social Science Review*, No. 11, p. 94.

Mbanefoh, G. I. and Egwaikhide, F .O. (1998). "Revenue allocation in Nigeria: Derivation principle revisited," in A. Kunle, R. Suberu, A. Agbaje, and G. Herault (eds.), *Federalism and political restructuring in Nigeria*, Ibadan: Spectrum Books Limited, pp. 213–246.

Naanen, B. B. B. (1995). "Oil producing minorities and the restructuring of Nigerian federalism: The case of the Ogoni people," *Journal of Common Wealth and Comparative Politics*, Vol. 33, pp.46–78.

Nafziger, W. (2008). "Nigeria's economic development and Niger Delta grievances," in Conference Proceedings, International Conference on the Nigerian State, Oil Industry and the Niger Delta, Organized by the Department of Political Science, Niger Delta University, in Collaboration with the Centre for Applied Environmental Research, Department of Geosciences, University of Missouri Kansas City, U.S., March 11–13, Yenagoa, Bayelsa State, Nigeria, pp. 147–156.

National Population Commission (NPC) and ICF Macro. (2009). *Nigeria: Demographic and health survey 2008.* Abuja, Nigeria: Authors.

Niger Delta Technical Committee Report (NDTCR). (2008). Report of the Niger technical committee established by the Nigerian government to review the recommendations of the reports of previous commissions and committees and determine appropriate policy options for the resolution of the Niger Delta Crisis, November.

Nna, N. J. (2001). *The Niger Delta: State legislation and disempowerment*, Owerri: Springfield Publishers.

Nwilo, P. C and Badejo, O. T. (2008). "Impacts and management of oil spill in Nigerian coastal environment," in Conference Proceedings, International Conference on the Nigerian State, Oil Industry and the Niger Delta, Organized by the Department of Political Science, Niger Delta University, in Collaboration with the Centre for Applied Environmental Research, Department of Geosciences, University of Missouri Kansas City, U.S., March 11–13, Yenagoa, Bayelsa State, Nigeria, pp. 1217–1232.

Obi, C. (2009). "Nigeria's Niger Delta: Understanding the complex drivers of violent oil-related conflict," *Africa Development*, Vol. 34, No. 2, pp. 103–128.

Obi, C. (2010). "Oil extraction, dispossession, resistance, and conflict in Nigeria's oil-rich Niger Delta," *Canadian Journal of Development Studies*, Vol. 30, Nos. 1–2, pp. 219–236.

Ogoni Bill of Rights. (1990). Adopted by general acclamation of the Ogoni People on August 26, 1990, at Bori, Rivers State.

Okoko, K. A. B. (1998). *Shell Petroleum Development Company (SPDC): Host community relations survey*, Report Submitted to the SPDC (Unpublished).

Okoko, K. A. B, Nna, N. J, and Ibaba, S. I. (2006). *The politics of oil and the underdevelopment of underdevelopment in the Niger Delta*, Port Harcourt: University of Port Harcourt Press.

OMPADEC (1993) OMPADEC Activities in Statistics: Statistics of Projects inherited from Presidential Task Force, Oil Minerals Producing Areas Development Commission (OMPADEC) Quarterly Report, Vol. 1, No. 1, October: pp. 15–44.

Onyekonwu, M. (2008). "Best practices and policies, the Nigerian oil and gas industry: Policy problems," *Port Harcourt Petroleum Review*, Vol. 1, No. 1, pp. 14–22.

Owugah, L. (1999). "Local resistance and the state," Paper presented at Oil Watch African General Assembly, Port Harcourt, Nigeria, February 9–14.

Resolutions of the First Urhobo Economic Summit Organized by the Urhobo Foundation. (1998). November 27–28, at Effurun, Warri, Delta State.

Salau, A. T (1993). "Environmental crisis and development in Nigeria," Inaugural Lecture, University of Port Harcourt, Nigeria.

Singh, J, Moffat, D. & Linden, O. (1995). Defining an environmental development strategy for the Niger, Delta: World Bank Report, Vol. 1.

State Government Report. (2008). *Bayelsa State statistical year book*, Yenagoa, Bayelsa State: Ministry of Finance and Budget & State Statistical Agency.

Tebekaemi, T. (1982). *The twelve-day revolution by Major Isaac Jasper Adaka Boro*, Benin City, Nigeria: Idodo Umeh Publishers.

United Nations Development Program (UNDP). (2006). *Niger Delta human development report*, Abuja, Nigeria.

Usman, S. (2008). Why Nigeria remains poor despite being rich," *Tell Magazine*, February 18, pp. 32–35.

Uzoma, M. R. (2008). "Gas flaring in the Nigerian petroleum industry," *Port Harcourt Petroleum Review*, Vol. 1, No. 1, pp. 29–31.

The Warri Accord. (1999). The Warri Declaration adopted after deliberations between Warri families at the Warri National Conference held on June 25–27, at Benin City, Edo State.

Watts, M. J. (2007). "Petro-insurgency or criminal violence? Conflict and violence in the Niger Delta," *Review of African Political Economy*, No. 114, pp. 637–660.

The Willinks Commission Report. (1958). *Report of the commission appointed to enquire into the fears of minorities and the means of allaying them*, London: Her Majesty's Stationery Office.

2 Because of Oil?

Understanding the Globalization of the Niger Delta and Its Consequences

Cyril Obi

INTRODUCTION: A TALE OF TWO "OILS"

Although the Niger Delta is a relatively small area of about 75,000 square kilometers in southern Nigeria, its significance transcends the country's borders, and the news and impact of violent events in this oil-rich region is felt across an oil-dependent world. The history and destiny of the Niger Delta and its relationship with the world appears to be intertwined with two types of oil: palm oil and crude oil. These two commodities among others have played a defining role in the trade, politics and society in the Niger Delta in the nineteenth, twentieth, and twenty-first centuries. Given the strategic geographical location of the region in the Gulf of Guinea as a natural entrepôt of the transatlantic trade for over 500 years, it is logical that the Niger Delta through contact, commerce, and international relations had been one of the earliest parts of Nigeria to be integrated into the global economic system.

This early integration of the Niger Delta into the global market was in part due to the fact that the region produced commodities that were in great demand in other parts of the world. Trans Atlantic mercantilism with its roots in the fifteenth century became the route for the early globalization of the Niger Delta, which also witnessed the rise of a local mercantilist class as the coastal region was socially reorganized in local response to the demands, pressures, and profits from the transatlantic trade. From the late fifteenth century to the early nineteenth century, when the trade in salt, textiles, spices, and slaves was largely replaced by the trade in palm oil or what was referred to as the "legitimate trade," the relationship between the Niger Delta and Europe was based on mutual respect for each other (Alagoa 1999). More so, the Europeans largely respected the sovereignty of the city-states and kingdoms of the region, and relied on their local partners for their personal safety and that of their goods.

Within the Delta, qualities such as business acumen and management, access to capital, shrewdness, bravery, and the ability to build "war canoes to convoy trade canoes" (Ikime 1977: 15) became salient factors in successful trade, local politics, and the formation, rise, and fall of coastal city-states and kingdoms. These qualities were also relevant in facilitating social mobility as well as political leadership. Indeed, in some communities, gifted individuals by virtue of their trading acumen and accumulation of wealth could overcome initially humble class origins.[1] The oil trade, partly based on a system of "trust," was both lucrative and conflictive as rival Niger Delta traders, and coastal Niger Delta and European traders, often disagreed over prices, goods, markets, and profit margins in what was also a violence-laden form of commerce (Ikime 1977, 1999; Alagoa 2004: 79).

Apart from its unique geographical location that made it a "natural" node of global trade, the region had rich natural endowments/resources that could be transformed by its enterprising people into commodities bound for the global market. Since this chapter is based on the two most critical commodities that defined the globalization of the Niger Delta through trade in the nineteenth, twentieth and twenty-first centuries, the analysis shall be limited to palm oil and crude oil or petroleum. Both commodities have been critical to the expansion and reproduction of global capitalism since the days of the Industrial Revolution. Palm oil was a strategic commodity in the emerging global market as an ingredient in the manufacture of lubricants for industrial machines, as well as a raw material for a range of household soaps and confectionaries.

The palm oil trade marked a new phase in the integration of the Niger Delta into the global economic system. While oil commerce was closely linked to Niger Delta politics, it also contributed to the quest of global actors (European traders and companies, adventurists, and colonial officials) to control the trade and maximize the profits for themselves. This was naturally resisted by the Niger Delta "merchant princes" and kings, who derived benefits from the trade and were determined to defend both their sovereignty and freedom, of which the control of the oil trade and their land were key components.

It was the bid of the European merchants backed by Imperial Britain to bypass the coastal traders and get to the source of the oil in the hinterland and control the trade in this precious commodity that resulted in conflicts, which culminated in the direct military intervention by the Royal Niger Company (RNC) and the colonial conquest of the Niger Delta and Nigeria. This guaranteed the RNC and British and European merchants direct access to the palm oil and natural riches of the region and its hinterland, after they put down the stiff resistance put up by the Niger Delta people. Thus, the global quest for the control of the trade in oil in the context of the scramble for Africa and the Berlin congress of 1884–1885 contributed to the "fall" of the Niger Delta in the late nineteenth century (Ikime 1977).

Throughout the colonial era, British and international traders and companies had access to, and profited from, the palm oil produced in the region. It was not until crude oil was discovered in Oloibiri in 1956 in present-day Bayelsa State, followed by the slump in the global market for agricultural produce in the mid-1960s, that the palm oil trade was gradually but steadily eclipsed by crude oil production and exports. After the Oloibiri discovery, more crude oil and gas was found in the Niger Delta, attracting the worlds most sophisticated and wealthy oil multinationals to the Niger Delta in another wave of globalization—more intense, ruthless, and extractive, integrating the region further into the global capitalist system as a source of highly valued, but cheap, oil. The processes of globalization also succeeded in separating the region as a site of production and pollution, from highly industrialized parts of the world that got most of the super-profits and consumed most of the oil produced from the Niger Delta (Obi 2009b).

Today, because of oil, the Niger Delta plays host to the world's most powerful oil multinationals as well as national and local actors. Petroleum is defined as a strategic source of one of the most highly priced (commoditized) forms of energy in human history. Because of its low-sulfur content, or "sweet oil," the Niger Delta is defined not just as a local space, but also as a globalized space of oil production and power, leading to new forms of alliances and relations between the local and the global actors (Obi 2001, 2007, 2009b). Like the old days of the palm oil trade, the petroleum commerce is laced with violence or what Watts refers to as the "worst forms of frontier capitalism" (Watts 1999: 1). In the last four decades of the twentieth century, and into the second decade of the twenty-first century, crude oil remains central not just to the survival of the Niger Delta and its peoples, but also as the lifeblood of the Nigerian state. Although an object of, and fuel for volatile politics and conflict, oil remains the glue holding Nigeria—a multi-ethnic social formation and Africa's putative hegemonic power together in a complex but rather fractious unity.

Oil makes the Niger Delta a site of oil extraction, production, and super-profits for a host of transnational, national, and local actors; it has also become a vortex of struggles over access to, control over, and distribution of oil wealth. Because of oil, and the greed that it has bred—globally as well as locally—violence and its production as a means of livelihood has mingled with the multiple inequalities and inequities and contradictions that mark daily existence in the villages, creeks, and cities of the region. Some commentators have referred to an "oil curse" that spells inevitable doom for those postcolonial countries endowed with its riches. They claim that such countries will continue to be afflicted by the paradox of poverty, corruption, waste, and violence conflict (Ross 2007). However, such deterministic positions are in my view based on spurious and ahistoric grounds (Obi 2010: 491–492). It should be emphasized that the issue of whether oil becomes a curse or blessing depends on the activities of several actors—local, national, and transnational, including the people—who ultimately determine what oil will represent for better or for worse. We cannot conceive of oil as a curse or a blessing outside of those forces that control it and thereby shape the structure of global economic and political power.

This chapter is divided into four broad sections. The introduction sets out the background of the place of the two "oils" in the political economy of the Niger Delta. It is followed by a conceptual and historical treatment of the globalization of the Niger Delta. The third section examines the conflicts revolving around the production of oil and the power and social relations that it spawns, while the concluding section suggests an alternative agenda for conflict resolution, inclusive democratization, and people-centered peace in the Niger Delta.

GLOBALIZATION AND THE NIGER DELTA: SOME CONCEPTUAL AND HISTORICAL ISSUES

The Niger Delta has been transformed by global processes since the latter part of the fifteenth century when European explorers (Portuguese), followed by merchants and missionaries (Portuguese, Dutch, French, and British), arrived at the coast, signaling the establishment of the region as an outpost of transatlantic commerce. The particular global processes that are relevant in our context relate to the local production of certain commodities destined for the global market, the presence of global actors in the region, and the impact of both processes on the local socioeconomic and political conditions. This early form of globalization linked the Niger Delta through trade relations to markets in Europe and the "new world" of the Americas. These initial trade links also meant that the region featured in the map of the world. The people of the Niger Delta were influenced by certain aspects of European cultures, some of which have survived till date.

There are records of people from rich or royal families in the Niger Delta that traveled to Europe to receive Western education in those days, underscoring the cosmopolitan outlook of some of the leading families in the region, and the extent to which they were already well integrated into global affairs and cultures. The interventionist logic of globalization, however, contributed to the eventual conquest of the region (to control the oil trade), and its subsequent inclusion in the Nigerian colonial state. This in turn defined the region in ethnic minority terms and introduced another element into the economics–politics interface and conflictive ethnic relations in a future Nigerian federation.

Several questions are relevant in the light of the foregoing: In what ways have the processes and actors linked to globalization transformed the Niger Delta? What kind of social and power relations has globalization spawned within the region, and between the region and the world? Who has benefitted from the relations spawned by the globalization of the region? Has the distribution of the benefits from the oil trade(s) been even, equitable, and sustainable? How can you explain the state of affairs in the region marked by high levels of poverty and conflict in spite of five centuries of local–global relations? In order to provide some answers, it is necessary to further explore the concept of globalization.

GLOBALIZATION: A CONCEPTUAL EXPLORATION

Although the concept of globalization gained traction after the Cold War, the sense of an interconnected and interdependent world dates back to the age of exploration. Initially framed with the context of the search for commodities, trade routes, trading partners, and markets, the expansionist and integrative logic of "early" globalization has survived until this day. Globalization is a contested concept and manifests in various dimensions as "a multicentric, multiscalar, multitemporal, multiform, and multicausal process" (Jessop 2002: 97). It is best captured in the context of growing transglobal "mixing" and interdependence of the various locales and levels of a global whole, which is also "present" in its component parts. For this reason, it is not difficult to fathom why various scholars and commentators have not agreed on a single definition of globalization.

While some commentators point to the ways globalization is erasing national borders, international boundaries, and accelerating the "withering away of the state," others counter by arguing that nothing has really changed except that a state-driven regionalism has assumed prominence across the world. Yet, there are others that focus more on the prominent role being played by non-state actors, the nature of global transformations and its implications for the various regions and peoples of the world. Whichever way we look at it, globalization is a complex, contested process, which manifests across different spaces, times, and intersections.

However, much evidence points to the changing nature and impact of globalization. In its current phase, globalization cannot be fully understood outside the transnational expansionist logic of capital (Gills 2000: 4–6). In other words, globalization thrives on the expansion and intensification of capitalist relations across spaces, times, and levels. Thus, it encompasses a "bundle," rather than one single set of issues. One therefore agrees with Mittelman's (2000: 3) view that "globalization is not a single unified phenomenon, but a syndrome of processes and activities." Globalization is also integrative. According to Mittelman (2000: 5), this is characterized by the "increase in interconnections, or interdependence, a rise in transnational flows, and an intensification of processes such that the world is, in some respects becoming a single place." Yet, the issue of the nodes or location of such interconnections and intersections, and the relationship between the various levels and actors should not be lost to the analysis. Increasingly, embedded in such growing interconnections are relations of inequality or marginalization between and within countries, regions, and even localities.

It is within this context that we can refer to a "globalization from above" and a "globalization from below." The interaction between both globalizations is both a product of history, transglobal actors operating from both ends of the global "social" spectrum, and suggests a dialectic that operates in "varying proportions above and below the territorial state" (Mittelman 2000: 5). Thus, while the forces of globalization from above penetrate and intervene in the locale, depending on their impact, whether they are empowering or disempowering, local social forces can connect with certain sections of the "global" to construct a globalization from below to counter those aspects of globalization from above that are perceived as being exploitative, alienating, and life threatening.

Globalization has far-reaching consequences for social life at the local level(s). Intersections between the global and the local can become flashpoints of conflict, where local forces pitch their battles against those aspects of globalization that exploit and impoverish local peoples. In such contexts, some local forces may seek to resist the hegemony of global capital over society. They do not do so alone, but tend to seek global partners that are supportive of local claims and mobilize global opinion and resources against hegemonic global extraction. In the Niger Delta, local forces have historically cooperated with, and then resisted, hegemonic forces of globalization when such have sought for the control of the region's vast resource wealth, and have excluded the people from gaining access to the wealth and benefits derived from the exploitation of their resources and the transfer of such wealth to distant places and people outside of the Niger Delta (Obi 2009).

Thus, the politics of local resistance becomes an instrument for those who are alienated by extractive globalized capitalist social relations, which tend to strip local people of their power, rights, and resources, and subordinate local interests to the extractive logic of globalized accumulation of wealth. Depending on the specificities of each moment, the balance of social forces and the organizational capacity of local resistance movements, they seek to forcefully upturn the inequities embedded in global–local relations, particularly the unequal relations of power around the local production of commodities destined for the global market.

It is important to note that local resistance to certain aspects or forces of globalization is not unproblematic. Indeed, in most cases, it is underpinned by blurred boundaries, complexities, contradictions, and ambiguities. This point echoes Gramsci's position on the "ambiguity of resistance" (Mittelman and Chin, 2005: 17–27) in seeking to explain the complex forces at play, and the fluid dynamics of the politics of resistance. Whether it is in the complex alliances in which some Niger Delta traders aligned with European traders to fight their local rivals during the days of the cutthroat competition that marked the "legitimate trade" or the divisions within the Movement for the Survival of Ogoni People (MOSOP) in the 1990s and the present-day Movement for the Emancipation of the Niger Delta (MEND) (Obi 2001, 2008: 417–434), the forces of local resistance continue to reflect some ambiguities.

While local resistance in the Niger Delta has evolved in response to the contradictions spawned by oil-led globalization, the struggles of the ordinary people of this oil-blessed region is by no means limited to their locality. For just as the nineteenth-century heroes of Niger Delta resistance such as King Koko of Brass, Jaja of Opobo, and Nana Olomu of Itsekiri blazed the trail for the likes of Isaac Adaka Boro and Ken Saro-Wiwa in the twentieth century, we note a continuity in the twenty-first century in the form of a locally rooted insurgent resistance, whose complex features still continue to defy full explanation. To further complicate the picture, a new set of global actors, state oil corporations from the East (China and India), have joined the international competition for oil in the Niger Delta. This has further raised the high stakes in the struggle for access to, and control of the oil in the region.

THE GLOBALIZATION OF THE NIGER DELTA AND ITS CONSEQUENCES

The Early Phase: Mercantilism

The early phase of globalization of the Niger Delta took place within a transatlantic framework, with the Atlantic Ocean as the "highway for the processes and external forces that radically transformed the course of the history of the Niger Delta" (Obi 2005: 189). As Dike (1965) notes, "During the seventeenth and eighteenth centuries the Delta was one of the most important, if not the leading slave market in West Africa." Through trade, European merchants introduced crops such as cassava and maize from South America into the Niger Delta. However, by the nineteenth century, Alagoa (1999: 249) informs us that while internal change was underway, external forces—merchants, missionaries, and British officials, including naval officers, consuls, and colonial administrators—intervened forcefully to alter the course of history in the region. The timing of international intervention coincided with the period following the abolition of the slave trade in 1807, the replacement of the trade in slaves with the "legitimate trade" in palm oil, and the upsurge in the industrial revolution in Britain.

Thus, rather than being driven by humanitarian considerations, international intervention was largely underpinned by the demand for palm oil from the Niger Delta by the British (Alagoa 1999: 249). Ikime (1977: 134) illustrates how much oil was exported from the region with the example of one source, Brass, which "exported a total of 2,280 tons of oil in the year 1856, and the figure increased to 2,800 tons by 1864." From this, the figures for the rest of the region could be extrapolated. Early globalization, particularly that which was linked to oil commerce, laid the basis for foreign intervention and the eventual conquest of the Niger Delta.

By the 1840s, British companies such as Horsefall, Harrison, and Hemmingway; Douglas Stewart; Miller Brothers; and James Pinnock established themselves as major players in the palm oil trade (Ikime 1999: 268). The patrolling of the waters of the Gulf of Guinea by the British Navy to stop ships suspected of carrying slaves also meant that the consuls could rely on force to protect the interests of British companies and traders. It became the practice for such consuls to enter into one-sided treaties with Niger Delta rulers, usually under the pretext of stopping the trade in slaves, but really to protect the interests of European and British traders.

Also of note were the activities of the United African Company (UAC), which later became the RNC. Under Tubman Goldie, the RNC became the de facto government of the Niger Delta Oil Rivers Protectorate after being granted a royal charter in 1886. It was not long before the RNC established a monopoly on the palm oil trade and also taxed the trade, leading to conflict with some Niger Delta kings and princes that were intent on protecting their sovereignty and the right to control trade in their own territory. During the last three decades of the nineteenth century, the entire region was forcefully brought under British rule, giving them unhindered access to the sources of the palm oil in the hinterland, and beyond that access to a vast territory that later became part of the Nigerian colonial state.

This interventionist phase of globalization led to the loss of sovereignty of the Niger Delta and foreign control of the oil trade. More instructive was the unequal nature of the trade between Europeans and the people of the Niger Delta. As Dike (1965), concluded with regard to the paltry gains that accrued to Niger Delta traders, "in return for superior labour force, the palm oil, ivory, timber, gold and other commodities, which fed and buttressed the rising industrialism, they received the worst type of trade gin and meretricious articles." As I have noted elsewhere, the real point is to note the "connection between the expropriation of Africa's wealth and the growth of industrial capitalism in Europe and North America" (Obi 2005: 196). The unequal character of the trade meant that the integration of the Niger Delta into global commerce as a source of palm oil did not benefit the region in any real terms; rather, it led to the violent subordination of the Niger Delta and the exploitation of its resources for the benefit of Europe and the New World.

The Niger Delta people were transformed into ethnic minorities in the context of a Nigerian colonial state, which introduced a new layer in their subordination by Imperial Britain, and marginalization by the forces of early globalization. It was partly the struggle against this subordination and "unjust" globalization that defined the early struggles of the people for self-determination (Tamuno 1970). Such struggles did not end with formal colonial rule, but continued in the postcolonial period. They continued in spite of the decline and collapse of palm oil commerce, which was overshadowed from the mid-1960s onward by that in crude oil, produced in the Niger Delta by foreign oil multinationals. However, like palm oil before it, the petroleum from the region was mostly destined for the highly industrialized countries of Europe and the Americas. This "petrolized" age of globalization, which coincided with the OPEC-led oil boom in the 1970s, brought with it even further serious consequences for the socio-economic and political life in the Niger Delta.

GLOBALIZATION AND PETROLEUM IN THE NIGER DELTA IN THE TWENTIETH AND TWENTY-FIRST CENTURIES

There is abundant evidence to show that petroleum has been a revolutionary commodity in global affairs in the twentieth and twenty-first centuries, transforming the nature of industrial production, mobility, war, and peace. Since crude oil is a unique commodity with high economic and strategic value and is increasingly found in the less-developed parts of the world, the issues of access to uninterrupted supply and the relationship between producing and consuming nations have remained a strategic issue in international political economy. For most of the twentieth century, Oil Multinational Corporations (OMNCs) nicknamed the "seven sisters"[2] wielded undisputed power over the world's oil fields up until the 1970s (Sampson 1975). From the 1970s, the "OPEC revolution" led to the reduction of OMNCs control over global sources of oil supply (which was taken up by OPEC member states), but they still continued to have substantial clout in the global political economy as some of the world's richest and most influential corporations, backed by the power of their home states. These global oil giants, though with less vigor, continue to act as energy monopolists, presiding over sophisticated transglobal oil operations that spanned both upstream and downstream sectors of the industry. Their key role in the processes of capitalist globalization and the reproduction of hegemonic power relations between global powers and third world oil producers is evident in Africa (Obi 2000).

The global reach and might of OMNCs is underlined and reinforced by recent mergers in which the "seven sisters" became "four": Exxon/Mobil, Royal Dutch Shell, BP-Amoco-Arco, and ChevronTexaco (Davis 2006: 3). OMNCs collectively constitute the richest and most powerful corporations in the world. In 2007, Exxon Mobil—the world's largest oil company—announced new record profits approximating $40.6 billion, with the total company sales put at more than $404 billion, exceeding "the gross domestic product of 120 countries" (Mouawad 2008). The same scenario holds true for Royal Dutch Shell, which operates in over 110 countries and made $27.56 billion in profits in 2007, and Chevron Texaco, which announced record profits of $18.7 billion in 2007 (BBC 2008; Porretto 2008). Although the global financial crisis adversely affected the annual turnover and profits of the companies in 2009, they still continue to make fairly good returns on their investments.

It is therefore no coincidence that, with regard to the Niger Delta, it was a partly-British owned OMNC, Shell-BP, that first struck oil in Oloibiri in 1956, began exports in 1958, and was joined by the world's other leading oil multinationals from 1959 onward. Shell has since maintained its head start over the oil multinationals. However, in a bid to gain ownership of the hitherto foreign-dominated oil industry, the Nigerian government indigenized the oil industry in the late 1970s and signed a series of Joint Venture Agreements and oil contracts with OMNCs to guarantee Nigerian interests. In spite of this, OMNCs still have considerable leverage in the Nigerian oil industry, not least because of their links to the Nigerian power elite, their control of oil technology, and the huge capital at their disposal.

Thus, oil production in Nigeria is still dominated by the global oil giants, which over time had become domesticated in the country, while remaining powerful transnational actors. The Shell group in Nigeria accounts for almost half of Nigeria's daily oil production, while other OMNCs such as Chevron-Texaco, Exxon Mobil, Total, and Agip-ENI mostly account for the rest. In spite of the recent entry of Chinese and other Asian and South American as well as indigenous oil companies, the OMNCs still dominate the Nigerian oil industry (Obi 2007a). As in the case of palm oil, most of Nigeria's oil exports (produced mainly from the Niger Delta) go to Europe and the Americas. According to the Energy Information Analysis (2010) figures, 40 percent of Nigeria's crude oil exports go to the United States, 24 percent to Europe, 20 percent to Asia, 10 percent to Brazil, and 4 percent to South Africa. Thus, the Niger Delta's role as a site of oil production by OMNCs continues to reinforce the region's integration into the global economy with far-reaching consequences both for the host communities, the inhabitants of the region, and Nigeria.

The enmeshment of "the global" and "national" in "the local" in oil production in the Niger Delta has been emblematic of a seamless transglobal capitalist accumulation process, which also defines the region as a "local" site of "global" oil production (mediated by the "nation-state") with its attendant contradictions, contestations, and crises (Obi 2009a, 2009b). At the heart of the emerging concerns is the question of what the Niger Delta gets in return for the export of the oil tapped from its land and waters. The answer is neither straight forward nor simple, but rather is embedded in the region's history of struggles for self-determination, the impact of the political economy of oil on its peoples and their land, which in the context of the Niger Delta have since the 1990s been increasingly confronted by the "paradox of plenty," protests and local resistance.

GLOBALIZED OIL PRODUCTION, PROTESTS, AND RESISTANCE IN THE NIGER DELTA

The impact of globalized oil production on the Niger Delta is visible as one traverses the region—its cities, villages, rivers, and creeks. Apart from the physical presence of the global oil industry in this largely rural setting, the socioeconomic impact of centuries of global–local relations has arguably left the Niger Delta holding the shorter end of the stick, hence the seething tensions, protests, and episodic outbursts of violent resistance against the perceived alienation, exploitation, and injustices perpetrated against the region and its ethnic minority people by the alliance of OMNCs and the federal government. Two questions are relevant. Is globalization the culprit for the situation of "poverty amid stupendous wealth" and the state of near neglect that typifies the situation in this oil blessed land? Why have OMNCs and the Nigerian federal government been the main targets of local protests and resistance?

Although so much has already been written in response to both questions, it is important to identify the link between oil globalization and the conflict in the region. Several issues underpin the oil-led globalization and its consequences for life in the Niger Delta, the main source of "global" oil in Nigeria. These include the widely held belief in the region that despite five decades of oil production, in which billions of dollars worth of the precious crude taken out of the region (by OMNCs and various governments), there is nothing substantial to show in terms of development, quality of life, and the integration of the local economy into the oil economy. Second, that the people of the Niger Delta have been largely alienated from oil production and marginalized with regard to the distribution of the benefits accruing from oil production, and third, that prolonged oil production has led to the destruction of the fragile environment, threatening the ecological basis of the livelihoods of the people in the region, with little compensation or remedial actions taken to reverse the unwholesome trend (Obi 2007; Douglas and Ola 1999; Okonta and Douglas 2001; Ibaba 2009).

Also relevant is the view that various Nigerian governments have failed to sufficiently address the contradictions arising from capitalist globalization, which has not only separated the source of wealth from the wealth produced, but also had undermined the basis of local livelihoods without adequate compensation or the provision of alternative means of sustenance. Rather than address the roots of these contradictions and their links to global oil production in the region, a lot of effort has gone into the use of "carrot and stick" policies that have turned out to be very expensive, but largely unsuccessful in stemming the tide of frustration, anger, opportunism and conflict.

The role of OMNCs in the globalization of the Niger Delta can be gleaned from the ways in which they act both as domesticated actors, and how their actions, implicate them in the deepening social contradictions, inequities, tensions, conflicts, and repression in the Niger Delta. Being physically present in the villages and creeks where oil extraction is done, they bring the face of global presence and might (globalization) home in sharp relief to the people of the Niger Delta who are alienated by the hegemonic power relations underpinning transnational oil production (Obi 2009b). Thus, globalized oil production becomes tantamount to dispossessing communities of the Niger Delta of their farmlands, crops, homes, and fishing grounds, without offering meaningful employment or viable livelihood alternatives to locals (Ashton-Jones, Arnott, and Douglas, 1998).

The implication of the foregoing scenario becomes clear when we observe according to the UNDP Niger Delta Report (2006). The region has a poverty rate of almost 70 percent alongside high levels of unemployment. The report also points to the high level of environmental pollution and degradation, partly linked to the operations of the oil industry, which has undermined the livelihoods and welfare of ordinary people—subsistence farmers and fishers. This rather sad state of affairs is further complicated by the relationship between OMNCs and the federal government, which results in the alienation and marginalization of the majority of the ordinary people, thus further fueling the politics of local resistance.

While it is important to note that not all the problems of the Niger Delta are the result or consequence of globalized oil production in the region, the contradictions arising from the presence of the "global in the local" is that internal problems have been further worsened. This is more so when we consider the ways in which the majority–minority ethnic relations have played out in Nigeria. What this means is that ethnic minorities of the Niger Delta have historically struggled against the domination of ethnic majority groups that control the federal government as well as the distribution of oil revenues. In this connection, the ethnic minorities have felt aggrieved on the grounds that the revenue allocation system takes away the bulk of the oil wealth produced from the region, while the people remain marginalized from the distribution of power at the federal level.

The combustible ethnic politics, within which the Niger Delta people have been engaged in and associated with struggle for self-determination and resource control, has been further compounded by the negative consequences of oil globalization. At certain levels, the Nigerian state and the OMNCs come together as a transnational alliance united around continued global oil extraction and profit making, while at another level, it is about the relationship between the federal and state governments, or one between the Nigerian state and its citizens in the Niger Delta. In several ways, this has fed into volatile politics and violent conflict in the region (Ikelegbe 2006; Omeje 2006) and as Ibaba (2009: 555–573) has shown, such conflicts do have adverse implications for development in the region.

This complex relationship explains why since the early 1990s, when MOSOP led the way in externalizing its local protest against the state–OMNC alliance by appealing to global rights advocacy networks and OMNC shareholders (Okonta 2008; Saro-Wiwa 1995), followed by campaigns of human and environmental rights groups, resistance has until very recently assumed insurgent proportions. The most recent insurgent turn has been led by MEND. By drawing on grievances within the region (Ukiwo 2007; Okonta 2007) and carrying out coordinated well-publicized attacks on oil installations and personnel, MEND posed a serious threat to globalized oil by forcing the shut-in of a third of daily production in the Niger Delta. However, the tensions in the area have somewhat eased considerably with the signing of most militia leaders up to an Amnesty Program put together by the federal government in October 2009 (Obi and Rustad 2011: 204). While it waged its campaign, MEND relied on global media and the Internet to draw global attention to its cause, even as its attacks had an instant impact on nervous global oil markets (Okonta 2007; Junger 2007).

Globalized oil production has led to the accumulation of wealth at the national and global levels, while simultaneously resulting in the dispossession, exploitation, and pollution of the Niger Delta (Douglas and Ola 1999; Okonta and Douglas 2001). The social relations spawned by globalized oil production is one that has largely resulted in the subordination of the Niger Delta to the imperatives of global oil extraction by a transnational oil alliance, and the disempowerment of the Niger Delta people. The OMNCs are the successors to, or the modern-day equivalent of the mercantile/trading companies that traded palm oil to satisfy the demand of the European, American and global markets. Except that in the case of OMNCs, theirs is a much larger and strategic mission that spans business and energy security considerations.

CONCLUSION: PLACING RE-GLOBALIZATION ON THE AGENDA

What the foregoing shows is that both "oils" have been central to globalization and violent resistance in the Niger Delta (International Crisis Group 2006; Obi 2007b, 2010). More recently, the centrality of crude oil has been reflected in the region, at different levels, and is underpinned by the high stakes involved and a deeply felt sense of grievance by the people arising from perceived injustices in the distribution of oil revenues and benefits. Resistance initially took the form of a struggle for self-determination before independence and after, culminating in an abortive attempt at secession from Nigeria led by Isaac Adaka Boro in 1966 (who proclaimed the region the Niger Delta republic). In the 1990s, the struggle for self-determination resurged and was linked to local ethnic/oil minority protests riding on the ascendancy of people's rights at the end of the Cold War, and demanding for redress, equity and justice, and seeking global support for their cause(s).

MOSOP used global media, rights discourses, and forums in taking the fight to the home of OMNCs and arenas of oil consumption in Europe and North America. In this way, it waged a moral crusade against oil multinationals in the dock of world public opinion as a strategy of forcing them to attend to the grievances of local people (Obi 2009b). For the first time in the recent history, a coalition of local ethnic minorities took on some of the world's most powerful and wealthy companies and sought the transformation of exploitative relations, albeit with limited success.

Nowhere else are contradictions linked to the globalization of the country as large as in the troubled Niger Delta region, which accounts for the bulk of Nigeria's oil production and exports. Although the "two oils" have historically shaped the extent and depth of the globalization of the region, the main issue is that the region has suffered underdevelopment while simultaneously contributing immense resources to the global market controlled by hegemonic mercantile and corporate oil actors. As the UNDP Niger Delta Human Development Report (2006: 15–16) concludes, the Niger Delta has "an appalling human development situation summed up in social instability, poor local governance, neglect of infrastructure, lack of access to fundamental services, environmental degradation and extreme economic deprivation." This situation has been brought about not only because of globalization or indeed the nature of oil, but also because of the character of the Nigerian state, the nature of politics, and the character of the political elites, which have all failed to transform the opportunities inherent in globalization into concrete steps towards equitable and people-centered national development.

Globalization has also meant that while the Niger Delta has become so important to the economies and stability of the world's powers, decisions taken far away in London, The Hague, Washington, DC, New York, Texas, Beijing and other centers of global oil commerce have direct implications for the lives of people in the oil region. There are so many ways in which the Niger Delta has become oil enclave or space serving the world market on account of its abundant oil endowments. This oil-rich region has unfortunately been treated more like a backyard, rather than the forecourt of global energy in the twenty-first century.

Equally significant since 9/11 has been the securitization of the Niger Delta on the basis of its being a major oil supplier to the United States and the Western powers. Securitization has meant increased militarization both on land (represented by the activities of the Joint military Task Force or JTF) and the adjoining Gulf of Guinea, where the U.S. Navy and AFRICOM patrol the Atlantic coast, both to check the activities of transnational criminal networks believed to be trafficking in oil stolen from the Niger Delta, and keeping international sea lanes safe and open for international commerce. The designation of the region as a strategic space of prime concern to the energy security calculations of the world's powers has also meant that the stakes in protecting globalized oil production against disruption by militant resistance forces continues to climb higher with dire implications for the people of the region.

What then is to be done? It would appear that the Niger Delta will have to be re-globalized on radically new terms as the present path of globalization is no longer sustainable and can only lead to more environmental degradation, misery, poverty, and violent conflict in the region. The question then is how, and by whom, can a project for the re-globalization of the Niger Delta be undertaken, and on whose terms? The first place to look to are the social forces of globalization from below—our people for whom our land means life, global allies and partners that believe in our people and our capacity to transform our lives and our resources for the common prosperity of all. We have to debate these issues in an open and frank manner, focusing on those things that unite us to free our land from forces that milk it in a non-sustainable manner. Even if crude oil is the current platform for the globalization of the Niger Delta, it will not remain so forever. Before oil, the region was being globalized, chances are that globalization in a different form may outlive oil in the region.

Just as the oil age started just over a hundred years ago, it will one day end, but our people will remain. The time to build a new equitable world for a post-hydrocarbon-based human civilization is upon us. Where else and who else knows this more than those who have paid a huge cost and suffered environmental pollution and marginalization to fuel the engines of global capital? Re-globalization will have to mean the empowerment and liberation of our people and the release of their energies to control their destinies. It is a call for a new developmental democratic state based on participatory democracy, equity and social justice at the local, national and global levels. A new and more just world is possible, and the Niger Delta may just well be its cradle!

NOTES

1. A good example of this was the case of Jaja originally an Igbo slave, who through his business acumen, rose to become the head of the Anna Pepple Trading House, and one of the most notable merchant-princes in the Niger Delta in the nineteenth century.
2. The "seven sisters" were Exxon (Standard Oil of New Jersey), Mobil (Standard Oil of New York), Socal (Standard Oil of California), Gulf Oil, Texaco, Royal Dutch Shell, and British Petroleum (BP).

REFERENCES

Alagoa, E. (1964). *The small brave city-state: A history of Nembe-Brass in the Niger Delta*, Ibadan and Madison: Ibadan University Press and the University of Wisconsin Press.

Alagoa, E. (1999). "The eastern Niger Delta and the hinterland in the 19th century," O. Ikime (ed.), *Groundwork of Nigerian history*, Ibadan: Heinemann Educational Books: pp. 249–261.

Alagoa, E. (2004) *The uses of hindsight: Reflections on Niger Delta and Nigerian history*, Port Harcourt: Onyoma Research Publications.

Ashton-Jones, N., with Arnott, S. and Douglas, O. (1998). *The human ecosystems of the Niger Delta*, Benin City: Environmental Rights Action (ERA).

BBC. (2008). "Shell sets new UK profits record," January 31, http://news.bbc.co.uk/2/hi/business/7219148.stm (accessed January 30, 2009)

Best, S. and von Kemedi, D. (2005). "Armed groups and conflict in rivers and plateau states, Nigeria," in N. Florquin and E. Berman (eds.), *Armed and aimless:*

Armed groups, guns and human security in the ECOWAS region, Geneva: Small Arms Survey: pp. 19–28.
Davis, J. (2006). "'And then there were four. . .': A thumbnail history of oil industry restructuring 1971–2005," in J. Davis (ed.), *The changing world of oil: An analysis of corporate change and adaptation*, Hampshire: Ashgate: pp. 1–10.
Dike, K. (1865). *Trade and politics in the Niger Delta*, London: Oxford University Press.
Douglas, O. and Ola, D. (1999). "Defending nature, protecting human dignity—conflicts in the Niger Delta," in M. Mekenkamp, P. van Tongeren, and H. Van de Veen (eds.), *Searching for peace in Africa: An overview of conflict prevention and transformation in Africa*, Utrecht: European Platform for Conflict Prevention, in cooperation with African Centre for the Constructive Resolution of Disputes.
Energy Information Analysis. (2010). *Country analysis briefs: Nigeria*, July, http://www.eia.doe.gov/cabs/Nigeria/Full.html (accessed December 22, 2010)
Gills, B. (2000). "Introduction: Globalization and the politics of resistance", in B. Gills (ed.), *Globalization and the politics of resistance*, Hampshire and London: Macmillan Press.
Human Rights Watch. (2002). *Niger Delta: No democratic dividend*, New York: Human Rights Watch.
Ibaba, S. (2009). "Conflicts and sustainable development in Bayelsa state," *Review of African Political Economy*, Vol. 36, No. 122, pp. 555–573.
Ikein, A. and Briggs-Anigboh, C. (1998). *Oil and fiscal federalism: The political economy of resource allocation in a developing country,* Aldershot: Ashgate.
Ikelegbe, A. (2006). "The economy of conflicts in the oil rich Niger Delta region of Nigeria," *African and Asian Studies*, Vol. 5, No. 1, pp. 23–56.
Ikime, O. (1977) *The fall of Nigeria*, Ibadan: Heinemann Educational Books.
Ikime, O. (1999). "The western Niger Delta and the hinterland in the nineteenth century," in O. Ikeme (ed.), *Groundwork of Nigerian history*, Ibadan: Heinemann Educational Books: pp. 262- 279.
International Crisis Group. (2006). "The swamps of insurgency: Nigeria's Delta unrest," *Africa Report*, Vol. 115, No. 3, August.
Jessop, B. (2002). "Time and space in the globalization of capital and their implications for state power," *Rethinking Marxism*, Vol. 14, No. 1, pp. 97–117.
Junger, S. (2007). "Crude awakening," *The Observer Magazine*, April 15.
Lawal, Y. (2008). "Crude shut-in hits 1m barrels per day," *The Guardian* (Lagos), February 18.
Mittelman, J. (2000). *The globalization syndrome*, Princeton, NJ: Princeton University Press.
Mittelman, J. and Chin, C. (2005). "Conceptualizing resistance to globalization," in L. Ammore (ed.), *The global resistance reader*, London and New York: Routledge.
Mouawad, J. (2008). "Exxon Mobil profit sets record again," *The New York Times*, February 1, http://www.nytimes.com/2008/02/01/business/01cnd-exxon.html?_r=1&hp&oref=slogin (accessed February 1, 2009)
Obi, C. (2000). "Globalised images of environmental security in Africa," *Review of Africa's Political Economy*, Vol. 83, pp. 47–62.
Obi, C. (2001). "Global, state and local intersections: Power, authority and conflict in the Niger delta oil communities," in T. Callaghy, R. Kassimir, and R. Latham (eds.), *Intervention and transnationalism in Africa: Global–local networks of power*, Cambridge: Cambridge University Press: pp. 173–193.
Obi, C. (2005). "Niger Delta: Trans Atlantic reflections on the colonial mirror," in T. Falola (ed.), *The dark webs: Perspectives on colonialism in Africa*, Durham, NC: Carolina Academic Press: pp. 189–212.

Obi, C. (2007). "The struggle for resource control in a petro-state: A perspective from Nigeria," in P. Bowles, H. Veltmeyer, S. Cornilissen, N. Invernizzi, and K. Tang (eds.), *National perspectives on globalisation*, Hampshire and New York: Palgrave Macmillan: 93–106.

Cyril O. (2008). "Enter the dragon? Chinese oil companies and resistance in the Niger Delta," *Review of African Political Economy*, Vol. 35, No. 117, pp. 417–434.

Obi, C. (2009a). "Nigeria's Niger Delta: Understanding the complex drivers of violent conflict," *Africa Development*, Vol. 34, No. 2, pp. 103–128.

Obi, C. (2009b). "Structuring transnational spaces of identity, rights and power in the Niger Delta of Nigeria," *Globalizations*, Vol. 6, No. 4, pp. 467–481.

Obi, C. (2010). "Oil as the 'curse' of conflict in Africa: Peering through the smoke and mirrors," *Review of African Political Economy*, Vol. 37, No. 126, pp. 483–495.

Obi, C. and Rustad, A. S. (2011). "Conclusion: Amnesty and post-amnesty peace, is the window of opportunity closing for the Niger Delta?" in C. Obi and S. A. Rustad (eds.), *Oil and insurgency in the Niger Delta: Managing the complex politics of petro-violence*, London: Zed Books: pp. 204–207.

Okonta, I. (2007). "Niger Delta: Behind the mask, Ijaw militia fight the oil cartel," *World War 4 Report*, http://ww4report.com (accessed January 30, 2009)

Okonta, I. (2008). *When citizens revolt: Nigerian elites, big oil and the Ogoni struggle for self-determination*, Trenton, NJ and Asmara: Africa World Press.

Okonta, I. and Douglas, O. (2001). *Where the vultures feast: 40 years of Shell in the Niger Delta*, Benin-city: Environmental Rights Action/Friends of the Earth.

Omeje, K. (2006). *High stakes and stakeholders: Oil conflict and security in Nigeria*, Hampshire: Ashgate.

Porretto, J. (2008). "Exxon, Chevron post record profits," *Washington Post*, February 2, www.washingtonpost.com (accessed February 20, 2009)

Ross, B. (2007). "News exclusive: Online interview with a terrorist," *ABC News*, January 3, http://abcnews.co.com (accessed February 20, 2009)

Sampson, A. (1975). *The seven sisters: The great oil Companies and the world they shaped*, New York: St. Martin's Press.

Saro-Wiwa, K. (1995). *A month and a day: A detention diary*, London: Penguin Books.

Tamuno, T. (1970). "Separatist agitation in Nigeria since 1914," *Journal of Modern African Studies*, Vol. 8, No. 4, pp. 563–584.

Ukiwo, U. (2007). "From pirates to 'militants': A historical perspective on anti-oil company Mobilization among the Ijaw of Warri, western Niger Delta," *African Affairs*, Vol. 106, No. 425, pp. 587–610.

UNDP Nigeria. (2006). *Niger Delta human development report*, Abuja: UNDP.

Watts, M. (1999). *Petro-violence: Some thoughts on community, extraction, and political ecology*, Institute of International Studies, Berkeley Workshop, September 24, Working Paper, WP 99-1, http://escholarship.org/uc/item/7zh116zd;jsessionid=49558B5D7B83639ECC93D3DE179673D8#page-1 (accessed December 22, 2010)

Watts, M. (2006). "Empire of oil: Capitalist dispossession and the scramble for Africa," *Monthly Review*, Vol. 58, No. 4, http://monthlyreview.org/0906watts.htm (accessed February 20, 2009)

3 Overcoming Tyranny and Underdevelopment in the Niger Delta Through Appropriate Human Resources Development and Utilization

Samson Ranti Akinola

INTRODUCTION

> The future place of democracies in human civilization will not just happen; it will be constructed and will require attentive care. Those concerned with the constitution of democratic societies are required to give critical attention to the development of a science of citizenship and civic enlightenment. That science should not be confined to the education of students in schools. It should be a science of association that is studied and applied by all as we assume responsibility for living our lives and learning how to work with others under variable and changing conditions that reach out to global proportions.
>
> —Vincent Ostrom (2000: 271).

There are strong theoretical reasons to think of democracy as the springboard of human development. However, the Niger Delta, the region that produces the lion's share of revenues for Nigeria, has been reduced to a basket of waste for the majority of its citizens. In democratic self-governing societies, environmental resources are directed toward the welfare of citizens because citizens are the deciders of resource utilization and distribution. However, under democratic tyranny in the Niger Delta, where "majority" carries the vote through the use of guns and cutlasses, proceeds from natural resources are used to repress the same citizens that are supposed to benefit from their resources. For more than two decades, ammunitions, warships, and air-raid equipments were purchased by the federal government to unleash genocidal attack on innocent people, in attempts to fight the militants. What a paradox!

Demographic features of Niger Delta confirmed that the decade of democracy has not benefited the vast population. In spite of its strategic economic importance, the Human Development Index (HDI) of the Niger Delta (0.453) is lower than nations with the same oil resources such as Norway (0.963), Kuwait (0.844), Libya (0.799), and Indonesia (0.697) (UNDP 2006). An important missing element in the conduct of public affairs in the region by the governments, oil companies, and other agencies is the involvement of self-governing people-oriented institutions that could check the excesses of elected officials. Consequently, the misuse of public resources, corruption, and low accountability of government officials in the region is rampant (Akinola 2008b: 94). Politics of exclusion neglect the development of human resources. Whereas human resources should be active agents who accumulate and exploit passive factors of production (capital and natural resources) and build social, economic, and political organizations for development, their neglect in the Niger Delta is largely responsible for lack of enlightenment. Consequently, politicians exploit the ignorance of the vast majority of the people at the community level in the Delta region, use the youth to rig elections, and later abandon them. In effect, people's aspirations are unfulfilled, and their potentials remain largely untapped.

This confirms the problem of "disconnect" that is caused by the absence of appropriate institutional mechanisms that could motivate the people (elite and non-elite) to work together as partners in developing the region. The stakeholders in development—governments, universities, oil companies, and the Deltans—operate on parallel lines, instead of collaboratively as colleagues with equal standing within governance and development arenas. This chapter, therefore, argues that human resources development that prioritizes citizens' enlightenment need to be adequately developed. This would enable citizens to pursue development agenda by drawing on their productive potentials and capabilities to achieve freedom and development.

Using the Institutional Analysis and Development (IAD) framework developed over the years by Vincent Ostrom and Elinor Ostrom and their colleagues at the Workshop in Political Theory and Policy Analysis, Indiana University, Bloomington, United States, this chapter examines the missing links in the operations of developers and users of human resources in the Niger Delta. It also suggests a Niger Delta Polycentric Human Resources Development and Utilization Model (NDPHRDUM) for bridging the gaps between developers and users of human resources in the region.

THEORETICAL UNDERPINNING

In order to contextualize the line of analysis in this paper, Public Choice Theory (PCT) is adopted. One of the important puzzles about the governance of human societies revolves around the relationship of federalism to the widely held aspirations of people for democracy. The term "democracy" implies that people govern. "The government," however, is plainly not the people. People vote and elect representatives who participate in the government. Voting is a very slender thread, hardly strong enough to let us presume that people, by electing representatives, govern. The ordinary use of language strongly implies that the government governs (Ostrom 1994:

5). But reality on ground in Africa confirmed that government governs in a limited sense as demonstrated by calamitous failure of the state in responding to the socioeconomic and political aspirations of the citizenry. The people also govern in the light of the resilience of self-organizing arrangements that the people of Africa have devised over the years in addressing problems of daily life, the same areas where governments have consistently faltered (Wunsch and Olowu 1995; Sawyer 2005; Gellar 2005; Akinola, 2000, 2004, 2005, 2007a, 2007b, 2008b, 2009a, 2010c, 2011d).

The failure of the liberal democratic paradigm and state-centered efforts in Africa requires a rethink with a view to finding alternative ways of effectively addressing African socioeconomic, technological, and political problems. Therefore, the specific variation used in this paper draws from the IAD framework. According to Sawyer (2005: 3), institutional analysis helps us to better understand how individuals within communities, organizations, and societies craft rules and organize the rule-ordered relationships in which they live their lives.

Relating institutions to the Niger Delta, the governance systems and rules that sustained them were inspired by European traditions, while the peoples in diverse language communities and ways of life in the region were ignored (Ostrom 2006) and their governance structures were denigrated. This is where elite leadership in the Niger Delta could not respond appropriately. Incidentally, the local people have been able to respond by exploring precolonial governance heritage to meet their daily needs (Akinola 2008b, 2009b, 2010c). How did these peoples cope and how are they coping? What lessons can we learn from these people-centered adaptation strategies? How can we align the efforts of the governments with that of the people through their institutions to resolve the lingering development crises and eradicate poverty in the Niger Delta? How can electoral system in the region be made democratic and people oriented?

Paraphrasing Hamilton's fundamental puzzle (Hamilton et al. 1961: 33) in human societies, the concern is "whether the Niger Delta as a society is really capable or not of establishing people-centered and true democracy from reflection and choice, or whether they are forever destined to depend for their political affairs on the outcomes of false and bloody electoral systems." If we understand society as a system of human cooperation, this puzzle can be formulated as two questions: Are people of the Niger Delta capable of cooperating with one another to organize people-oriented elections that will produce accountable leaders of their choice? If the answer is "yes," under what conditions can they cooperate to achieve such a goal?

Though there is a growing awareness of the need to strengthen community institutions that have existed and have facilitated self-reliant development at the local level, these institutions in oil communities of Nigeria exist at grassroots without official connection with the state-based institutions. They operate on parallel line with governments, their agencies (oil commissions), and oil companies (Akinola 2008b). If these institutions are viable (though not perfect), the question then is how do we connect them to the formal government structure?

The major concern of this chapter, therefore, is to design Niger Delta polycentric human resources development and utilization framework that would provide platform for connecting the formal structure with informal institutions in the region. However, the people should be regarded as important resources in development system. Scholars of human resources development and utilization (HRDU) have reminded us that human resources, not capital, not income or material resources constitute the ultimate basis for the wealth of nations. Capital and natural resources are passive factors of production. Human beings are the active agents who accumulate capital; exploit natural resources; build social, economic, and political organizations; and carry forward national development (Harbison 1973: 63; Ndiomu 1992: 34).

There is Eurocentric definition and Africentric perspective of human resources. Eurocentric definition excludes informal sector where the majority of Africans belong, while Africentric perspective considers informal role that Africans play in HRDU. For example, both in the public and private sectors, there were no serious efforts to develop indigenous staff in specialized knowledge during the pre-independence era. The only training took the form of formal education in administrative and clerical service (Bur 1992: 51). Colonial administration put priority on white-collar jobs at the expense of proper and adaptive education that could have elevated and harnessed the potentials of the citizenry (Eleazu, 1977: 117; Akinola 2005: 239). Africentric perspective emphasizes the convergence of formal and informal activities in the community. It emphasizes the availability of basic infrastructure and services for citizens to be trained to enhance their skills and entrepreneurial capability so that they can be productively engaged in socioeconomic activities.

HRDU, though very nascent, is a dynamic and vibrant field. Without guided and realistic policies on how to treat the most important productive human resources, there will be underdevelopment and human misery. There is the need for coordination and cooperation between developers and users of human resources. But experience shows that the vital links between developers and users are missing or not appropriately harmonized (Mbat 1992: 159). This may be caused by factors such as the following: (a) colonial syndrome and intellectual poverty; (b) defective planning process and procedure; (c) lack of research incentives; (d) poor data base; and (e) defects in the communication system. Considering the wealth in the Niger Delta, these missing vital links between developers and users in the region have engendered governance crisis and made development elusive.

DEMOCRATIC TYRANNY AND ELUSIVE DEVELOPMENT IN THE NIGER DELTA

Democratic tyranny, an offshoot of false electoral system and governance crisis in the Niger Delta, cannot be divorced from the persistent gap between elite leadership and ordinary individuals. This confirms that "elected" officials are often not chosen by the people and are, therefore, not accountable to the electorates after elections (Ake 1996; Fawole 2005; Akinola 2004, 2010b, 2010c, 2010d). The essence of democracy resides in the relationship between the state and the people, especially on how much control the latter has over the former (Chole 1995: 3). The gap between elite leadership and citizens, which manifests in structural disconnect, generates crisis that revolves around contention of power over the allocation, distribution, and control of human, financial, and material resources. The challenges in the region arising from structurally defective pattern of governance include (a) large amounts of money flowing to the Niger Delta region regularly but with little or no impact on the lives of the people; (b) party patronage and "godfatherism" predominating the political system in the region; (c) using false electoral system (based on money-bags politics) to induce unenlightened citizens to vote for the wrong candidate and against their own interest/well-being; (d) the use of armed gangs, thugs, and hooligans to intimidate opponents or rig elections and later abandon these thugs after winning elections, letting the thugs terrorize the masses; (e) an electoral system that results in winner-takes-all situation; (f) unemployed and disgruntled youths resulting in militancy as a means of survival; (g) widespread poverty among the people; (h) failure of local governments in the region to meet the aspirations of the citizenry make the political system irrelevant to the grassroots; (i) the "disconnect" and alienation between the leaders and the rest of the society, resulting in crisis and high level of insecurity; and (j) the local people through self-organizing arrangements, shared strategies, and problem-solving interdependencies are more effective in responding to community needs and aspirations than governments and their agencies.

The configuration of interactions between leadership and the people in the region portend ruler-rule-ruled relationship as against the ideal rule-ruler-ruled relationship that is more congenial to democracy. In a ruler-rule-ruled configuration, the ruler is above the law/rule, while in a rule-ruler-ruled configuration, the law/rule is above the ruler and the ruled. Democratic societies depend on self-organizing and self-governing capabilities of citizens. That is why Ostrom (2000: 225) raises a fundamental question: Where do we turn to explore potentials for the emergence of self-organizing and self-governing capabilities and the development of creative potentials in crafting mutually productive ways of life?

Exclusions and deprivations are seeds of aggression and violence planted in the Niger Delta by oil explorers, and these constitute strong barriers to mutually productive ways of life. For example, a total of ₦44.9 billion as monthly allocation to the Niger Delta in August 2009 confirms the fact that colossal amount of money is flowing to the region regularly.[1] However, politicians and public officials in the region loot public funds for personal aggrandizement (Aluko 2006: 59–66). For example, the Oil Mineral Producing Areas Development Commission (OMPADEC) paid ₦6.6 million as mobilization to contractors who embezzled the money (Ibaba

2008: 535). Between 1999 and 2004, a total of ₦1 billion and ₦9.1 billion were embezzled in Bayelsa and Delta States, respectively, while ₦25 million was diverted to private pockets in Akwa-Ibom State in 2007 (Philips 2008: 893). It has been observed that the Ministry of Niger Delta Affairs (MND) did not perform due to the activities of some lawmakers in the region (Ochayi 2009). Akinola (2010d) confirms the high level of public immorality of politicians on constituency projects in Ondo State, one of the Niger Delta states. The pillage and plundering in the region, invariably, have made development in the region to be elusive.

Indicators of elusive development in the region are sundry. Educational attainment at primary and secondary levels in the region suffers from a high teacher–pupil ration—1:42, compared with the national average of 1:36. This high ratio, invariably, reduces the teachers' ability to impart knowledge (FGN 2008: 221). In turn, lack of teachers, the poor inculcation of knowledge, and consequent poor academic performance of pupils invariably result in large number of dropouts (Akinola 2009b: 85). Average life expectancy in the Niger Delta is decreasing, from 46.8 years in 2008 (FGN 2008:221) to 43 years in 2009 (Osagie et. al. 2009:17). This is mostly due to high mortality of young children—of every 1,000 new born, 200 die by the age of five. This is one of the poorest among developing countries (FGN 2008: 221). Statistics also confirms that poverty measured by income and food intake stands at 71.22 percent in the region (Osagie et al. 2009: 17). Access to health care was estimated to be available to only 56.5 percent of the population and with one hospital bed available per 1,277 people (Okaba 2005: 55). According to Watts (2009: 45), there is one doctor for every 150,000 inhabitants of the oil-rich states of Bayelsa and Delta. At the same time, unemployment is about 30 percent in the region (FGN 2008: 212) compared to the national average of 20 percent (Ogoh-Mesarawon 2009). Similarly, transportation cost in island communities in the region is about ten times higher when compared with the same distance on land in other parts of the country (Akinola 2009b: 85).

HUMAN RESOURCES DEVELOPMENT AND UTILIZATION IN THE NIGER DELTA

In order to overcome tyranny and underdevelopment in the Niger Delta, citizens need to be politically enlightened and socioeconomically empowered so as to (a) know their rights; (b) defend their rights in a civil manner; (c) work together as colleagues to make meaningful contributions towards development; and (d) be active agents of positive change in the socioeconomic, technological, and political arenas. To this end, an HRDU strategy is imperative. HRDU ensures citizens' enlightenment by setting up institutional mechanisms that focus on community where both formal and informal activities converge for knowledge generation and application. This, in turn, requires the establishment and maintenance of institutions that can assure an effective formal and informal learning environment. While governments and private and social organizations help in establishing and running institutions that provide for the learning process, there is the need to reorient these institutions toward adaptive learning culture in order to induce socioeconomic, technological and political development.

Since society is a system of human cooperation, people in any society should collectively relate to and deal with their exogenous variables. Exogenous variables are those conditions that affect human livelihoods and that humans have to work on through appropriate planning and institutional arrangements to better their conditions of existence. However, there are some fundamental imperatives of collective action within the development arena. These are collegiality, mutual trust, reciprocity, and shared understanding. It is the realization of these imperatives through constitutional reforms, effective planning, and institutional arrangements that can enable the people and their leaders to work together to achieve meaningful progress.

Cooperation requires deliberation. That is why deliberative democracy is considered more appropriate for the Niger Delta. For example, one of the proud inheritances of South Africa's democracy is public dialogue in the form of community forums, negotiations, and *imbizos* (gathering in Zulu Language) which have been part of social movements in the fight against both apartheid and postapartheid inequalities (Hartslief 2005:1). The equivalent of *imbizo* in the Niger Delta is *opuwari* (village court of legislators) among the Ijaw in Bayelsa State and *mbogho* among the Efik and Ibibio of Cross River and Akwa Ibom States. It is high time the Deltans looked back in retrospect to learn from their roots by harnessing certain self-governing principles that are inherent in their cultural/traditional heritage to address the present challenges. That is why Alagoa (2005) reminds us that the basic Ijaw political system was a stateless organization based on the autonomous settlement without central political authority (Alagoa 2005: 17).

If we agree that institutions matter in terms of their influence on cooperation, then self-organizing and self-governing arrangements that the people of the Niger Delta have adopted in cooperating mutually in responding to their common problems are imperatives as the first condition to be met for the attainment of people-oriented elections, good governance, viable democracies and sustainable development. Recent studies support the fact that the Niger Delta people through self-organizing and self-governing arrangements have been responding appropriately to the needs and aspirations of the citizenry. By exploring precolonial governance heritage, the people have been able to respond to social challenges that the state has effectively dodged over the years (Akinola 2008b, 2009b, 2010c). Considering the good performance of the local people through self-governing institutions in the region (Akinola 2009b: 87–89), the people of the Niger

Delta are capable of cooperating with one another to organize people-oriented elections that will produce accountable leaders of their choice. This is because the configuration of relationships that bind the people together in these institutions is cultural value that enables them to sustain cooperation by building and sustaining trusted institutional arrangements (Akinola 2009b: 87–89).

It is this type of self-governing and self-organizing local arrangement that can be integrated into the formal system of government at the local level in the Niger Delta. This, invariably, will lead to effective cooperation and deliberation between public officials and citizens at community level, thereby eliminating gaps between the two groups.

NIGER DELTA POLYCENTRIC HUMAN RESOURCES DEVELOPMENT AND UTILIZATION MODEL

In order to bridge the gaps between leaders and the Niger Delta citizens, on the one hand, and between developers and users of human resources, on the other, NDPHRDUM has been designed (Figure 3.1). However, NDPHRDUM is predicated on the restructuring of the public sphere (Akinola 2010c). The model conceptualizes HRDU as a process of bridging the gaps between developers and users of human resources. It puts in place vital links between developers and users—intellectual relevance, effective planning process and procedure, research incentives, and database and efficient communication systems. This will ensure problem-solving scholarship as well as citizens' enlightenment, which is *sine qua non* to people-centered democracy and development. This is because enlightened citizens pursue development agenda by drawing on their productive potentials and capabilities to achieve freedom and development. The HRDU process has seven stages: (1) theoretical reasoning, (2) empirical analysis with sound "footing" in the community, (3) communiqués drawn from robust conferences, workshops, and seminars, (4) responsive policies leading to innovation (a planned change), (5) pragmatic actions through experimentation and pilot cases, (6) cybernetics/feedback system, and (7) replication.

The first part of the model in Figure 3.1 shows that the three major stakeholders (developers, users, and beneficiaries) operate on parallel lines. Both developers (educational institutions) and users (governments and industries) of human resources are physically located in the community but psychologically outside the community because of Eurocentric tendencies that permeate their operations. This is engendered by colonial mentality syndrome with the consequence of intellectual poverty. Only the community (supposed beneficiaries) is partly inward looking and partly outward looking.

A good example of community's inward-looking practices that utilize local knowledge and skills in the informal sector are found in

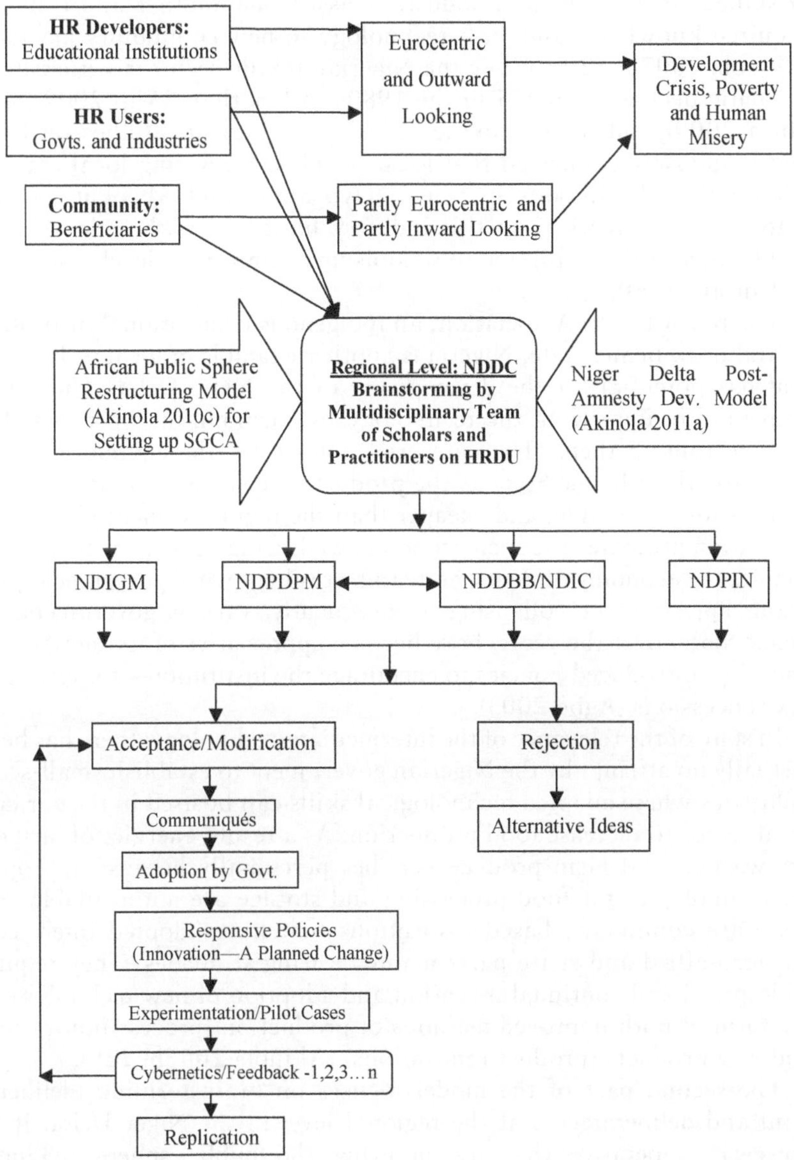

Figure 3.1 Niger Delta Polycentric Human Resources Development and Utilization Model (NDPHRDUM).

Saki, Oke-Ogun area of Oyo State in Nigeria. On the ground, grass-roots innovations include the transformation of inherited indigenous knowledge. People in intermediate technology institutions (notably the fabrication of aluminum cooking utensils), blacksmiths and iron-smelters, iron-benders and welders, inherited their skills. Associations of skilled workers in these industries assist one another and transmit acquired knowledge and craft technology to new community members (Akinola 2007b: 229). While the Nigerian textile sector is witnessing a dramatic decline from 175 in the 1980s to less than 25 in 2009 (Shosanya 2009), indigenous textile industry is resilient. Studies on local textile industry confirmed that local people are reviving local craft to sustain their livelihoods in Iseyin, Oyo State, and Abeokuta, Ogun State, Nigeria. Workers in this industry built houses, bought vehicles and land, sent their children to schools up to university level, and so on (Adediran 2000).

The Burnt Bricks Association, an indigenous occupational institution in Makurdi, Benue State, Nigeria is another example of local technology that has potential for the development of the Niger Delta. The entrepreneurs are improving the technology by surmounting obstacles that are confronting them. The enterprise constitutes the engine of industrial growth in Benue State as the products are stronger, more durable, more readily available, and cheaper than the regular cement block. The institution promotes the socioeconomic well-being of their members and enables the economy of Benue State to be resilient when government programs appear to be collapsing. Consequently, various governments of Benue State, over the years, have become appreciative of its significance and, thus introduced policies to encourage the institution—for example, tax concessions (Agbo 2003).

In spite of the relevance of the intermediate-technology, there has been virtually no attempt by the Nigerian government to establish small-scale industries where adapted technological skills can be used in the agricultural sector to increase food production. As a result, energies of farmers are wasted, and farm produce perishes perennially because appropriate technologies for food processing and storage are not available. Yet there are community-based institutions that have adopted intermediate agro-allied and spare-parts manufacturing strategies. They require widespread and continual invention and adoption of new technology in the form of both improved methods of production (process innovation) and new products (product innovations) (Akinola 2007b: 229).

The second part of the model focuses on brainstorming (deliberation) and deliberateness at the regional level in the Niger Delta. It is, however, imperative that restructuring the public sphere (Akinola 2010c) and Amnesty Program (Akinola 2011a) are factored into the brainstorming exercise. The essence of the brainstorming by a multidisciplinary team of scholars and practitioners on HRDU is to examine the workability of the proposed model. The NDPHRDUM derives inspirations and workability mechanism from three models that focus on intellectual relevance (Akinola 2010b), development planning (Akinola 2008a, 2010a) and information networking (Akinola 2008a: 188–189; 2009b: 94–95).

NIGER DELTA INTELLECTUAL GAP MEASUREMENT MODEL (NDIGMM)

The Niger Delta Intellectual Gap Measurement Model (NDIGMM) is derived from African Intellectual Gap Measurement Model to measure intellectual potentials and relevance of universities and other higher educational institutions with the aim of reforming educational curriculum and making scholarship problem solving and solution seeking. Knowledge-management tools and techniques as well as effective planning and institutional framework that can make knowledge generated by scholars relevant to the needs and aspirations of the peoples of the Niger Delta would need to be employed (Akinola 2010b).

NIGER DELTA POLYCENTRIC DEVELOPMENT PLANNING MODEL (NDPDPM)

The Niger Delta Polycentric Development Planning Model (NDPDPM) is a multidisciplinary and stage-wise poverty reduction process. NDPDPM can function effectively in Niger Delta Innovation Centre (NDIC) where Niger Delta Development Brain-Box (NDDBB) (Fig. 3.1) (Akinola 2008a, 2010a) could be applied and operationalized. Niger Delta Polycentric Development Planning (NDPDP) is the process of conceptualizing, initiating, executing and monitoring people-centered and community oriented development. It deviates from centralized and state-centered development planning that characterizes failed state.

NDPDP, as an adaptation strategy, helps in matching the output/product of scholars and industries with the needs of the grassroots. This bottom-up development strategy has been experimented in Irepodun Local Government area of Osun State, Nigeria (Akinola 2007b, 2008a, 2010a). The Niger Delta Development Brain-Box (NDDBB) / Niger Delta Innovation Center (NDIC), as a control unit for the four development stakeholders (governments, universities, industries and the people) is conceived as an intellectual center where innovations and new ideas generated by scholars are adapted through experimental stations on a pilot scale and then send its output to the community where they will benefit the people. The NDDBB can be operationalized through six steps (Akinola 2008a: 186–187).

Since it has been proved that people of the Niger Delta are capable of cooperating with one another to resolve challenges of daily life (first condition), the kind of incentives that promote cooperation, mutual relationships, and collective action among the people is the second condition that needs to be met before the Niger Delta people can cross the hurdles in their passage to mutually productive ways of life, democratic society and development. The incentives are collegiality, mutual trust, reciprocity and shared understanding. The model suggests that the four key stakeholders in development should operate as colleagues with equal standing in rule making, policy formulation, execution and maintenance of projects. It is also important at this juncture to emphasize that the language that is clearly understood by the people should be used in all interactions and activities in the region.

NIGER DELTA POLYCENTRIC INFORMATION NETWORKING SYSTEM (NDPIN)

The Niger Delta Polycentric Information Networking (NDPIN) can help in strengthening linkages and interactions between individuals and self-governing institutions in the Niger Delta. The beauty of polycentricity is in its multifarious connections and interactive links that all members of a particular community have to receive information, interact, and make contributions to decision making and conflict resolution. The networks once established can be useful at various domains of human interactions in the Niger Delta, from regional to state and then to local/community levels (Akinola 2008a: 188–189; 2009b: 94–95).

RESEARCH INCENTIVES

The first thing that Nigerian governments should do is to increase education fund to the Niger Delta. Apart from the general funding that covers salaries and emolument, and capital projects, task-specific funding in forms of incentives should be directed at scholars who are assigned specific tasks to find solutions to specific problems. Universities in the region should establish linkages with industries for fabrication and production of agricultural machines and equipment (Akinola 2011c). For Nigerian universities to be organic, they have to learn how to be problem solving and solution seeking, constantly operating in synergy with public authorities as well as the people at community level. This will find practical expression through the establishment of a proposed Niger Delta Innovation Centre (NDIC) where Niger Delta Development Brain-Box (NDDBB) could be operationalized.

THE OUTCOME OF BRAINSTORMING

The outcome of the brainstorming (Figure 3.1) will be either to reject the idea or accept it with some modifications. If the idea is rejected, the group should come up with alternative ideas on how to address the crisis in the Niger Delta. On the other hand, if the idea is accepted with some modifications, the next step is to take deliberate action. In this sense, the communiqués that emanate from brainstorming sessions should lead to responsive policies by government and, thus, leading to innovation (a planned change). It is expected that pragmatic actions through experimentation and pilot cases should follow. It is important that cybernetics/feedback system be carried out for modification (if need be) before replication of the projects across the region (Figure 3.1).

The contention of this chapter is that the people-centered creativities and adaptation strategies (Akinola 2008b) should form the basis for reconstructing adaptive education system in the Niger Delta. Citizens' education and enlightenment are imperative for deliberative democracy, and these form part of the second condition that needs to be met before the Niger Delta people can cross the hurdles in their passage to mutually productive ways of life, democratic society and development. This is because enlightened citizens will not sell their votes for a morsel of meal like Essau; nor will they allow themselves to be used by politicians that will later abandon them. It is, therefore, imperative to set up a system of checks and balances through Self-Governing Community Assembly (SGCA) as contained in Akinola (2010c).

SELF-GOVERNING COMMUNITY ASSEMBLY (SGCA), CIVIC ENLIGHTENMENT, AND CITIZENS' RESPONSIBILITIES/TASKS

The SGCA should be patterned after *opuwari and mbogho* but modified to include representatives of governments with their agencies, higher institutions, community institutions, occupational groups, women groups, youth, and so on. Since SGCA is a multitasks assembly, one of its operations will have to do with education and enlightenment of citizens so that public officials and the people operate within shared communities of understanding. This is because people are the human resource for the supply of physical labor, technical and professional skills that are germane to effective and efficient planning and implementation of development policies, programs, projects, and daily activities. Some of the critical questions that citizens need to address at the SGCA include the following:

1. What should governments do in terms of human resources development and utilization, and how should they do it?
2. What can people do alone without government intervention?
3. What can people do in tandem with government?
4. What can people do in conjunction with industries?
5. What can people do with agricultural and other natural resources in their communities?

6. How can people handle these issues in numbers 1 to 5?
7. Since oil is a finite resource, how should people relate with it, especially with regards to future generations?
8. What should be the role of local people in shaping an electoral system before, during and after elections?

Similarly, citizens should be prepared to engage in productive economic activities as they are made to open up through the operations of SGCA. Professionals who are indigenes (but reside outside their communities) need to be encouraged to come home and share their experiences with their people on project management and other issues of life that pertain to governance of community affairs. Both leaders and citizens need new orientations in governance of community affairs, which require some training at the level of SGCA. Leaders should come down to the level of citizens (as proposed in African Electoral Reform and Democratisation—Akinola 2008a: 192–193; 2010d), while citizens need to be prepared for regular dialogues with their leaders to ensure that the problem of corruption is addressed (Aluko 2006: 121).

When citizens are able to realize that they can and should take full responsibilities in shaping and reshaping socioeconomic and techno-political configurations to suit their daily aspirations and yearnings through active and constructive interjections, then shared communities of understanding will be established. This will provide fertile ground for the adoption of successful practices elsewhere such as the Alaska solution (Akinola 2011b).

ENTREPRENEURIAL DEVELOPMENT, TECHNO-ECONOMIC OPPORTUNITIES, AND CITIZENS' EMPOWERMENT

Entrepreneurial development, an offshoot of adaptive education, requires knowledge-based environment with some imperatives:

1. A socioeconomic and institutional regimes that provides incentives for the efficient use of existing knowledge, the creation of new knowledge, the dismantling of obsolete activities, and the start of new and more efficient ones;
2. An educated and entrepreneurial population that can both create and use new knowledge;
3. A dynamic information infrastructure that can facilitate the effective communication, dissemination, and processing of information; and
4. An efficient innovation system comprising science and research centers, universities, think-tanks, specialist professional firms and bodies, and other organizations' that can interact and tap into the growing stock of global knowledge, assimilate and adapt it to local

needs, and use it to create new knowledge and technologies (DBSA 2006:4).

The activities and operations of NDIC will be carried out at the community level where SGCA plays prominent role (Figure 3.2). Local entrepreneurs, craftsmen and artisans with potentials in diverse areas should be recognized by the NDIC and links be established with them. According to Figure 3.2, in order to develop homegrown technology in the Niger Delta, it is imperative to establish some Intermediate Technology Centers (ITCs) across the region, drawing some lessons from Saki Initiatives (Akinola 2007b). In addition, the type of Technology Incubation Centre (TIC) at Calabar and Kano (Eni 2011: 34) should be replicated across the Niger Delta region. ITC/TIC will synergize the efforts of both formal and informal educational institutions. Under this new arrangement, students will find it easy to familiarize themselves with local skills and knowledge that reside with the local people. For example, what lessons can the students learn from local auto repairers, rewires, panel beaters, beekeeper, weavers, blacksmith, and so on? Knowledge adaptation in the engineering sector will produce appropriate technology that can help in manufacturing equipment and implements for farming activities and other micro-enterprises. Similarly, electrical engineers should design communication and other electrical gadgets that can be refined and produced for the needs of the people. At the same time, students on internship programs or student industrial work experience scheme (SIWES) controlled by Industrial Training Fund (ITF) should relate with ITC/TIC where they can benefit from local and endogenous artisans.

These new arrangements require understanding between elite and non-elite in the Niger Delta while individuals are given opportunities to demonstrate their skills. It might be helpful to listen to the words of Vincent Ostrom when he cautions that "science should not be confined to the education of students in schools. It should be a science of association that is studied and applied by all as we assume responsibility for living our lives and learning how to work with others" (Ostrom 2000 271).

If this is done, NDIC will utilize potentials—natural, human, institutional, and entrepreneurial resources—to generate employment; reduce poverty; create wealth; secure food; protect environment; detect, prevent, and resolve conflict; and enhance security of lives and property. Findings and experiences gathered from its pilot projects (after some modifications) will provide good platform for practical application of innovative ideas generated in diverse disciplines in the Niger Delta. Entrepreneurial skills that are derived from NDIC and ITC/TIC are meant to develop students who will be employers of labor rather than job seekers. With such entrepreneurial skills, Niger Delta youths will become problem solvers through various avenues and platforms that will be facilitated by the NDDC and NDDBB/NDIC such as turning waste to wealth, food production, and so on.

A comprehensive list of innovative ideas by Nigerians can be seen in Akinola (2007b). There are sundry cases of talented people in the Niger Delta who due to financial constraints could not pursue their education to higher institutions. What do we do with this group of youth? How do we empower them so that their potentials and skills can be harnessed toward economic development? It is strongly believed that efforts to develop the region should not be concentrated on government alone. Some stakeholders (scholars, patriotic individuals, community leaders, etc.) might need to spearhead the implementation of these strategies on a pilot scale instead of waiting for government and oil companies. This view is reinforced by the fact that there exists on the ground already self-governing arrangement that is democratic and self-regulating (Akinola 2008b, 2009b, 2010c, 2011b).

Under the proposed institutional arrangements (Figure 3.2), interactions and discussions at SGCA will avail the people great opportunities to open new channels of innovative ways of thinking and development. By engaging in some specific economic activities such as food security, employment generation, and local share holding (Akinola 2007b, 2008a: 190–195, 2009b, 2011a), some avenues to develop and enlighten the people will be opened up. Such avenues with examples are l isted here:

1. Establishment of formal and informal creativity centers that are linked to ITC/TIC: These creativity centers will cater for those in school and those not in schools. Such centers should be designed, equipped and saddled with responsibilities of food production and processing of raw materials for local consumption and export (Akinola 2007b, 2008a, 2011c, 2011d: 46–47).
2. Development of craft centers: Upgrade existing craft centers and create new ones by equipping and connecting them to ITC/TIC (Akinola 2007b, 2008a).
3. Training for the Niger Delta youth and local people: The emphasis of training here is on establishing a program for personal development of youth and local people in the Niger Delta. Good examples are: Benjamin Franklin, Richard Branson, and the two Wright brothers who were dropouts but, through an enabling environment and personal creativities, became publishers, authors, inventors, and scientists (Oyedepo 2006: 75, 77).
4. Security of lives and property: The Niger Delta people should follow the example of Saki initiatives in Saki, Oyo State, Nigeria, where local people used adaptation strategy to transform the Oodua Peoples' Congress (OPC) in their community from violent orientation to positive result (Akinola 2009a).

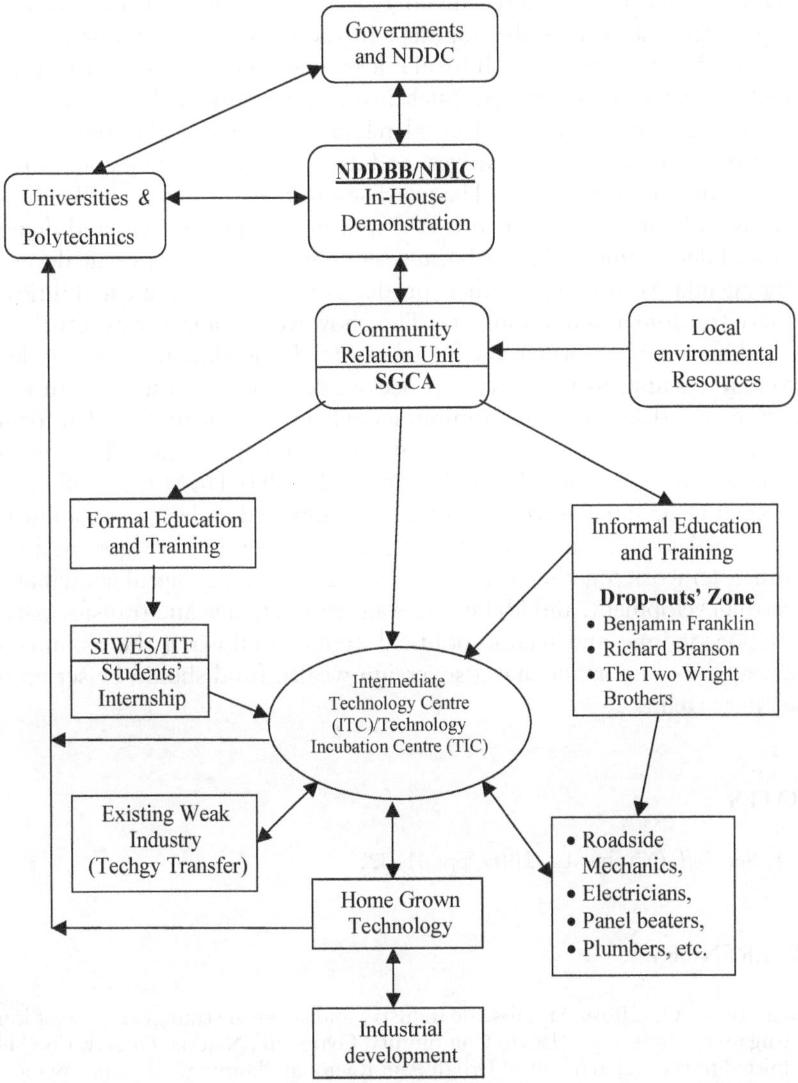

Fig. 3.2 Illustration of the mechanism of NDDBB/NDIC in evolving homegrown technology.

Source: Adapted from Akinola (2008a: 187, 2010a).

CONCLUSION

Since state-centered democracy has not delivered as expected in the Niger Delta, and the people have generally relied on self-organized institutions to solve their problems, it is imperative to use these local and community initiatives and self-governing arrangements as building blocks for the emergence of people-centered democracy in the region. In order to overcome tyranny and underdevelopment in the region, institutions that can provide effective formal and informal learning atmospheres must be established and effectively serviced. Such institutions must make provision for the missing vital links—intellectual relevance, effective planning process and procedure, research incentives, and database and efficient communication and interaction systems. The provision of these essentials will enhance citizens' enlightenment, which is *sine qua non* to people-centered democracy and development. This is because enlightened citizens pursue development agenda by drawing on their productive potentials and capabilities to achieve freedom and development. This, however, requires restructuring of the public sphere to bridge the gaps between leadership and the people. It also requires appropriate HRDU processes designed to ensure institutional mechanisms that focus on community where both formal and informal activities converge for knowledge generation and application. The restructuring will pave way for the application of NDPHRDUM that will enable the Niger Delta citizens to be politically enlightened and socioeconomically empowered so as to (a) know their rights, (b) defend their rights in a civil manner, (c) work together as colleagues and make meaningful contribution toward development, and (d) be active agents of change and transformation in socioeconomic and techno-political arenas. Following the example of Norway, it is important that a sovereign wealth fund should be set up for the Niger Delta.

NOTES

1. See *Tell*, October 12, 2009, pp. 31–32.

REFERENCES

Adediran, G. O. (2000). Small-scale industry and survival strategy: A case of knitting textile industry in Iseyin Community, Oyo State, Nigeria. Dissertation Submitted to the Department of Urban And Regional Planning, Obafemi Awolowo University, Ile-Ife, Nigeria.

Agbo, M. (2003). "Indigenous institutions in Benue State." Ph.D. term paper submitted to the Department of Public Administration, Faculty of Administration, Obafemi Awolowo University, Ile-Ife.

Ake, C. (1996). *Is Africa democratizing?* Lagos: Centre for Advanced Social Sciences (CASS) and Malthouse Press Limited.

Akinola, S. R. (2000). "Balancing the equation of governance at the grassroots." In A. Adedeji and B. Ayo (Eds.), *People-centred democracy in Nigeria? The search for alternative systems of governance at the grassroots*, Ibadan: Heinemann, pp. 171–197.

———. (2004). "Local self-governance as an alternative to predatory local governments in Nigeria," *International Journal of Studies in Humanities*, Vol. 1, No. 3, pp. 47–60.

———. (2005). "Structural transformation and polycentric governance: Complementary strategy towards Nigeria's reform agenda," *Proceedings of the 14th General Assembly of Social Science Academy of Nigeria, Abuja, Nigeria*, pp. 238–250.

———. (2007a). "Coping with infrastructural deprivation through collective action among rural people in Nigeria," *Nordic Journal of African Studies*, Vol. 16, No. 1, pp. 30–46, http://www.njas.helsinki.fi

———. (2007b). "Knowledge generation, political actions and African development: A polycentric approach," *International Journal of African Renaissance Studies*, Vol. 2, No. 2, pp. 217–238.

———. (2008a). "Alternative planning models for development in Africa." In The Development Bank of South Africa (Ed.), *Knowledge to remobilise Africa*, Johannesburg: Knowledge Management Division, pp. 169–202.

———. (2008b). "Coping with social deprivation through self-governing institutions in oil communities of Nigeria," *Africa Today*, Vol. 55, No. 1, pp. 89–107.

———. (2009a). "The failure of central policing and the resilience of community-based security institutions in Nigeria." In A. Amuwo, H. A. S. Pul, and I. O. Adadevoh (Eds.), *Civil society, governance and regional integration in Africa*, Development Policy Management Forum (DPMF), Nairobi, Kenya, pp. 257–274.

———. (2009b). "Polycentric planning and community self-governance as panacea to the Niger Delta crisis," *African Journal of Development*, Vol. 11, No. 2, pp. 79–104.

———. (2010a). *Institutional crisis, resources governance and economic prosperity in Africa: Crossing the great divide through polycentric development planning.* Social Science Research Consultancy Trust, Monograph Series, Vol. 1, No. 2.

———. (2010b). "The nexus between spirituality, intellectualism and development in Africa: A problem-solving perspective." Conference paper for the International Conference on "Politics, Poverty and Prayer: Global African Spiritualities and Social Transformation" scheduled to hold at Africa International University/NEGST, Nairobi, Kenya, July 22–25, 2010.

———. (2010c). "Restructuring the public sphere for social order in the Niger Delta through polycentric planning: What lessons for Africa?" *Journal of African Asian Studies*, Vol. 9, Nos. 1–2, pp. 55–82.

———. (2010d). "The roles of civil society in elections and democratisation in Africa: A polycentric planning perspective," *Zimbabwe Political Science Review*, Vol. 1, No. 1, pp. 6–31.

———. (2011a). "Post-Amnesty Plan, Peace-Building and People-Centred Development in the Niger Delta: A Polycentric Planning and Poverty Reduction Strategy (PPPRS)" *Journal of Sustainable Development and Environmental Protection*, Vol. 1, No. 2, pp. 52–75.

———. (2011b). "Community self-governance as a panacea for environmental and social injustice in the Niger-Delta of Nigeria." In A. Alao and R. Taiwo (Eds.), *Perspectives on African studies: Essays in honour of Toyin Falola*. LINCOM Europa (Lincom Academic Publishers), LINCOM GmbH, Gmunder Str. 35, D-81379 München, GERMANY, pp. 220–248.

———. (2011c). "Institutional analysis, peasant farmers and food security paradigm in Africa: A polycentric planning and poverty reduction perspective," Submitted to *South African Journal of International Affairs*.

———. (2011d) "Restructuring the public sphere for democratic governance and development in Africa: The polycentric planning approach." In A. Bujra (Ed.), *Political culture, governance and the state in Africa: Development policy management forum (DPMF)*, Nairobi, Kenya, pp. 1–61.

Alagoa, E. J. (2005). *A history of the Niger Delta*, Port Harcourt: Onyoma Research Publications.

Aluko, J. O. (2006). *Corruption in the local government system in Nigeria*, Ibadan: BookBuilders.

Bur, A. (1992). "The case for human resources development and utilisation policy for Nigeria." In A. D. Yahaya and C. I. Akinyele (Eds.), *Human resources development and utilisation: Policies and issues*, Administrative Staff College of Nigeria, Topo, Badagry, Lagos. Ibadan: Spectrum Books Ltd., pp. 51–69.

Chole, E. (1995). "Introduction." in E. Chole and J. Ibrahim (Eds.), *Democratization process in Africa: Problems and prospects*, Dakar, Senegal: CODESRIA, pp. 1–4.

DBSA. (2006). *Knowledge to address Africa development challenges*. Edited Proceedings of the Inaugural Knowledge Management Africa (KMA), organized by the Development Bank of South Africa (DBSA) held in Johannesburg, South Africa, March 2005.

Eleazu, U. O. (1977). *Federalism and Nation building: The Nigerian experience, 1954–1964*, Ilfracombe, Stockwell.

Eni, H. (2011). "Stifling small business." *Tell*, No. 24, June 20, pp. 34–37.

Fawole, W. A. (2005). "Voting without choosing: Interrogating the crisis of 'electoral democracy' in Nigeria." in T. Lumumba-Kasongo (Ed.), *Liberal democracy and its critics in Africa*, Pretoria: University of South Africa Press, pp. 149–171.

Federal Government of Nigeria (FGN). (2008). *Sustainable development in the Niger Delta: The master plan road map 2020 (1960–2007)*. A Consolidation of Democracy.

Gellar, S. (2005). *Democracy in Senegal: Tocquevillian analytics in Africa*, New York and Basingstoke: Palgrave Macmillan.

Hamilton, A., Jay, J., and Madison, J. (1961). *The federalist*, ed. Edward M. Earle. New York: Modern Library. [1788]

Harbison, F. H. (1973). "Objective machinery and methodology of manpower planning." In T. M. Yusufu (Ed.), *Manpower problems and economic development in Nigeria*, Oxford: Oxford University Press, p. 63.

Hartslief, O. (2005). *The South African presidential participation programme (Presidential Imbizo): Engaging communities for a better life*. An unpublished paper, http://www.engagingcommunities2005.org/abstracts/S14-hartslief-o.html (accessed May 25, 2009)

Ibaba, S. I. (2008). "State intervention in the Niger Delta: A critical appraisal of the ideology of development commission." Unedited conference proceedings, International Conference on "The Nigerian State, Oil Industry and the Niger Delta," held in Yenagoa, Bayelsa State, Nigeria, March 11–13, 2008. Port-Harcourt: Harey Publications Company, pp. 530–558.

Mbat, D. O. (1992). "Issues and problems facing national agencies and institutions responsible for human resources development." In A. D. Yahaya and C. I. Akinyele (Eds.), *Human resources development and utilisation: Policies and issues*, Administrative Staff College of Nigeria, Topo, Badagry, Lagos. Ibadan: Spectrum Books Ltd., pp. 154–167.

Ndiomu, C. B. (1992). "Human resources development and utilisation in the Nigerian Armed Forces." In A. D. Yahaya and C. I. Akinyele (Eds.), *Human resources development and utilisation: Policies and issues*, Administrative Staff College of Nigeria, Topo, Badagry, Lagos. Ibadan: Spectrum Books Ltd., pp. 34–50.

Ochayi, C. (2009). "Niger Delta ministry's budget hijacked—inserted their constituency projects." *Vanguard*, November 30, http://allafrica.com/stories/200911300110.html (accessed December 1, 2009)

Ogoh-Mesarawon, J. (2009). "Unemployment in Nigeria: World Bank study shows high unemployment in Nigeria." *Voice of America*, http://www.voanews.com/english/Africa/2009-03-12-voa20.cfm (accessed March 13, 2009)

Okaba, B. O. (2005). *Petroleum industry and the paradox of rural poverty in the Niger Delta*, Benin City, Nigeria: Ethiope Publishing Corporation.

Osagie Sylvester O., Ibaba, I. S., and Watts M. J. (2009). "Reflections on the Nigerian state, oil industry and the Niger Delta," *African Journal of Development*, Vol. 11, No. 2, pp. 9–26.

Ostrom, V. (1994). *The meaning of American Federalism: Constituting a self-governing society.* San Francisco: Institute for Contemporary Studies.

Ostrom, V. (2000). *The Meaning of democracy and the vulnerability of democracies: A response to Tocqueville's challenge*, Ann Arbor: The University of Michigan Press.

Ostrom, V. (2006). "Citizen-sovereigns: The source of contestability, the rule of law, and the conduct of public entrepreneurship," *Political Science and Politics*, Vol. 39, No. 1, pp. 13–17.

Oyedepo, D. O. (2006). *Success systems*, Canaanland, Ota: Dominion Publishing House.

Philips, S. (2008). "Corruption and the Niger Delta crisis." Unedited conference proceedings, International Conference on "The Nigerian State, Oil Industry and the Niger Delta," held in Yenagoa, Bayelsa State, Nigeria, March 11–13, 2008. Port-Harcourt: Harey Publications Company, pp. 891–901.

Sawyer, A. (2005). *Beyond plunder: Toward democratic governance in Liberia*, Boulder, CO: Lynne Rienner, Inc.

Shosanya, M, (2009). "Why textile sector collapsed." *Daily Trust*, July 27, http://allafrica.com/stories/200907270892.html (accessed July 28, 2009)

United Nations Development Programme (UNDP). (2006). *Human development report 2006*, http://www.nationmaster.com/graph/eco_hum_dev_ind-economy-human-development-index (accessed June 25, 2009)

Watts, M. J. (2009). "The rule of oil: Petro-politics and the anatomy of an insurgency," *African Journal of Development*, Vol. 11, No. 2, pp. 27–56.

Wunsch, J. S. and Olowu, D. (1995). *The failure of the centralised state: Institutions and self-governance in Africa*, Boulder, CO: Westview Press.

4 Assessing the Human Development Efforts of the Niger Delta Development Commission

Augustine Okhobo Dokpesi and Michael Irabor Ibiezugbe

INTRODUCTION

Human elements are the greatest levers of societal transformation as they provide two-edged effects for the society. While on the one hand, it can lead to societal transformation, on the other, it can lead to the underdevelopment of the society. However, this is a function of the manner in which it is harnessed and utilized. A society that places emphasis on human capital development creates the conditions for sustainable development. In human development, the individuals are the focus of development effort. It looks beyond economic growth and enlarges the social, economic, cultural, and political choices of individuals. This entails that the focal individuals' needs are captured in the process of sustainable development (UNDP 2006).

Human development requirements, on a general note, include "increased skill and capacity, greater freedom, creativity, self-discipline, responsibility, and material well-being" (Rodney 1990: 9). The acquisition of knowledge and skill, and the opportunity to express this, creates the condition for sustainable livelihood. This is the bedrock of human development. Sustainable livelihood provides a holistic approach to development in the sense that it leads to self-reliance. It also creates the conditions for environmental sustainability as well as intensifies the process of infrastructure development. The foundation of social and economic transformation of any society, and the creation of a decent standard of living for its people, is tied to how well individuals have been economically empowered to be able to contribute to the process of societal transformation.

Therefore, if the mandate of the Niger Delta Development Commission (NDDC) is to facilitate rapid and sustainable development of the Niger Delta region into one that is economically regenerative and prosperous, socially stable, and politically peaceful, empowering affected groups should be a key part of its priority. This is necessary because of the worsening poverty level of households—a condition aggravated by the high incidence of unemployment.

CONDITIONS OF HUMAN CAPITAL UNDERDEVELOPMENT IN THE NIGER DELTA REGION OF NIGERIA

The continuous destruction of the environment by oil-related activities, indifferent attitudes of government to strict enforcement of environmental laws, policy failure, and neglect have created conditions of underdevelopment and poverty, especially in the oil-bearing communities in the region. According to the United Nation Development Programme (UNDP 2005), whereas the human development index of other oil-producing states like Indonesia and Saudi Arabia are put at 0.70 and 0.78, respectively, the oil-bearing local areas of Bakassi, Burutu, Brass, and Bonny have human development index of 0.392, 0.433, 0.458, and 0.471, respectively.

More so, maternal and infant mortality rates in this region are high (UNDP 2006). The region has the least percentage of people with access to health care provision. While it has 44.6 percent access, the South-West, North-West, and North-East have 72.3 percent, 60.1 percent, 54.2 percent, and 47.3 percent, respectively (Eneh 2011). This implies that there are inadequate health-care systems to cater for the health needs of the growing population. Furthermore, the region has low local economic activities, since the advent of oil, as the traditional occupations—namely, fishing and farming—have been undermined by oil economy. Even with such declining fortune, these traditional occupations still account for about 44 percent of employment in the region (UNDP 2006).

In the areas of infrastructure and social services, the Niger Delta region has poor records. According to Watts (2005: 67), in Ogoni land,

> Few Ogoni households have electricity, there is one doctor per 100,000 people, child mortality rates are the highest in the nation, unemployment is 85 percent, 80 percent of the population is illiterate and close to half of Ogoni youths have left the region in search of work. Life expectancy is barely 50 years, substantially below the national average.

Generally, statistical reports from the region show that only 45.5 percent of the people in the region have access to safe drinking water, compared to the 50.2 percent and 48.5 percent in North-West and the North-Central regions of Nigeria, respectively (Eneh 2011). Although there is growing enthusiasm to send children to school, educational facilities are inadequate. The NDES (2000) report shows that there is 1 primary school to 3,700 people, serving 2 settlements, while the ratio of secondary school is 1 to 14,679 people, representing 1 school to every 7 settlements. This is buttressed further by the 2009 statistical reports on access to education. Whereas the 70.3 percent access to primary school education is relatively high in the Delta region, the 47.1 percent access to secondary school education is relatively low (Eneh 2011).

Studies have shown that the poverty level of households in the region is worsened by the rising situation of unemployed dependants. For instance, 5.8 percent of households have one or two unemployed members; 15.3 percent have three or four unemployed members; while 72.5 percent of households have five to more members who are unemployed (DPC 2001). In other words, approximately 94 percent of the Niger Delta households have one or more unemployed dependant.

Urban unemployment for the year 2000 in Akwa-Ibom, Bayelsa, Delta, and Rivers States were 12.6 percent, 13.0 percent, 16.2 percent, and 18.2 percent, respectively—against a 7.2 percent national average. Rural unemployment rates in these states were 18.3 percent, 5.5 percent, 8.8 percent, and 19.3 percent, respectively—against a national average of 3.7 percent in the same year (UNDP 2006). Even in 2009, the level of absolute poverty in the region was higher than what obtained in other geopolitical zones of Nigeria. Household poverty in the Niger Delta region, in its absolute terms, was put at 18.5 percent, as against 12.5 percent in the North-East, 9.5 percent in the North-West, and 7.2 percent in the North-Central regions of Nigeria (Eneh 2011).

While the emergent oil industry undermined agriculture through disorientation, its attendant environmental challenges on fishing and farming activities generated discouragement for the people of this region. Consequently, "the Niger Delta people observed helplessly as their youths lost interests in traditional occupations and got no substitute" (Anikpo 1993: 48). Many youths, even those still residing in rural areas, are more interested in rent-seeking from the oil companies in the form of stand-by money or oil bunkering, hostage-taking, and sabotage (UNDP 2006: 298).

GOVERNMENT DEVELOPMENT INITIATIVES IN THE NIGER DELTA REGION

Following the development challenges in this region, the then Colonial Government instituted the Willinck Commission in 1957 (Omene 2003; Ugochukwu 2003; Okaba 2005; Watts 2005). Having acknowledged the fears and conditions of these ethnic minorities, the commission recommended that a special attention should be paid to the region because of its peculiar development problems. Consequently, through an act of parliament of 1961, the federal government established the Niger Delta Development Board (NDDB). Its mandate was to redress injustice and provide human and infrastructure development in the region. However because of politics, "this ideal and mission of a special development effort for the Niger Delta merely transformed into sordid mockery" (Okaba 2005: 72). Constitutionally, "It was practically impossible for the Board to engage in project execution since the enabling instrument limited its assignment to advisory capacity in planning and designing of projects" (Etekpe 2007: 46). More so, the major ethnic groups opposed the establishment of "a special Development Commission' for the ethnic minorities of this region (Okaba 2005: 72). This was perhaps informed by the low revenue from oil at this period.

What resulted from this ethnic politics was the proliferation of Basin Development Authorities across the country. Consequently, the NDDB was renamed as the Niger Delta River Basin and Rural Development Authority (NDBRA) in 1976. However, by mid-1982, it became clear that the NDBRA could not meet the aspirations of its target groups. Its failure was due to the fact that those appointed to run it were more interested in personal gains rather than addressing the problems of development of the target groups (UNDP 2006: 30). This ruined the region, particularly as some of the negative consequences of oil production had manifested in the lives of the people (Nyong and Oladipo 2003: 113).

In the early 1980s, the federal government established the Presidential Task Force (PTF), to utilize the 1.5 percent allocation from the Federation Account for development process, following rising tension in the region. However, "there was no indication that money was released out of the 1.5 percent allocation to the Task Force" (Nyong and Oladipo 2003: 113) before the Shagari regime was sacked. For the better part of the 1980s, successive military regimes in Nigeria did not show much concern about development agenda for this region, in spite of its increasing economic relevance.

However, in 1992, the Oil Minerals Producing Areas Development Commission (OMPADEC) was instituted by the government. Again its mandate was the rehabilitation and development of the region (Ikporukpo 2000: 25). In terms of implementation, not only were projects imposed on supposedly beneficiary communities, but "all projects associated with OMPADEC were abandoned half way" (Onyeonoru and Aborishade 2001: 54). Besides project abandonment, Ikporukpo (2000) observed that corruption and ineptitude of OMPADEC officials, and deceit and corruption in the Nigerian leadership that set it up, were responsible for its failure. In a related development, Sada (2001: 6) asserted that OMPADEC failed because of lack of funds. Between 1992 and 1996, the commission got less than 12 percent of the statutory funds approved for it from the 3 percent derivation fund. OMPADEC got only ₦10.9 billion out of about ₦86.4 billion allocated to it between 1992 and 1996 (Akanimo, 2004: A8). However, the four-man panel constituted by the government to investigate the commission submitted that there were indeed incidence of inflated contracts, misappropriation of funds, problem of accountability, and awarding of dubious contracts. Instructively, these problems were a function of a defective policy structure. The United Nations Fact-Finding Mission to Nigeria within this period noted that Decree 23 of 1992, which established OMPADEC, created room for inefficiency and mismanagement because of defective management structure. It did not create room for checks and balances because members of the board were both policy makers and implementers (Onyeonoru and Aborishade 2001).

One of the fundamental issues that have arisen over the years in the development of this region has been who takes responsibility for development initiatives in the region. In the 1980s, for instance, while the federal government accused Bendel and Rivers States for neglecting the oil-bearing communities, through the diversion of money to develop the non-oil-bearing communities within the states; the indigenes of these states and their various governments accused the federal government for employing their oil wealth in the development of non-oil-producing states (Omoweh 2001). This exploitation by forces within and outside the region has left the oil-bearing communities in poverty. This buck-passing tactic perhaps explains why previous attempts at developing the region have often experienced deliberate starvation of funds from the central government.

Another fundamental problem has been the lack of opportunity on the part of the recipient communities to participate in their process of development. Policy instruments put in place by successive governments in Nigeria to address the problems of the region had often failed to meet their objectives partly because they were imposed without being collectively owned by the Delta people (CDD 2000). The consistent failure of these development instruments has heightened the tension and crises in this region.

COMMUNITY RESENTMENT TO NEGLECT AND POLICY FAILURE

The underdevelopment of this region has, partly, been attributed to its difficult physical terrain. Ironically, the oil companies create worker settlements, equipped with modern facilities such as electricity, water, housing, telecommunication, and recreation, within installations in an attempt to create comfort for their employees. This sharply contrasts the dearth and decay witnessed in host communities that adjoin these oil companies' facilities. This unequal access to modern infrastructure and social services within the same environment, coupled with neglect on the part of government, has attracted resentment from members of these oil-bearing communities (Chokor 2005). What resulted from this situation was the emergence and proliferation of ethnic militias. Even the death of Ken Saro-Wiwa could not abate this crisis of social relations. Instead, it fanned the embers of militancy. In a bid to taking their collective destiny in their hands, community youths resorted to acts of vandalism, seizure of oil installations, hostage-taking, and kidnapping in order to draw attention to their plight.

THEORETICAL ANCHORAGE: RELATIVE DEPRIVATION THEORY

For Runciman (1972), relative deprivation is based on the axiom that "people's attitudes, aspirations and grievances largely depend upon the frame of reference within which they are conceived." Following the oil boom in the

1970s, the Nigerian government shifted emphasis from the farmlands to the oil fields with excessive exploitation of the Niger Delta resource endowment. While it created excessive wealth for the national economy, the oil-bearing communities were left with socioeconomic and ecological crises. Their aspirations for a better treatment, on the part of government, became high. However, because previous government policies failed to realize these expectations, inhabitants expressed their discontentment, as signs of their perceived neglect and deprivation. In other words, because these problems have festered over time, they have led to the formation of negative attitudes and perceptions.

He further argued that "a man who has been led to expect, shall we say, promotion in his job will be more aggrieved if he fails to achieve it, than a man whose ambitions have not been similarly heightened." As far as oil related environmental problems are concerned, the oil-bearing communities feel more deprived and neglected than any other community in Nigeria. Over the years, the intervention programs of the federal government had led them to expect that their conditions of underdevelopment would soon be a thing of the past. However, the failure of these programs "left this region battered, desolated and ruined" (Odje 2000: 63). This has heightened their feeling of severe deprivation. According to him, "The magnitude of a relative deprivation is the extent of the difference between the desired situation and that of the person desiring it (as he sees it)." This underscores that relative deprivation is a function of the perception of the affected human actor/actors. The degree to which this feeling is expressed is based on the degree to which actors see their situation(s) as far away from their expectation(s). In terms of oil production, from the initial 12,000 barrels per day (bpd) in 1959 to the over 2 billion bpd at present, the expectations of the Niger Delta people are high while the conditions of underdevelopment subsist.

The substance of his argument rests on the assumption that if people have been led to see as a possible goal the relative prosperity of some more fortunate community with which they can directly compare themselves, then they will remain discontented with their lot until they have succeeded in catching up. Over the years, the people of the oil-bearing communities had felt severely deprived and neglected as they compared their situation to those of other groups within Nigeria and beyond. The 1960 constitution of Nigeria provided for 50 percent deprivation formula that enabled the regions to have access to a reasonable amount of money for development projects. However, following the 1970s oil boom, emphasis on revenue allocation formula was shifted from deprivation to equity. This did not favor the Niger Delta people in spite of the contribution of oil to the federation account.

Thus, "when expectations are rising faster than the likelihood of their fulfillment violent changes may result" (Runciman 1972). While their expectations are rising, their conviction that government can solve their problems diminishes. In an attempt therefore to take their collective destiny into their hands a lot of ethnic militias emerged.

Following the continuous environmental deterioration in the midst of consistent policy failure, and the continuous agitations of community groups, the NDDC came on board as a new intervention paradigm, in the year 2000. Its mandate, like its predecessors, is to provide even and sustainable human and infrastructure development. Therefore in order to examine its implementation attitudes, a study was designed to provide a systematic assessment of the human development efforts of the NDDC by the beneficiary communities.

METHODOLOGY

Survey design was employed to collect both the quantitative and qualitative data. Afiesere, Koko, Olomoro, and Oporoza communities in Delta State were chosen to reflect ethnic representation. One thousand two hundred (1,200) respondents were systematically selected, using union registers, among vulnerable groups such as farmers, fishermen, traders, and youths. Separate sets of questionnaires were administered to members of these groups in order to be able to gather both general and specific information from them. Qualitative data were collected from twenty opinion leaders across these communities, while a representative each from the Nigerian Petroleum Development Company and Chevron oil firm, and an NDDC official, were interviewed using the in-depth interview method for detailed information.

NDDC HUMAN DEVELOPMENT EFFORTS IN SELECTED OIL-BEARING COMMUNITIES IN THE NIGER DELTA REGION

In order to determine the expectations of vulnerable groups from the NDDC, respondents were asked to list their groups' specific needs as presented in Table 4.1.

From Table 4.1, the three prominent needs of the farmers across these target communities are subsidization of farming inputs such as fertilizers, tools, seedlings, and so on; loan facility; and good road network and transportation. The most common needs of the fishermen, across these communities are similar to that of the farmers. This is because they are both exposed to similar environmental hazard. In the case of the market women, the most listed needs are loan facility, market stalls, and good road network and transportation. Job creation, infrastructure development, skill acquisition, and scholarship and education were listed, respectively, as the prominent needs of youths. The fundamental remedy to the vandalistic attitudes of youths in particular and youth restiveness in general, in the region rests on the provision of means of livelihoods, as suggested by majority of the youth respondents. This implies that the solution to the problem lies in the problem itself. Put differently, job creation was listed the highest number of times, by community youths, across target communities as

Table 4.1 Percentage Distribution of Groups Expectations from the NDDC

Expectations	*Groups*							
	Farmers		*Fishermen*		*Market Women*		*Youths*	
	Freq.	*%*	*Freq.*	*%*	*Freq.*	*%*	*Freq.*	*%*
Loans	54	26	76	36.0	122	50.6	32	6
Subsidized Facilities	93	44.7	102	48.3	-	-	-	-
Training/ Skill Acquisition	11	5.3	6	2.8	-	-	84	16
Market Stores	4	1.9	-	-	73	30.3	-	-
Storage Facilities	12	5.8	-	-	-	-	-	-
Environmental Protection	5	2.4	27	12.8	-	-	-	-
Road Network/Transport	23	11.1	-	-	43	17.8	10	1.9
Factory	1	0.4	-	-	-	-	-	-
Extension Services	5	2.4	-	-	-	-	-	-
Price Reduction	-	-	-	-	1	0.4	-	-
Clearing of Refuse	-	-	-	-	2	10.8	-	-
Job Creation	-	-	-	-	-	-	217	40
Scholarship/Education	-	-	-	-	-	-	68	13
Infrastructure	-	-	-	-	-	-	119	22.3
Recreational facilities	-	-	-	-	-	-	1	0.2
Sensitization	-	-	-	-	-	-	3	0.6
Total	**208**	**100**	**211**	**100**	**241**	**100**	**534**	**100**

Source: 2008 fieldwork by the authors

a panacea for sustainable peace which is likely to reduce the vandalizing of oil installations and the general restiveness in the region. For instance, in Afiesere, Koko, Olomoro, and Oporoza communities, job creation was listed the highest number of times, that is, 73 (55.7 percent), 66 (44 percent), 44 (65.7 percent), and 65 (73 percent) times, respectively. The establishment of industry had the second highest listing in Afiesere community, that is, 12 (9.2 percent), skill acquisition 24 (16 percent), and government improvement of the local economy 8 (11.9 percent) had the second highest listing in Koko and Olomoro communities, respectively. Similar views were expressed by a representative of the oil firms in one of the IDIs conducted in the course of the study. For him, "Restiveness is due to uneven development and unemployment; plus Government insensitivity to the plight of the ordinary men."

In terms of the solution, he provided a comprehensive summary of all the remedies suggested by others. According to him,

> Empower the people by creating employment, building factories/industries; and developing the grassroots. Government should provide infrastructure and an enabling environment for all to develop and excel individually.

All these point to the need for the economic empowerment of affected individuals as a condition for the attainment of sustainable livelihoods. In terms of the efforts the NDDC has made in providing for these needs, the proceeding table provides the relevant data.

Table 4.2 shows that the majority of the respondents, across groups, asserted that the NDDC has not done anything yet to impact positively on their groups' needs. The assessment visitations to these communities revealed that no effort has been made yet by the NDDC in the area of economic empowerment for vulnerable groups within these selected communities. This explains why a majority of the farmers, fishermen, traders and youth—representing 85.9 percent, 72.2 percent, 70.5 percent, and 72.4

Table 4.2 Percentage Distribution of Responses on Whether or Not the NDDC Has Met Groups Expectations

Communities	*Groups*	*Responses*								*Total*
		Yes		*No*		*Don't Know*		*No Response*		
		Fr	*%*	*Fr*	*%*	*Fr*	*%*	*Fr*	*%*	
Afiesere	Farmer	1	2	43	86	4	8	2	4	50 (100%)
	Fishermen	1	7.7	12	92.3	-	-	-	-	13 (100%)
	Mkt. Women	5	8.8	38	66.7	-	-	14	24.5	57 (100%)
	Youths	5	5	81	81	9	9	5	5	100 (100%)
Koko	Farmers	2	5.7	31	88.6	2	5.7	-	-	35 (100%)
	Fishermen	3	8.3	31	86.1	1	2.8	1	2.8	36 (100%)
	Mkt. Women	3	4.8	54	85.7	-	-	6	9.5	63 (100%)
	Youths	9	9.9	69	75.8	7	7.7	6	6.6	91 (100%)
Olomoro	Farmers	4	8	32	64	14	28	-	-	50 (100%)
	Fishermen	9	18	16	32	24	48	1	2	50 (100%)
	Mkt. Women	15	21.4	30	42.9	-	-	25	35.7	70 (100%)
	Youths	13	21.7	24	40	22	36.7	1	1.7	60 (100%)
Oporoza	Fishermen	2	2.2	76	86.4	5	5.7	5	5.7	88 (100%)
	Mkt. Women	-	-	48	94.1	3	5.9	-	-	51 (100%)
	Youths	6	8.3	60	83.3	-	-	6	8.3	72 (100%)
	Total	78	8.8	645	72.8	91	10.3	72	8.1	886 (100%)

Source: 2008 fieldwork by the authors.

percent, respectively—reported that the NDDC had not yet met their economic empowerment needs. Although the NDDC in Delta State claimed to have generally provided computer literacy programs for 1,450 youths, 134 buses on hire purchase basis for mass transit, and skills-acquisition centers under which 1,006 youths are being given vocational skills training in various trades between 2000 and 2005 (NDDC 2005), the manner in which these schemes are handled does not create the opportunity for human development, especially as it relates to the affected groups. Politics and favoritism equally come to play in the determination of who benefits from such gestures. According to one of the opinion leaders in the IDIs, for instance, "Some of the beneficiaries of the Mass Transit Buses are already established transporters; or politicians and their friends and relatives thereby depriving the real target (unemployed people) access to this opportunity."

Furthermore, to examine the NDDC efforts in meeting the specific infrastructural needs of communities, respondents were asked to state their community expectations from the NDDC. Findings are presented in Table 4.3.

Table 4.3 Responses on Community Expectations from the NDDC.

	Communities							
	Afiesere		*Koko*		*Olomoro*		*Oporoza*	
	Freq.	%	*Freq.*	%	*Freq.*	%	*Freq.*	%
Industry and Job Creation	70	15.9	44	11.0	58	15.8	11	3.1
Loan	09	2.1	21	5.3	08	2.2	-	-
Water	76	17.3	27	6.8	59	16.1	73	21.0
Health Care	54	12.3	19	4.8	36	9.8	79	22.7
Roads/Bridges	105	24.0	116	29.0	68	18.5	61	17.6
Schools	45	10.3	45	11.3	32	8.7	35	10.1
Market Stalls	23	5.2	27	6.8	43	11.7	-	-
Skill Acquisition Center	11	2.5	49	12.3	04	1.1	-	-
Roads/Water Transport	-	-	19	4.8	-	-	-	-
Electricity	39	8.8	-	-	58	15.8	71	20.4
Town Hall	03	0.7	-	-	-	-	-	-
Scholarship	03	0.7	05	1.2	-	-	-	-
Drainage	01	0.2	-	-	-	-	-	-
Jetty	-	-	15	3.8	-	-	11	3.1
Shoreline Embankment	-	-	05	1.2	-	-	0.2	0.6
Housing Unit	-	-	07	1.7	-	-	0.5	1.4
Stop Spillage	-	-	-	-	0.1	0.3	-	-
Total	439	100	399	100	367	100	348	100

Source: 2008 fieldwork by the authors.

Each respondent was allowed to list as many of his community needs as he could remember. One of the expectations, which cut across the four target communities, is the issue of roads/bridges. The essence is to open up the area for efficient socioeconomic activities. This is so because "it is generally understood that poor accessibility in the Niger Delta Region has been responsible for the high cost of providing adequate social services and infrastructure to communities in the region" (NDDC 2006: 8). Worst hit by this phenomenon are the riverine areas, most of which are cut away from the urban areas. For instance, the journey from Warri to Oporoza, which is about 60 kilometers, attracts ₦1,500 on a speedboat, whereas the journey from Benin City to Warri, by road, which is over 100 kilometers, attracts less than ₦1,000. The implications of these are glaring for the poor villagers. The necessity for access roads/bridges is high since it will make the cost of development lower. This was buttressed by the views of an opinion leader in the course of the interviews:

> In the year 2000, I happened to be in the team that saw Mr. President in Abuja. We presented a paper to him. The easiest way to bring development that will stop all this restiveness is through road network. We've told the government, we've written a series of papers that government should take a bold step to link the riverine areas to the urban. If they want to construct a bridge from Warri to Oporoza, it is not going to be as long as the third mainland bridge. If they do that naturally, ordinary people will go and develop this land. Strangers will also go there. Maybe tourist industry will now take off here. The problem we have is lack of infrastructure . . . Without road it is difficult to actually develop the riverine areas.

In addition, given the importance of pipe-borne water to human health and industry, it is not surprising that respondents listed it as one of the most pressing needs of the communities. Considering the negative effect of petroleum on the aquatic resources of oil-bearing communities, the necessity for clean water can never be overemphasized. Furthermore, industry and job creation are central to the sustainable development of this region in that economic empowerment ensures human development, environmental friendly attitude as well as infrastructural sustainability.

In summary, series of challenges confront the NDDC's efforts in meeting identified needs. Implementation is problematic because there is an uneven distribution of infrastructural facilities among the oil-bearing communities in the study area. Afiesere community, for instance, with thirty-four oil wells, and Oporoza community with ten oil-wells, do not have any presence of the NDDC projects. Besides the selected communities, the NDDC has actually executed projects in several other communities in Delta State. Between 2001 and 2005, for instance, sixty-two building projects, four canalization projects, twenty-two electrification projects, eighteen jetty projects, twenty-one road projects, and forty-two water projects were completed by the Commission across communities (NDDC 2005). However, non-oil-bearing communities like Kiagbodo, Ovu, Agbarha-Otor, Emuhu, Oko, Owa-Oyibo, Adonta, Idumujeunor, Imbiri, Agbor, and others had all benefitted from the NDDC, whereas oil-bearing communities like Atiesere, Oporoza, and many others have not yet benefitted. Further, even where the commission supplied communities with infrastructure, they were contrary to their preferred needs. This is illustrated by the case of Koko community where only 3.8 percent of the respondents identified with the jetty supplied by the NDDC, whereas 29.0 percent preferred bridge construction.

It was only in Olomoro community that infrastructure was supplied in abundance. The reason(s) for this could be adduced from the comments and counter-comments of the NDDC official and community leaders. According to the NDDC official,

> We consider the oil-producing communities before allocating projects. If there are oil-producing communities that have not benefitted, it could be because they have not made request. It is only a group that comes to tell you what they want that you can do something for.

However, this assertion is at variance with comments of the opinion leaders from Oporoza and Afiesere communities. When asked if they had made any request to the Commission, an opinion leader said, "Yes! This Oporoza Federated community has once written a letter to the NDDC, telling them about our needs. But up till now nothing has been done." According to another opinion leader from Afiesere community, "Ah! We have written and written, we have gone there, not once, not twice. They have not done anything about it." This, perhaps, shows that project implementation is bedeviled by the politics and favoritism expressed by those in charge of NDDC policy implementation. Communities that do not have the political muscles to fight for the implementation of their desired expectations are not favored by project execution. Apart from creating lopsided development, this implementation attitude equally generates a feeling of social deprivation. This is expressed by one of the opinion leaders thus:

> If you go to the NDDC they always tell us that things are shared according to the ratio of production. Ughelli town has NDDC projects yet does not produce oil. We are the highest oil-producing community in the area, yet we have nothing to show from the NDDC.

Furthermore, arising from the effects of environmental degradation on traditional livelihoods and lack of access to capital, the subsidy of occupational inputs was listed most by farmers (44.7 percent) and fishermen (48.3 percent). Loan facility was listed second by farmers (26.0 percent) and fishermen (36.0 percent), as a preferred need, yet the commission has not demonstrated any commitment to granting loans. According to the NDDC officials, "We do not give loans because repayment is difficult." Consequently, unemployment remained rife among the youths, and joblessness, rated 61.12 percent, largely accounts for the resort to pipeline vandalism. Because of lack of consultation and fairness in project allocation to oil-bearing communities, the NDDC has not yet been able to confront the critical issues of development in this region.

Another critical challenge associated with government's effort at providing development assistance to oil-bearing communities in this region, through its development instrument, is the starvation of statutory funds. This is where the major problem with the NDDC implementation drive lies, just like the previous agencies before it. The sources of funds of NDDC include 15 percent contribution from the federal government, 3 percent from the oil and gas industries, 50 percent ecological fund allocation to the Niger Delta member states, and proceeds from other NDDC assets. The federal government, which set up the NDDC, only released a total sum of ₦136.234 billion, out of the total budgeted amount of ₦436 billion between 2001 and 2009 (Etekpe 2009: 32). What the commission gets in any fiscal year does not correspond with the contribution of oil to the federation account. In 2005, for instance, while the commission's budget was put at ₦63.5 billion, it got only ₦17 billion from the statutory transfer, whereas ₦2.902 trillion was the collectible revenues from oil. In 2006, whereas the commission had a budget estimate of ₦57.418 billion, it was allocated only ₦26 billion, despite the ₦2.8 trillion contributions from the petroleum industry. Even the 2007 budget followed the preceding budgetary allocations. Within this period, oil contributed ₦3.2 trillion, that is, 84 percent of the total budget. However, in the statutory transfer, only ₦24 billion was set aside for the Commission as against the ₦26 billion it got in 2006 budget (see Obasanjo 2005, 2006, 2007). This explains why many critics see the funding of the commission as deceptive, poor, epileptic, unrealistic, and unjust. The NDDC spokesperson in Delta State, during the interview session for this study, acknowledged this problem thus: "Funds are not available. If every stakeholder does his own NDDC will work well."

Furthermore, impeding the effectiveness of government development efforts in the region is the problem of misappropriation of funds. Ojameruaye (2003) asserted that "some critics have raised the issues of transparency, accountability, corruption, political interference etc. They cite the replacement (in 2002) of the first Managing Director / Chief Executive Officer of the Commission as a case in point." There is a point in making such an assertion, especially when you judiciously examine the cost of projects awarded by the NDDC. In Delta State, for instance, NDDC findings show that the cost of awarding a six classroom block is between ₦11 million to ₦13 million. While in Koko community, it was awarded for ₦11 million because it is an upland community, Oporoza's six classroom project was awarded for ₦ 13 million because it is a riverine community. The "Nigerian factor" of over-inflation of contract by government officials for the purpose of collecting 10 percent gratification in the award of contract is clearly seen here. While lesser amount is used in the actual execution of the project, what is left to be shared among the individuals connected with the project far exceeds the amount actually used. If well managed and well accounted for, the same amount for which a particular project is awarded can be used in the execution of at least two similar projects. For instance, in Koko community, ₦11 million can be used to build at least four 6-classroom blocks, instead of one. Premo (2005: 20) observed that the NDDC is only a conduit pipe through which officials unsparingly defraud the government of huge sums of petro-dollars with little or no efforts made to achieve the set objectives of ameliorating the suffering of the people of Niger Delta. The simple fact that these corrupt policy implementers are mainly replaced, instead of being prosecuted, underscores the institutionalization of corruption in Nigeria. This is premised on the fact that those assigned to replace them often continue the cycle of corrupt practices.

One of the serious human development challenges, which the study identified outside the NDDC, is the problem of sub-cultural value orientation. The oil economy, by undermining traditional livelihoods has created a culture of monetization and dependence. The insistence on the performance of traditional rites by some community leaders, for instance is to some extent a function of the desire of some community leaders to reap some financial benefits from a proposed community project. According to the NDDC spokesperson in Delta State during one of the interview sessions for this study,

> Some communities insist you carry out some traditional rites before carrying out a project. One community, for instance, insisted a contractor must carry out a traditional rite at night before a road project could be executed in the community. We had to stop that project.

This leads us to a related attitudinal problem, that is, the culture of "sharing the cake for personal use." The NDDC spokesperson in Delta State in the same interview said,

> Initially jobs (contracts) were given to non-indigenes. The indigenes complained bitterly about this. Even now those jobs are given to the indigenes; they will refuse to mobilize to site. They think the NDDC is a cow to be milked. They feel that they should have a piece of the action.

This attitude is influenced by the common perception of some indigenes regarding how much oil revenues contribute to the national purse. That some community youths and leaders often ask for settlement before any community project is embarked upon, as claimed by the NDDC, is not surprising in that community members have been exposed to a monetized culture by virtue of the social experiences they have had over the years. In order to remain in operation, some oil companies, for instance, have resorted to divide and rule methods, through the award of bogus contracts and bribe to some selected community leaders. More so, community members live in an environment in which the oil workers display their affluence as it manifests in their life styles. The tendency to meet up with these affluent lifestyles generates monetized culture in which almost every relation revolves around money. The political economy of kidnapping is understood within this context.

HUMAN CAPITAL DEVELOPMENT AGENDA FOR THE NIGER DELTA REGION

For any intervention instrument to be able to make any quick and meaningful impact within the shortest possible time, in the area of human capital development, it must involve three quick intervention schemes that will operate simultaneously. The essence is to solve the problems of monetized culture informed by joblessness and poverty and infrastructural decay. These schemes include: traditional occupations revival scheme; youth empowerment scheme and Infrastructure development scheme.

Traditional Occupations Revival Scheme

This scheme addresses the problems of traditional occupations, especially fishing and farming, in the region. The essence is to win back public confidence in the traditional livelihoods that sustained the people in pre-oil era. It is therefore necessary that any attempt at providing human development must take cognizance of vulnerable groups if it must produce meaningful results. This revival scheme requires a participatory approach that will begin with the involvement of the vulnerable groups in the identification of their felt needs and in the formulation of program designed to address such needs in ways that also engages the hitherto unemployed in gainful employment. Socio-psychologically, this is likely to make individuals and communities feel a sense of recognition and belonging. What will result from this is a commitment to addressing community-based restiveness induced by frustration and deprivation, which will in turn ensure quick and desired impact. This is crucial, in the sense that in spite of the deteriorating conditions of these occupations many inhabitants still participate in fishing and farming, perhaps because of the inability of the people to adequately fit into the emergent oil economy. To achieve this, vulnerable groups should be encouraged to form co-operative society, where it does not exist, in order to have a platform on which bailout funds could be disbursed to members so as to redeem these ailing occupations.

However, the success or failure is ultimately tied to the nature of environmental attitude. Therefore, there must be urgent and strict enforcement of existing environmental laws, if the expected gains of consultations and economic empowerment of vulnerable groups must lead to sustainable human development. Economic empowerment solves the problem of environmental sabotage due to poverty and frustration. However, so long as environmental standards are not maintained by the oil establishments, the agricultural and aquatic resources of this region will continue to be exposed to degradation and contamination. When this happens, no development strategy will be able to sustain any effort at improving the quality of lives of the target population.

Youth Empowerment Scheme

This should normally begin with the massive injection of funds into education and skill acquisition. Education develops the human mind and actualizes human and societal potentials. To understand education as a veritable tool for change is to understand its relevance to the human society. It helps in the process of human capital development in that it generates knowledge and skills for sustainable livelihoods. It influences human attitudes, perceptions, interactions, and systems of values. A society that neglects and underplays the relevance of education hardly develops.

More so, to help those who may not wish to further their education, the provision of skill acquisition should be encouraged in order to give them a sustainable means of livelihood. However, this must be followed by access to capital and the establishment of non-oil industries. These are necessary because sustainable livelihood rests not only on knowledge and skills acquired, but also on how well the opportunities are created for the individuals to earn a living. The establishment of non-oil-manufacturing industries will reduce joblessness and its associated problems of terrorism and restiveness. It will also reduce the over dependence on oil; this helps in the process of human and community development.

The relevance of youth economic empowerment can never be overemphasized because of its social and economic effects on the individuals, the family and the entire community. It provides empowerment for the individuals in several ramifications as well as enhancing status and self-esteem. It also provides support for the family. This is more so in African societies in which extended family system is still a common phenomenon. Gainful employment for a youth member of a family means (to some extent), insurance at old age for the parents, as well as a means of support for siblings to be able to realize their potentials as well. This has some positive implications for the reduction of youth restiveness and vandalization of oil installations.

The economic empowerment of youths should be taken very seriously. To this end, skill acquisition must be supported with access to capital to ensure sustainable livelihoods and reduce negative youth culture. In its efforts to grant micro-credit loans, the NDDC should work closely with cooperative societies and other organizations where they exist and encourage the establishment of such bodies in communities where they do not exist in order to have a structure through which micro-financial support could be channeled. This would help to develop individual potentials, provide jobs for restive youths, encourage those with technical skills to be productively engaged by providing subsidiary services to the industries, and assist in the process of community development through wealth creation, which in turn encourages infrastructure development as well as the improvement of the local economy. In the same vein, there should be massive disbursement of funds for the establishment of non-oil-manufacturing industries in the oil-bearing communities. The essence is to reduce the over dependence on oil.

Infrastructure Development Scheme

If the gains recorded in the first two schemes must be meaningful there is need to also focus on the provision of infrastructure. This is imperative because human development is very much tied to the state of infrastructure. An environment provides the opportunity for individuals to develop when the state of its infrastructure is relatively conducive for individuals to enjoy the basic standards of living. This is indeed a test of the extent of human capital development. An individual may be economically empowered, but if basic amenities like electricity, water, transportation, good roads, and health centers, and so on are not provided, it may be difficult for him to live a worthy life or achieve a sustainable livelihood. This explains why the youths are interested in these factors as their general expectations.

CONCLUDING REMARKS

Human development and attitudinal change in the Niger Delta region require a holistic approach to tackle the issue of economic empowerment and infrastructure development. Attitudinal change must involve some economic empowering measures (i.e., training, skill acquisition and job creation) to keep the idle youths busy. It must equally take cognizance of factors that are creating a feeling of deprivation that generates destructive tendencies. Infrastructure development is expected to provide the enabling environment for improvement in quality of life. This creates conditions for investment opportunities and the creation of job opportunities. The provision of economic empowerment is expected to positively affect environmental protection, leading to a reduction in pipeline vandalism and other antisocial tendencies by the youths.

For any intervention agency to be able to achieve sustainable human development in this region it should design a pyramid-shape approach to implementation. In this approach the specific needs of communities and groups are considered first before the general needs; and the oil-bearing communities are considered first before the non-oil bearing communities through a participatory approach.

Each of these schemes above should have both internal and external monitoring, evaluation and audit committees that would ensure that implementation corresponds with policy. They should equally ensure that appropriate projects are awarded at reasonable cost and executed according to specification.

REFERENCES

Akanimo, S. (2004). "Omuike: A community tired of oil spills." *Daily Independent*, Thursday, May 13, A7.

Anikpo, M. (1993). "Sociology of oil areas: Imperatives for development." In M. A. C. Odu (Ed.), *Toward enduring symbiosis in oil producing areas: The rating of oil properties*, Lagos: Princes Communication, pp. 29–46.

Centre for Democracy and Development (CDD). (2000). Report on the Consultative Conference on the Niger-Delta held in Benin City, March 29–April 1, Lagos: CDD.

Chokor, B. A. (2005). "Humanistic approach to environmental assessment with case study from the Niger Delta." In A. G. Onokerhoraye and G. E. D. Omuta (Eds.), *Perspectives on development*, Benin City: Centre for Population and Environmental Development, pp. 350–377.

Development Policy Centre (DPC). (2001). *Socio-economic mapping of the Niger Delta: A report prepared for Shell Petroleum Development Company*. Ibadan: DPC.

Eneh, O. C. (2011). "Crippling poverty amidst corporate social actions: A critique of peripheral corporate community involvement in the Niger Delta Region of Nigeria," *Asian Journal of Rural Development*, Vol. 1, No. 1, p. 1–20.

Etekpe, A. (2007). *Politics of resource allocation and control in Nigeria: The Niger Delta experience*, Port Harcourt: Harey Publications.

Etekpe, A. (2009). "The Niger Delta Development Commission and peace-building in the Niger Delta," *National Development Review*, No. 1, April.

Ikporukpo, C. O. (2000). "Petroleum, fiscal federalism and environmental justice in Nigeria." A Paper Presented at the IFRA Seminar Series, University of Ibadan, Nigeria.

Niger Delta Development Commission (NDDC). (2005). NDDC in Delta State June 2001–September 2005: Corporate Affairs Department, Port Harcourt: NDDC.

———. (2006). *Niger Delta regional development master plan*, Port Harcourt: NDDC.

Niger Delta Environment Survey (NDES). (2000). *Niger Delta development priorities and action, Phase II report*, Vol. 2.

Nyong, E. E. and Oladipo, E. (Eds.). (2003). *Creating an enabling environment for the sustainable development of the Niger Delta Region*, Lagos: Green Edge Resources.

Obasanjo, O. (2005). Budget speech presented at the Joint Session of the National Assembly. Abuja, Tuesday, December 6.

Obasanjo, O. (2006). Budget speech presented at the Joint Session of the National Assembly. Abuja, Wednesday, December 11.
Obasanjo, O. (2007). Budget speech presented at the Joint Session of the National Assembly. Abuja Wednesday, October 11.
Odje, A. M. (2000). "The Niger Delta and expropriatory laws: Time for resources control," *The Guardian*, October 17.
Ojameruaye, E. (2003). "Deploying oil wealth to reduce poverty in the Niger Delta Region of Nigeria: Lessons from the Chadian model." http://www.nigerdeltacongress.com/darticles/deploy-o-wealth-o-reduce-p.htm
Okaba, B. O. (2005). *Petroleum industry and the paradox of rural poverty in the Niger Delta*, Benin City: Ethiope.
Omene, G. E. (2001). "Overview of NDDC Interim Action Plan." Pre-International Conference Workshop Organized by the NDDC in Port Harcourt, Monday, October 22.
Omene, G. E. (2003). "Interim Action Plan and framework for the development of the Niger Delta Region." In E. E. Nyong and E. Oladiopo (Eds.), *Creating an enabling environment for the sustainable development of the Niger Delta Region*, Lagos: Green edge Resources.
Omoweh, D. A. (2001). *Shell, the state and underdevelopment of the Niger Delta of Nigeria: A study in environmental degradation*, Trenton, NJ: AWP.
Onyeonoru, I. and Aborishade, F. (2001). "The remote causes of the oil workers' 1994 strike in Nigeria," *Africa Development*, Vol. 26, Nos. 3–4, pp. 43–65.
Premo, D. (2005). "Niger Delta sitting on a time bomb!" *National Standard* (Port Harcourt), Vol. 1, No. 9, March.
Rodney, W. (1990). *How Europe underdeveloped Africa*, London: Bogie-L Ouverture Publications.
Runciman, W. G. (1972). *Relative deprivation and social justice*. London: Routledge & Kegan Paul.
Sada, P. (2001). "Why OMPADEC failed," *Nigerian Tribune*, August 6.
Ugochukwu, O. (2003). "Delivering on our mandate." In A. Usen (Ed.) *The journey so far: June 2001–November 2003*, Port Harcourt: Corporate Affairs Department, NDDC.
United Nation Development Programme (UNDP). 2005. *Human Development Report 2005: International cooperation at a crossroads: Aid, trade and security in an unequal world*. New York: Oxford University Press.
———. (2006). *Niger Delta Human Development Report*. Abuja: UNDP.
Watts, M. (2005). "Resource course? Governmentality, oil and power in the Niger Delta, Nigeria." In P. L. Pillon (Ed.), *The geopolitics of resource wars: Resource dependence, governance and violence*, London: Frank Cass, pp. 50–80.

5 Entrepreneurship Development and Poverty Reduction in the Niger Delta

Gordon M. Bubou and Nimiye A. Egai

INTRODUCTION

Entrepreneurship is a burgeoning global phenomenon (Higher Colleges of Technology 2010), and the entrepreneur has been described as the single most important player in the modern economy (Lazear 2002). Equally, entrepreneurship is frequently pinpointed as the most effective way for those without much experience or political clout to engage in their country's economic development (CIPE 2010). Consequently, within the last decades, entrepreneurship has ascended to the centre stage in the public policy arena of most countries (Reynolds et al. 1999). On the other hand, public expenditure and poverty issues have occupied frontline position in Nigeria's quest for development (Akpan 2007). Unfortunately, the language of "poverty reduction" itself has done more harm than good, for it has laid emphasis on short-term interventions such as relief efforts at the expense of long-term competence-building programs that raise economic productivity and expand opportunities for wider access to productive assets (Juma 2007).

The current situation of the people of Niger Delta Region (NDR) of Nigeria can be likened to that of the American Blacks during their struggles to free themselves from poverty after the abolishment of the slave trade. Then, the theme of the struggle for Black consciousness was centered on redistributing wealth through welfare programs. But such measures were at best palliative and therefore could not completely address the issues of poverty and unemployment among the Blacks. This situation was blamed on a missing ingredient needed for economic development which was entrepreneurship (Green and Pryde 1990). Similarly, the people of the NDR can be said to be coming out of economic subjugation imposed upon them by the majority ethnic groups of the Nigerian Federation. Notably, after nearly six decades of the exploration, discovery, and exploitation of petroleum resources as well as the appropriation of the revenue derived from petroleum, which is principally found in the NDR, the people of the region have little or no access to that wealth up till today. This chapter therefore highlights the role entrepreneurship can play in socioeconomic development of a region like the Niger Delta. It starts with a review of the regions followed by some conceptual clarifications and discussion of entrepreneurial frameworks. Next, it examines the status and challenges of the Niger Delta entrepreneur. Finally, the chapter proposes a sustainable poverty-reduction strategy (SPRS) for socioeconomic development of the region and ends with recommendations for policy makers.

THE NIGER DELTA REGION

Prospecting for petroleum resources in Nigeria is recorded to have begun as far back as 1908 when the German Bitumen Corporation started exploration activities in the Araromi area of present Ondo State of Nigeria. Shell D'Arcy, one of the prominent oil exploration companies in the NDR over the years, commenced its own exploration activities in the country in 1937. However, it was not until 1956 that petroleum was first discovered in commercial quantities in Nigeria at Oloibiri in Bayelsa State of Nigeria (Chima et al. 2002). The core of the petroleum industry in Nigeria is in the Niger Delta, including Akwa Ibom, Bayelsa, Cross River, Delta, Edo and Rivers States, the South-South geopolitical zone, and the neighboring oil-producing states of Ondo, Abia, and Imo. The industry covers about 112,110 square kilometers (12 percent of Nigeria's total surface area) and goes well into the offshore of the country's territorial waters in the Gulf of Guinea (Niger Delta Development Commission 2006). Petroleum resources are said to have accounted for approximately 80 percent of government revenues, 90 percent of foreign exchange earnings, and 24 percent of Gross Domestic Product (GDP) (Shell International 2006; SPDC 2006). Going by the 2006 census figures, the NDR accounts for about 25 percent of the total population of Nigeria with an estimated population of about 36.6 million people, and over 60 percent of this population is rural. An overview of rural areas in the region reveals the absence of large-scale industries, difficult terrain, absence of good roads, absence of portable water, and lack of power supply, which is an indication of poverty.

Contrary to standard demographic data where females usually outnumber males, there are many idle young males than their female counterparts in the NDR according to the 2006 census figures. This can be seen as a clear situation of "youth bulge," and findings from other countries with youth bulges have a markedly higher risk of having conflicts (Urdal 2005), as violent conflicts mostly involve young people. Again, unresolved social issues between the local community and the petroleum industry plague the NDR (Bubou et al. 2009). Expectedly, the NDR was ripe for the militancy to thrive as, according to Sharma and Ruud (2003), global environmental change or the social problems of desperate poverty can stimulate antisocial behavior and terrorism. Evidently, the NDR witnessed an unprecedented level of violent agitations from armed militant youths who were demanding for a fair share of the region's rich petroleum resources. Such violent agitations took the form of wanton destruction of life and property, mostly targeted at the oil industry. This lasted for a couple of years until the government of President Yar'Adua introduced the Amnesty Program in 2009.

The NDDC (2006) aptly observed that developmental challenges of the region include "widespread poverty; severe death of infrastructure and amenities in the rural areas; being the world's third largest wetland with fragile ecosystems; high unemployment, rural-urban migration, urban decay; and environmental degradation and pollution." This is clearly poverty in the mist of plenty in the Niger Delta region. Besides petroleum resources, access to the Atlantic Ocean, both brackish and fresh water bodies provided rich breeding grounds for fishes, while the rich alluvial plains provided fertile farm lands for the people of the NDR. Thus, the predominant occupations of the people of the region over the ages have always been in the primary extractive industries characterized by farming and fishing activities, mostly on a subsistence scale.

The discovery of petroleum in the region changed this scenario completely. The people rather turned their attentions to the potential benefits petroleum could bring to them. Regrettably, overdependence on the promised wealth of petroleum resulted in high unemployment levels, and unacceptably high levels of poverty and social inequality—both in terms of assets and income which have now become the most persistent problems. Against this background, this chapter discusses the position of Niger Delta entrepreneurs. But first we shall provide operational definitions or clarifications of the following selected terms and concepts used in this chapter.

CONCEPTUAL CLARIFICATIONS

Entrepreneur

There appears to be confusion as to a specific definition of the term "entrepreneur" (Gray 2002). But the term entrepreneur is said to have originated in French economics in the seventeenth and eighteenth centuries and suggests that the entrepreneur shifts economic resources out of an area of lower productivity and into an area of higher productivity and greater yield (Dees 1998; Mort et al. 2003); it was first coined by the French economist Jean Baptiste Say around 1800 (Drucker 2004; Dees 1998). However, Joseph Schumpeter is seen to have given greater prominence to the term entrepreneur in the twentieth century as noted by researchers (Dees 1998; Nijkamp 2000).

Entrepreneurship

The concept of entrepreneurship is defined as the process of using private initiative to transform a business concept into a new venture or to grow and diversify an existing venture or enterprise with high growth potential. Entrepreneurs identify an innovation to seize an opportunity, mobilize money and management skills, and take calculated risks to open markets for new products, processes, and services (UNDP 2003). Entrepreneurship is self-employment through business ownership that includes significant elements of risk, control, and reward. It is the process through which entrepreneurs create and grow enterprises to provide new services or products, or add value to services or products (Emery et al., 2006). For purposes of clarity for this study, entrepreneurship also includes the simplest form of self-employment, which is petty trading that is common in Nigeria.

Small- and Medium-sized Entrepreneurs

According to Okowa (2008), what defines small- and medium-sized entrepreneurs (SMEs) depends on the authority proffering the definition and the basis for the definition. Okowa goes on to illustrate this definition by classification with the aid of a chart (see Table 5.1).

Table 5.1 Definitions/Classifications of SMEs

Employment-Based Classification			
Organisation	*Micro-Enterprise*	*Small Enterprise*	*Medium Enterprise*
IFC	< 10	10–50	50–100
CBN	-	< 50	< 100
NASSI	-	< 40	-
Asset-Based (Excluding Real Estate) Classification			
IFC	-	< USD 2.5M	< =N=150.0M
CBN	-	< =N=40.0M	-
NASSI	-	< =N=50.0M	< =N=200.0M
FMI	-	< =N=10.0M	-
NERFUND			

CBN: Central Bank of Nigeria
FMI: Federal Ministry of Industry
IFC: International Finance Corporation
NASSI: National Association of Small-Scale Industries
NERFUND: National Economic Reconstruction Fund

Source: Okowa (2008 as found in Nigeria Business Info website).

Entrepreneurship Development

According to the UNDP (1999),

> Entrepreneurship development (ED) refers to the process of enhancing entrepreneurial skills and knowledge through structured training and institution-building programs; it aims to enlarge the base of entrepreneurs in order to hasten the pace at which new ventures are created. This accelerates employment generation and economic development. Entrepreneurship development focuses on the individual who wishes to start or expand a business.

Why entrepreneurship development? Because attempts at addressing the challenges of underdevelopment in the NDR have failed. One approach to overcoming the persistent problems of unemployment, poverty, and social inequality is to create an abundance of "grassroots" support for enterprising behavior (Beaulieu and Barefield 2006). Consequently, most countries have placed significant emphasis on entrepreneurship as an impetus for growth and economic prosperity and the foundation for transformation into innovative societies. For instance, SMEs account for about half of all U.S. jobs and nearly 70 percent of all new jobs created in the United States (CNN 2009), and in India, small-scale industries are said to have provided employment for nearly 20 million persons, accounted for 40 percent of the value added in the manufacturing sector, 34 percent of total national exports, and 7 percent of GDP during 2002–03 (Kamesam 2003).

Like the case of the American Blacks, all the efforts geared towards development of the region will remain palliative and cosmetic unless the main ingredient needed for their socioeconomic development, which is entrepreneurship development, is deliberately embedded in such packages. Therefore, investments in massive infrastructure in the NDR to bring about sustainable development must be complemented with entrepreneurship development. This is imperative as the spirit of entrepreneurship continues to shape and define our small world, fostering hope and opportunity. Developing economies are especially seeing small businesses as potential instruments for the alleviation of poverty and regional development (Harvie 2008).

Natural Resource Abundance and Entrepreneurship

This study was not an attempt to further research on the resource curse hypothesis debate. There have been empirical studies that linked levels of economic activities, growth, and the failure of natural-resource-abundant nations to catapult their economies to international limelight. Phenomenon researchers refer to this as resource curse hypothesis (Papyrakis and

Gerlagh 2004, 2007; Sachs and Warner 2001; Alayli 2005; Esanov et al. 2003). According to Papyrakis and Gerlagh (2007), there is indeed no obvious reason why natural resources should frustrate economic growth per se but that plentiful fertile land, rich fishing banks, diamond mines, and vast oil and gas reserves should drive economic growth rather than restrain it. Unfortunately, resource riches such as the ones mentioned have became associated with a slowdown in economic growth across the world during the last three decades. Natural resources may crowd out entrepreneurial activity and innovation by encouraging potential innovators to work in the resource sector (through a wage premium) and it thus directs funds away from the research and development sector into the primary sector (Sachs and Warner 2001). On the other end of the spectrum, since the state sector tends to dominate, citizens have less incentive to form a healthy "civil society," an independent middle-class fails to develop, and technocratic and entrepreneurial talent remains captive of state largesse in terms of employment and advancement opportunities and technocratic entrepreneurial talent is stifled (Alayi 2005).

History is replete with countries that have prospered no matter what the initial natural resource base of those countries was, only because they evolved social conditions favorable to their long-term social, environmental, and economic survival (Sirolli 2008). For instance, countries such as Japan, South Korea, and Switzerland have experienced remarkably high rates of economic growth despite their lack of natural resources; on the contrary, countries, such as Mexico, Nigeria, Venezuela, and the so-called oil states in the Gulf became examples of development failures despite their extensive reserves of natural wealth (Papyrakis and Gerlagh 2007). With the discovery and subsequent exploitation of petroleum resources in the NDR, the petroleum industry should have promoted the establishment of prestigious educational institutions to generate and disseminate knowledge across other industrial sectors like what happened in the United States with mining. But that did not happen in Nigeria.

One model posits that motivation and skills drive entrepreneurial behavior and that availability of resources has a moderating effect on both entrepreneurial behavior and achievement (Sriram et al. 2007). In some cases, resources may create a false sense of security and weaken the perceived need for investments, skilled labor force, and growth-promoting strategies (Papyrakis and Gerlagh 2007). In effect, activities that could have led to innovations or entrepreneurship are crowded out (Papyrakis and Gerlagh 2004, 2007; Sachs and Warner 2001). Evidence shows that natural resources can drive civil conflict as parties struggle to gain control over resource revenues and in some cases fueling internal grievances that cause conflict and civil war as excluded groups have an incentive to try and wrest control, while dominant groups have an incentive to take a disproportionate share of benefits (Alayli 2005). These seem to be the exact scenarios that are replicated in the NDR.

Culture and Entrepreneurship

Over two decades ago, Shapero and Sokol (1982) implicated sociocultural factors as potential inducers of entrepreneurship. Culture bears a profound impact on all facets of entrepreneurship in societies (Licht and Siegel 2006) and is one of the most important framework conditions that can inhibit or enhance the level of entrepreneurial activity in a country (Stephan et al. 2003). In the Nigerian context, most of the country's ethnic groups place so much emphasis on family relationship, which ultimately results in nepotism and limited initiative (Nwanchukwu 2003). Such close extended family support system is evident in all parts of the NDR, especially amongst the Ijaws. However, crosscultural comparisons of entrepreneurs and nonentrepreneurs indicate that entrepreneurs are similar in their characteristics and in their cultural values regardless of their national affiliation (McGrath et al. 1992). This means that culture should not be an impediment to entrepreneurship development in the NDR.

Entrepreneurship and Socioeconomic Development

The contributions of entrepreneurship to socioeconomic development have been well documented. The Global Entrepreneurship Monitor (GEM) hypothesized that the entrepreneurship conditions in a country will stimulate every entrepreneurial activity, which in turn stimulates national economic growth as the entrepreneur is an important engine for the growth of the economy (Khanduja et al. 2008; Blanchflower 2007; Sriram and Mersha 2006). Thus, entrepreneurism is a viable option for spurring local economic development in downtimes (Beaulieu and Barefield 2006). Hence, governments all over the world have gone to great lengths to transfer practices from more entrepreneurial nations to their own institutional environments (Parhankangas and Lindholm-Dahlstrand 2006). Small businesses have been recognized as key to economic regeneration. They also provide a substantial share of employment and growth prospects (Oviatt and McDougall 2005). Moreover, entrepreneurial ventures are the economic backbone even among economically developed countries, accounting for over 95 percent of the businesses and almost 70 percent of employment in OECD countries (Sriram and Mersha 2006).

Barriers to Entrepreneurship in Developing Countries

Empirical research seems to suggest that one of the greatest possible impediments to entrepreneurship is lack of capital (Blanchflower and Oswald 1998; Sriram and Mersha 2006; Nwanchukwu 2003). Another commonly recognized constraint to entrepreneurship in the developing world is the external environment, which not only does not actively encourage business start-ups but also frequently acts as a hurdle (Sriram and Mersha 2006).

The business environment include—physical, economic, sociocultural, political, and legal (Ubom 2003). Education (or lack thereof) in most developing countries can possibly inhibit entrepreneurship (Singh 1990) as it is in Nigeria when early entrepreneurs lacked prestige compared to their more educated counterparts (Nwachukwu 2003).

Others factors limiting entrepreneurship are lack of (a) market-augmenting governments, that is, a government that is not strong enough to enforce private contracts and protect property rights or one that is too strong and tramples them can both create insurmountable barriers to entrepreneurship; and (b) a legal property system that discourages people from unleashing their innovative potential because of lack of marketable titles and the institutional infrastructure that enables fluid trade in those titles (Sarasvathy 2004).

ENTREPRENEURSHIP DEVELOPMENT FRAMEWORKS

As economic turbulence across the world has led to new business strategies to meet sustainability challenges (Khanduja et al. 2008), a reassessment of the role of SMEs in sustainable development of nations became imminent. Such reassessment of the role of SMEs in the sustainable development of a sound and growing economy commenced in United Kingdom as far back as 1971 as documented in the "Bolton Report" (Gray 2002). Thus, countries all over the world have adopted various frameworks for entrepreneurship development within their domains. Analysis of some of these models are carried out here to encourage learning and benefiting from the experience of other countries in entrepreneurship development (Kropp and Zollin 2005).

Enterprise Facilitation®

The Enterprise Facilitation® model was founded by the Sirolli Foundation. According to Sirolli (2008), Enterprise Facilitation focuses on the "people" side of economic development through a grassroots approach to local development, and teaching civic leaders how to establish a programme that transforms individual passion and community activism into rewarding sustainable local enterprises. Enterprise Facilitation® works on the principle that economic development walks on two legs: The first leg is concerned with the creation of infrastructure for development, while the second has to deal with building the capacity of people to utilize such infrastructures (Sirolli 2008).

Rural Business Hubs (RBHs)

The Rural Business Hubs (RBHs) concept was adopted in India (Khanduja et al. 2008). This framework involves rural friendly ventures, including using rural resources, employing rural work force, preferring rural sites, and utilizing rural expertise. Further, the framework, among other things, ensure equitable development of the country, optimal utilization of natural endowments, social awakening of rural masses, optimal utilization of academic talent and expertise, downsizing of technology to rural people, and improvement in national industrial productivity.

Business Incubators

National Business Incubation Association (NBIA, 2008) defines a business incubator (BI) as an economic development tool designed to accelerate the growth and success of entrepreneurial companies through an array of business support resources and services by nurturing the development of entrepreneurial companies, helping them survive and grow during the start-up period, when they are most vulnerable. BIs provide not only basic services such as inexpensive space, but also provide various services to incubatees in early stages to effectively connect abilities, technology, capital, and the know-how of entrepreneurs, thereby promoting development of start-ups and transfer of technologies (Kim and Ames 2006).

The BI concept is now very popular in the industrialized world and in developing countries with particular focus to specifically identified key sectors (industries) of need like agribusiness, technology business, services, manufacturing, bio-resources, and so on. Nigeria has equally embraced BI concept with emphasis on the technology-business incubator. However, the impact of such incubators on the creation of new technology-based businesses is yet to be seen.

Enterprise in Action EiA®

Enterprise in Action® was developed in Botswana by Mellalieu (2006), who determined that the University of Botswana required significant investment in human capacity building to devise and expand learning environments appropriate for mass-scale development and deployment of innovators, entrepreneurs, and entrepreneur enablers throughout the country.

Scottish Enterprise Program

There are similarities between the Enterprise in Action® model and the Scottish Enterprise Program, as both models use educational approach to creating entrepreneurial societies. However, the Scottish Enterprise Program tended to impact entrepreneurship on a national basis through education from elementary school through university, plus public relations and financing initiatives. And it collects tracking data on the effects of those efforts (Vesper 1998).

Venture Capital

In light of the fact that the greatest barrier to starting or growing an SME is capital and with the level of poverty in the NDR, it is worth mentioning the Venture Capital (VC) model. VC model is not really an entrepreneurial development model, but rather a financial support platform for SMEs, mostly start-up firms. Venture capitalists bring money to the table and also help groom start-ups into multinational institutions. They do this by selecting business proposals that have strong potentials for survival and then buy into the investment as equity partners. They also help nurture the business. Introducing VC markets to developing countries may help ensure the sustainability of the companies in which they invest. A study by Gaspar (2009) confirmed that venture capital and business incubation contribute positively to the creation and survival of new enterprises.

RESEARCH METHODOLOGY AND DATA ANALYSIS

This study, conducted in September 2009, was limited to Yenagoa City in Bayelsa State. Yenagoa is considered the core of the NDR and has witnessed large influx of persons from the other Niger Delta states and elsewhere. The instrument of the study was a questionnaire that contained structured questions. It was first piloted before the main survey. A purposive sample size of 220 was selected. Consequently, 220 questionnaires were administered with 10 questionnaires given out to each of the about twenty-two identified entrepreneurial activities (see Table 5.2); 154 questionnaires were retrieved, which accounted for about 70 percent of total administered questionnaires.

The questionnaire comprised of two broad sections. Section 1 contained personal information such as age, sex, state of origin, marital status, level of education, and so on. Section 2 was designed to establish the reasons for choosing self-employment and barriers to start-up or growth. The main objectives were to

1. identify problems related to entrepreneurship in the NDR;
2. ascertain the level of entrepreneurialism in the NDR; and
3. propose a model for entrepreneurship development in the region.

Results

Forty-six respondents, accounting for about 30 percent of total returned questionnaires, were female entrepreneurs. Fifty-one respondents fell within the 18–30 years age bracket, 70 respondents fell within the 31–40 age bracket, while the remaining 33 were more than 41 years of age. Out of the 154 respondents that returned their questionnaires, 21 indicated that they have first degree, while 85 passed or attempted the School Certificate

Examination (GCE/SSCE), and 28 passed or at least attended primary school. The remaining 20 persons admitted not to have attended any formal schooling. This distribution of entrepreneurs in the study areas with respect to age, sex, and level of education can be seen as relatively fair considering the statistics provided above.

Table 5.2 indicates that, of the thirty-six artisans that returned their questionnaires, only eleven of them were from the NDR, 47.4 percent of them engaged in petty trading, and a paltry 27.8 percent were involved in

Table 5.2 Distribution of Entrepreneurial Activities and Proportion of Niger Delta People Engaged in the Activities

Entrepreneurship Category	*Total Number of Questionnaires Returned*	*Number of Respondents That Are Niger Deltans*	*Proportion of Niger Deltans*
Artisans	36	11	30.6%
-Welders	6	2	
-Carpenters	10	4	
-Auto mechanics	10	2	
-Electrical/electronic equipment repairers	10	3	
Manufacturing	20	11	55.0%
-Water packaging	3	2	
-Food and beverages	5	3	
-Block making	4	2	
-Upholstery making	8	4	
Wholesale/retail	18	5	27.8%
-Supermarket owners	8	2	
-Major shops	10	3	
Hospitality	24	17	70.8%
-Hoteliers	10	7	
-Restaurant operators	9	7	
-Bar owners	5	3	
Services	37	20	54.1%
-Transporters	7	3	
-Tailoring services	10	4	
-Cybercafé	4	2	
-Telecoms operator	1	1	
-Call-center business	10	7	
-Business support services	5	3	
Petty trading	19	9	47.4%
-Roadside small store owners	5	3	
-Kiosk operators	10	5	
-Street traders (hawkers)	4	1	

the wholesale/retail business. However, people from the region, especially the people of Bayelsa State, dominated both the hospitality and services industries. Surprisingly too, a little more than half of the people interviewed that are engaged in some form of manufacturing activities are from the region.

With respect to the challenges encountered by entrepreneurs in the study area, an overwhelming 97 percent of all respondents ranked finance as the greatest challenge they faced when starting-up or trying to expand their businesses. The second-most ranked challenge faced by entrepreneurs or would-be entrepreneurs in the region was stable electricity supply. Energy accounts for the greatest part of their operational cost. Respondents equally mentioned the lack of government support by way of providing the enabling environment. They equally decried the lack of training support and that even when entrepreneurial training workshops were organized, beneficiaries were mostly cronies of top politicians and government functionaries. With respect to determining whether or not a link existed between natural resource abundance and the presence or lack of entrepreneurialism, no specific question was asked as this could form the basis for another detailed study. However, the trend in the NDR is consistent with other resource-rich regions. When money can be extracted from the ground, people simply don't develop the DNA of innovation and entrepreneurship (Friedman 2008).

Proposed Model

In view of these results, we hereby propose the following model titled "Niger Delta Entrepreneurship Development for Sustainable Development Strategy (NDESDS)." The model represents an integration of the various models we have discussed earlier. It embraces both the people side and the infrastructural side of development. As literature and empirical finding indicate, the area not only lack basic infrastructure, it equally lacks institutional structures necessary for the growth of entrepreneurship. Therefore, the NDESDS factors in all the issues raised by the models discussed earlier. It does this by looking at both the short-, medium-, and long-term measures for the development of entrepreneurship in the region (see Figure 5.1).

As shown in Figure 5.1, the focus of the short term strategy is on creating awareness about entrepreneurship by organizing trainings/workshops for people of the region while the infrastructural development of the region is equally ongoing. Granted that some awareness generation is already taking place, the scale advocated here should be providing trainings and support to at least 100,000 indigenes of the region annually for the next five years. After five years, the situation can be reviewed.

The medium-term strategy is supposed to include the steps advocated for the short term. However, the emphasis here will be the establishment of RBHs and BI centers as well as a VC fund. These centers will provide a

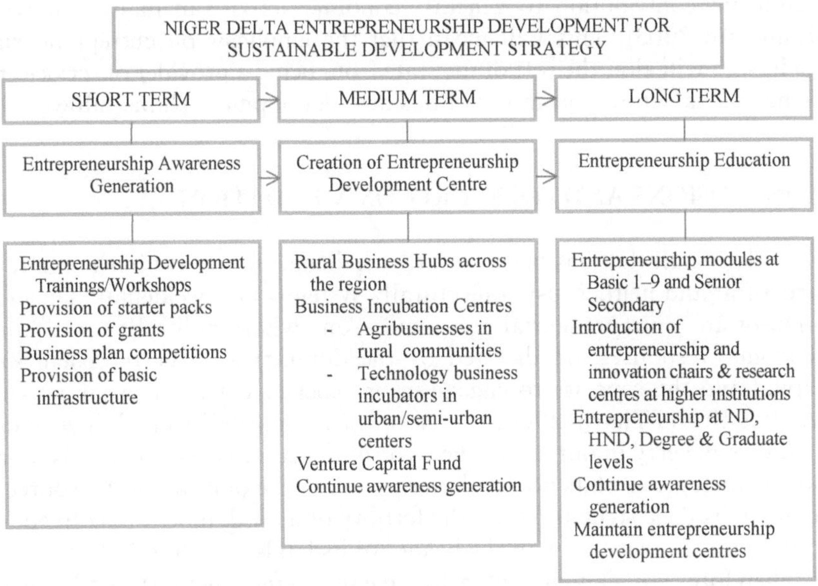

Figure 5.1 Niger Delta entrepreneurship development model.

platform for SMEs to share knowledge and experiences, form alliances and partnerships both local and abroad, since the center will provide further training and support. The VC fund may take the form of a public–private partnership arrangement with the NDDC and other development partners providing contributory equity.

The long-term strategy focuses on a systemic entrepreneurial education that will see the introduction of the subject at the basic through the senior secondary school to the introduction of programs at National Diploma, Higher National Diploma, Degree, and Graduate levels in the higher institution. This strategy is premised on the fact that one of the most challenging implications of new institutional economics is that the relationship between entrepreneurship and education matters (Aligica and Florian 2008). Entrepreneurial education and pedagogy plays an important role in the development of the cognitive capital of society, as a high level of awareness would enrich various aspects of social and economic development (Yamin and Tanas 2006). The long-term strategy equally advocates the continuation of the activities of the earlier two strategies.

However, since the NDR is part of the Nigerian nation, it means that whatever strategy adopted for its development will only work if the right institutional frameworks exist in the country, as strong and effective institutional frameworks encourage productive entrepreneurship (Baumol 1990; Karabegović et al. 2008). Therefore, government needs to take initiatives to ensure that the overall policy environment encourages industrial activity in general, and SME activity, in particular, given the latter's significant contribution to general economic activity in many countries (Kamesam 2003). This will mean that the emphasis on entrepreneurial leadership will alter the role of the state from being a provider of services to being an enabler and promoter of business development (Juma 2006).

CONCLUSIONS AND POLICY RECOMMENDATION

Considering all that has been said, the challenge of poverty in the NDR is structural and neither just conjecturally systemic nor accidental. The creation of an "entrepreneurial economy"—one whose political, social, and economic responses are dictated by the dominance of entrepreneurship capital and the capacity to engage in or generate entrepreneurial activity (Audretsch and Thurik 2004)—must be the responsibility of all, if we must eradicate poverty in our land. The wealth of a country itself depends more on the intelligence of its people than the abundance of its natural resources, more on its civic structure than the fertility of its soil, more on its freedom to invent and create than on the beauty of its landscape (Sirolli 2008).

Therefore, government's plan for massive infrastructural development in the region should go side-by-side with entrepreneurship development. And if truly the NDR forms part of the 7-Points Agenda of government, and if Vision 20:2020 envisions the eradication of poverty in Nigeria, then the proposed NDESDS framework offers a handy strategy. No matter how sophisticated the local infrastructures may be, without people using them, they are useless. We therefore hope our work stimulates honest self-examination and provides a useful roadmap for new, more entrepreneurship-development perspectives among the people of the NDR, other parts of Nigeria, and beyond.

Given the positive importance of entrepreneurship in the socioeconomic development of regions and the lack thereof of the spirit of entrepreneurism in the NDR, we make the following recommendations:

- Entrepreneurship development should go side-by-side with the massive infrastructural development plan of government for the NDR.
- In promoting entrepreneurship, entrepreneurial courses should be fully embedded in the school curricula at all levels of our educational system. However, emphasis should be placed on technical colleges and polytechnics, and university offering science and engineering programs.
- Entrepreneurial training organizations outside the formal academic setting (e.g., SMEDAN, National Directorate of Employment, NGOs providing such trainings) should be strengthened to provide adequate training to those who may not be privileged to be in school.
- Efforts at promoting entrepreneurship development should be coordinated, such that government should be able to determine how many entrepreneurs she is willing to groom at every point in time.

- Since lack of capital remains the most critical challenge to the growth of entrepreneurship, government should collaborate with the organized private sector to set up venture capital funds primarily for the funding of viable enterprises.
- The NDESDS proposed in this chapter be adopted by government as a significant effort in developing local capacity (both human and material) to empower the next generation of home-grown business leaders for the benefit of the region, Nigeria and society at large.

REFERENCES

Akpan, P. L. (2007). "Public expenditure and poverty alleviation in Nigeria," *Development Studies Round Table*, Vol. 3, No. 1, pp. 140–161.

Alayli, M. A. (2005). "Resource rich countries and weak institutions: The resource curse effect," http://are.berkeley.edu/courses/EEP131/fall2006/NotableStudent05/Resource%20CurseM_Alayli.pdf (accessed December 8, 2008)

Aligica, P. D. and Florian, B. (2008). "Entrepreneurship and education: The missing link in international development theory and practice," *International Journal of Business and Globalisation*, Vol. 2, No. 1, pp. 28–38.

Audretsch D. B. and Thurik A. R. (2004). "A model of the entrepreneurial economy," *International Journal of Entrepreneurship Education*, Vol. 2, No. 2, pp. 143–66.

Baumol, W. J. (1990). "Entrepreneurship: Productive, unproductive, and destructive," *The Journal of Political Economy*, Vol. 98, No. 5, pp. 893–921.

Beaulieu, L. J. and Barefield, A. (2006). *The voices of the people: Strategies for expanding entrepreneurship in the rural south*, Southern Rural Development Centre, Barbara Ray, HiredPen, Inc.

Blanchflower, D. G. (2007). "Entrepreneurship in the UK," Speech delivered at the Max Planck Summer Institute on Entrepreneurship Research, July 9, 2007, Berlin, Germany.

Blanchflower, D. G. and Oswald, A. J. (1998). "What makes an entrepreneur?" *Journal of Labour Economics*, Vol. 16, No. 1, pp. 26–60.

Blanchflower, D. G., Oswald, A., and Stutzer, A. (2001). "Latent entrepreneurship across nations," *European Economic Review*, Vol. 45, Nos. 4–6, pp. 680–691.

Bubou, G. M., Brent, A. C., and Tredoux, C. (2009). "Towards assessing the social sustainability performance of the petroleum industry in the Niger Delta Region of Nigeria," *South African Journal of Industrial Engineering*, Vol. 20, No.1, pp. 119–131.

Chima, R. I., Owioduokit, E. A., and Ogoh, R. (2002). *Technology transfer and acquisition in the oil sector and government policy in Nigeria*, African Technology Policy Studies Network (ATPS) Working Paper Series No. 32, Nairobi.

CIPE. (2010). "Take off the band aid: Healing social wounds in MENA." Centre for International Private Enterprise (CIPE) Development blog, http://www.cipe.org/blog/?p=5258 (accessed May 26, 2010)

CNN. (2009). Morning edition, March 17, 2009.

Dees, J. G. (1998). "The Meaning of 'Social Entrepreneurship'," Stanford University: Draft Report for the Kauffman Center for Entrepreneurial Leadership. Available online at: http://www.caseatduke.org/documents/dees_sedef.pdf (accessed December 10, 2008)

Drucker, P. F. (2004). *Innovation and entrepreneurship: Practice and principles* (2nd rev. ed.), Amsterday: Elservier Butterworth-Hennemann.

Emery, M., Zuiches, J. J., and Flora, C. B. (2006). "Rural entrepreneurship development program and the National Coalition for Rural Entrepreneurship," Iowa State University, North Carolina State University, USA.

Esanov, A., Raiser, M., and Buiter, W. (2003). *Nature's blessing or nature's curse: The political economy of transition in resource-based economies. Successes and failures in real convergence—National Bank of Poland, 23–24 October 2003*. European Bank for Reconstruction and Development.

Fiet, J. O., Norton Jr., W. I. and Clouse, G. H. (2007). "Systematic search as a source of technical innovation: An empirical test," *Journal of Engineering and Technology Management*, Vol. 24, pp. 329–346.

Friedman, T. L. (2008). *Hot, flat, and crowded: Why we need a green revolution and how it can renew America*, New York: Farrar, Straus and Giroux.

Gaspar, F. C. (2009). "The stimulation of entrepreneurship through venture capital and business incubation," *International Journal of Entrepreneurship and Innovation Management*, Vol. 9, No. 4, pp. 396–415.

Gray, C. (2002). "Entrepreneurship, resistance to change and growth in small firms," *Journal of Small Business and Enterprise Development*, Vol. 9, No. 1, pp. 61–72.

Green, S. and Pryde, P. (1990). *Black entrepreneurship in America*, Piscataway, NJ: Transaction Publishers.

Harvie, C. (2008). "Regional integration in Asia and the contribution of SMEs: A review of the key issues and policy imperatives," The Asia Pacific Economic Forum (APEF) Conference Programme, November 2–5, 2008, Isfahan, Iran.

Higher Colleges of Technology. (2010). "Fostering and inspiring the next generation of entrepreneurs," HCT Global Entrepreneurship Conference 2010, http://e2010.hct.ac.ae/ (accessed August 3, 2010)

Juma, C. (2006). "Reinventing growth: Science, technology and innovation in Africa," *International Journal of Technology and Globalisation*, Vol. 2, Nos. 3–4, pp. 323–339.

Juma, C. (2007). "Linking knowledge and business," *Business Daily* (Africa), March 9.

Kamesam, V. (2003). "Financing for entrepreneurship and SMEs: An Indian perspective," *BIS Review*, Vol. 40, pp. 1–5.

Karabegović, A, McMahon, F. Ashby, N. J., Dowd, A. W., and Sobel, R. S. (2008). *Economic freedom of North America: 2008 annual report (US Edition*, Calgary: Fraser Institute.

Khanduja, D., Khanduja, J., and Singh, S. S. (2008). "The ambience of incubated entrepreneurship in Indian economy," South East Asia, Australia and New Zealand (SEAANZ) 2008 Conference Proceedings http://wms-soros.mngt.waikato.ac.nz/NR/seaanz/docs/proceedings/677.pdf (accessed December 11, 2008)Kim, H. and Ames, M. (2006). "Business incubators as economic development tools: Rethinking models based on the Korea experience," *International Journal Technology Management*, Vol. 33, No. 1, pp.1–24.

Kropp, F. and Zolin, R. (2005). "Technological Entrepreneurship: The Role of Small Business Innovation Research," *Programs Academy of Marketing Review*, available at: http://www.amsreview.org/articles/kropp07-2005.pdf (accessed December 20, 2009)

Lazear, E. (2002). *Entrepreneurship*, National Bureau of Economic Research Working Paper No. 9109, Cambridge, MA: NBER.

Licht, A. N. and Siegel, J. I. (2006). "The social dimensions of entrepreneurship," in M. Casson and B. Yeung (Eds.), *Oxford handbook of entrepreneurship*, Oxford: Oxford University Press, pp. 511–539

McGrath, R. G., MacMillan, I. C., and Scheinberg, S. (1992). "Elitists, risk-takers, and rugged individualists? An exploratory analysis of cultural differences between entrepreneurs," *Journal of Business Venturing*, Vol. 7, No. 2, pp. 115–135.

Mort, G. S., Weerawardena, J., and Carnegie, K. (2003). "Social entrepreneurship: Towards conceptualization," *International Journal of Non-profit and Voluntary Sector Marketing*, Vol. 8, No. 1, pp. 76–88.

NBIA. (2008). "Business incubation facts," http://www.nbia.org/resource_center/bus_inc_facts/index.php (accessed February 26, 2009)

Niger Delta Development Commission (NDDC). (2006). *Niger Delta Regional Development Master Plan—popular version*. Port Harcourt, NDDC.

Nijkamp, P. (2000). *Entrepreneurship in a modern network economy*, Serie Research Memoranda, Faculteit der Economische Wetenschappen en Econometrie, vvije Universiteit, Amsterdam.

Nwachukwu, C. C. (2003). *The practice of entrepreneurship in Nigeria* (Reprint), Owerri: Springfield Publishers Limited.

Okowa, W. J. (2008). "Secrets of successful SME entrepreneurs: Simple specific, proven methods to ensure entrepreneurial success," Paper delivered at the 9th Advancement and Continuous Educational Programme of the Institute of Chartered Economists of Nigeria, June 6, 2008, Abuja, Nigeria.

Oviatt, B. M. and McDougall, P. P. (2005). "Defining international entrepreneurship and modeling the speed of internationalization," *Entrepreneurship Theory and Practice*, Vol. 29, No. 5, pp. 537–553.

Papyrakis, E. and Gerlagh, R. (2004). "Natural resources, innovation, and growth," In DEGIT Conference Proceedings, available at http: http://www.degit.ifw-kiel.de/papers/degit_10/C010_054.pdf (accessed December 17, 2009).

Papyrakis, E. and Gerlagh, R. (2007). "Resource abundance and economic growth in the United States," *European Economic Review*, Vol. 51, pp. 1011–1039.

Parhankangas, A., and Lindholm-Dahlstrand, Å. (2006). "Spin-offs to stock markets as an alternative form of entrepreneurship: An institutional approach," Paper presented at the Academy of Management Conference, Atlanta, August.

Pavlovich, K. and Corner, P. D. (2006). "Knowledge creation through co-entrepreneurship," *International Journal of Knowledge Management Studies*, Vol. 1, Nos. 1–2, pp. 178–197.

Petrakis, P. and Bourletidis, K. (2004), "How and what we shall teach in an Entrepreneurship Educational Program: The dilemmas of Entrepreneurship Curriculum Development", Paper presented at the Economic Education Conference—What we teach and how we teach it: Perspectives on Economics from around the Globe, Adelaide, Australia, (13–26 July 2004).

Reynolds, P. D., Hay, M. and Camp, S. M. (1999). *Global Entrepreneurship Monitor: 1999 executive report*, London: Global Entrepreneurship Monitor.

Sachs, J. D. and Warner, A. M. (2001). "Natural resources and economic development: The curse of natural resources," *European Economic Review*, Vol. 45, pp. 827–838.

Sarasvathy, S. D. (2004). "The questions we ask and the questions we care about: Reformulating some problems in entrepreneurship research," *Journal of Business Venturing*, Vol. 8, pp. 183–195.

Shapero, A. and Sokol, L. (1982). "The social dimensions of entrepreneurship." In C. Kent, D. Sexton, and K. Vesper (Eds.), *The encyclopaedia of entrepreneurship*, Englewood Cliffs, NJ: Prentice-Hall, pp. 72–90.

Sharma, S. and Ruud, A. (2003). "Editorial on the path to sustainability: Integrating social dimensions into the research and practice of environmental management," *Business Strategy and the Environment*, Vol. 12, pp. 205–214.

Shell Foundation. (2005). *Enterprise solutions to poverty: Opportunities and challenges for the international development community and big business*, London: The Royal Dutch Shell plc.

Shell International. (2006). *The Shell sustainability report 2005: Meeting the energy challenge*, London: Royal Dutch Shell plc.
Singh, J. B. (1990). "Entrepreneurship education as a catalyst of development in the Third World," *Journal of Small Business and Entrepreneurship*, Vol. 7, No. 4, pp. 56–63.
Sirolli, E. (2008). *Enterprise, entrepreneurship and their role in the local, regional and national economy*, Sirolli Institute. available at: http://www.sirolli.com
SPDC. (2006). *Shell Nigeria annual report 2005: People and the environment*, Shell Petroleum Development Company of Nigeria Limited, Port Harcourt.
Sriram, V. and Mersha, T. (2006). "Facilitating entrepreneurship in Sub-Saharan Africa: What governments can do," *Journal for International Business and Entrepreneurship Development*, Vol. 3, Nos. 1–2, pp. 136–151.
Stephan, U., Lukes, M., Pawlowska, A., and Richter, P. G. (2003). "Conditions for entrepreneurship in Germany, Czech Republic and Poland: Is culture the crux?" XIth European Congress on Work and Organizational Psychology, May 14–17, 2003, Lisbon.
Sutela, P. (2002). "How to escape the trap of resource-based development: contrasting experiences," *HSE Economic Journal*, Vol. 6, No. 3, pp. 315–323.
Ubom, E. E. (2003). *Entrepreneurship, small and medium enterprises (theory, practice and policies)*, Lagos: Sendina Limited.
UNDP. (1999). *Essentials: Entrepreneurship development*, New York: Author.
UNDP. (2003). *Human Development Report 2003—Millennium Development Goals: A compact Among nations to end human poverty*, Oxford: Oxford University Press.
Urdal, H. (2005). "People vs. Malthus: Population pressure, environmental degradation, and armed conflict revisited," *Journal of Peace Research*, Vol. 42, No. 4, pp. 417–434.
Vesper, K. H. (1998). "Unfinished business (entrepreneurship) of the 20th century," United States Association for Small Business and Entrepreneurship (USASBE) Address, San Diego, January.
Yamin, S. and Tanas, J. K. (2006). "Entrepreneurial education in Poland for the new millennium: a social capital perspective," *International Journal of Business Innovation and Research*, Vol. 1, Nos. 1–2, pp. 73–91.

6 Nongovernmental Organizations and Conflict Resolution in Niger Delta

The Yakubu Gowon Centre's Peace Process in Ogoni

Ambily Etekpe

INTRODUCTION

The Niger Delta crisis became violent when after several decades of unfruitful dialogues, Isaac Boro introduced "armed struggle" on February 23, 1966 (Boro 1982). Whereas Boro's rebellion was "crushed" by the federal government after twelve consecutive days of gun battle, the cycles of violence continued and peaked in Ogoni Kingdom in 1995. It started with the killing of four prominent second-generation Ogoni leaders, namely, Albert T. Badey, Edward Kobani, Samuel N. Orage, and Theophilus Orage allegedly by members of the National Youth Council of Ogoni People (NYCOP). Those killed are popularly referred to as the "Ogoni 4." This was followed by the arrest, trial, and execution of nine other leaders, including Ken Saro-Wiwa by Justice Auta's Panel on November 10, 1995. The second group is further referred to as the "Ogoni 9."

This singular action of the youths under the auspices of NYCOP at Giokoo in 1994 not only cost Ogoni the avoidable loss of thirteen leading elites, but plunged the entire kingdom into "darkness" and bitter acrimony. Dumpe (1997: 15–20) described it as the "sunset in Ogoni Kingdom." The death of especially the "Ogoni 9" attracted several negative reactions from the international community. The Commonwealth of Nations, for example, expelled Nigeria from the organization. Several human rights and civil society organizations within and outside Nigeria regarded it as a disgrace to civilization. Nigeria became a pariah state as the crisis generated more problems for the principal parties in conflict, that is, the Ogonis, Shell Petroleum Development Company of Nigeria Ltd (SPDC), and the Nigerian government.

What was, perhaps, more problematic was how to rescue Ogoni and the country from the "darkness," bitter acrimony, and pariah status created by the crisis. After several unsuccessful attempts by government and private sector organizations, including the Rivers State Peace Conference

Committee (RSPCC), National Council of Inter-Governmental Relations (NCIGR), National Reconciliation Committee (NARECOM), and World Council of Churches (WCC), General Dr. Yakubu Gowon (GCFR), under the auspices of Yakubu Gowon Centre (YGC), secured the consent of the three principal parties (Ogoni, SPDC, and federal government) in the conflict. YGC, a nongovernmental organization (NGO) committed to peace and international cooperation, commenced a tedious peace process in 1997 that has become a landmark in the region and country. This chapter, therefore, aims at examining

1. the strategies employed in the peace-building process, and whether or not they were successful;
2. the experiences and lessons learned, and their implications for the future; and
3. the lessons to offer suggestions for a lasting peace in the Niger Delta.

The chapter is divided into five parts, beginning with this introduction. It is followed by an in-depth analysis of the historical background, the crisis (problem), and the theoretical and methodological challenges. The chapter then progresses to examine the mediation strategies employed in the peace process, followed by three lessons, and their implications for the future. The chapter highlights an emerging destructive role of corrupt local leaders, adoption of a pan-Deltaic approach to issues of the region, and vigorous pursuance of constructive dialogue. It also suggests incorporation of the local people into the oil business, and massive community action against local leaders and bureaucrats who loot our resources with impunity.

HISTORICAL BACKGROUND

The Ogoni Kingdom or Clan in the present day Rivers State is about 414 square miles with 126 towns and villages. It became one of the five divisions when the Rivers Province was created in 1946. Its headquarters was, and still is, at Bori. Prior to becoming a division, the people formed the Ogoni Central Union (OCU) in 1945. The union became the think-tank of Ogoni development until it was replaced by the Ogoni State Representative Assembly (OSRA) in 1950. The President and Secretary of OSRA were Messrs Paul Birabi and F. W. A. Saron Wiyor, respectively. OSRA adopted democratic principles in its operations and mobilized the warrant chiefs of each of the five clans of the kingdom to support it.

In 1962, the second generation of Ogoni leaders regrouped and formed another union, the Ogoni Divisional Union (ODU) at Bori with Edward Kobani as President and Kenule Saro-Wiwa as Secretary. In the mid-1970s, another group, KHAGOTE (an acronym for Khana, Gokana, Tai and Eleme), sprang up and continued the struggle for the autonomy and development of the kingdom. The high point of KHAGOTE was the preparation of the Ogoni Bill of Rights (Etekpe 2007a: 111–113) and inauguration of the Movement for the Survival of the Ogoni People (MOSOP) in 1990. The OBR was like a social contract that attempted to tie oil exploration and exploitation to the provision of social infrastructure and human capacity development for the people. The essence was for the oil producing communities to benefit from the resources found in their land.

The OBR points out that SPDC discovered crude oil in Bomu, and Korokoro-Tai and Afam in Ogoni land in 1958 and 1966, respectively, and by 1990, the kingdom was said to have provided the Nigerian state with a total revenue of US $40 billion. This spurred the people to demand for corresponding benefits from SPDC and federal government, especially as there were no potable water, good network of roads, social amenities, or infrastructural development to compensate for the amount of sacrifice in sustaining the national economy.

Amid the agitations, the federal government contracted Wilbros West Africa Inc., an American oil servicing company located in Choba, Port Harcourt, to bury pipelines from the Bomu oil field to Kaduna Refinery (Etekpe 2007b: 168–169). Without an environmental and social impact assessments, Wilbros West Africa Inc. commenced work by destroying the farmlands and economic trees of Biara village in Gokana LGA. As the people resisted, Wilbros West Africa contacted the police headquarters in Port Harcourt and about 1,900 armed mobile policemen were dispatched under the instruction of Colonel Dauda Komo, the then military administrator of the state to protect Wilbros West Africa's activities. They shot indiscriminately and killed twenty, and arrested and detained thirty prominent sons of Ogoni land. In the funeral ceremony of the victims, Ken Saro-Wiwa said, "We are not fighting war with the federal government to attract the attention of policemen or soldiers; we are prepared to cooperate with them while we continue to demand what is due us."

The unprovoked police action propelled the need to prepare the Ogoni Bill of Rights (OBR), and form MOSOP to implement it. The OBR was signed by all the six first-class traditional rulers and thirty opinion leaders from the 126 towns and villages in Ogoni in the proportion of six (Babbe), six (Tai), six (Ken-Khana), six (Gokana), and six (Nyo-Khana) clans and submitted to the federal government (during General Ibrahim B. Babangida's administration), the then military administrator of the state Colonel Dauda Komo, SPDC, and other multinational corporations operating in the Ogoni land. In the preamble, the OBR states,

> The Ogoni case is that of a district of 500,000 ethnic minority people who feel so suffocated by the existing condition that they have to form an organization that will struggle for their survival . . . The purpose of OBR is not to confront the people and Government of Nigeria but to focus world attention on the plight of Ogoni people, proffering a

> way out of our collective dilemma. The OBR is a call for social justice (social contract) and resource control(Etekpe 2007a:115)

The principal officers of MOSOP were Dr. Garrick B. Leton, an eminent scientist and later politician as president; Chief Edward N. Kobani, a businessman, career civil servant and later politician as vice-president; and Mr. Ken B. Saro-Wiwa, a writer and social activist as spokesman. As the movement went on to make positive impact, the three officers found it difficult to work as a team because their individual ambitions and ideologies conflicted with those of one another, plunging Ogoni into crisis.

THE CRISIS AND CASUALTIES

We traced the genesis of the crisis to when Ken Saro-Wiwa proposed to boycott the ill-fated June 12, 1993, presidential election in Nigeria as a way of expressing the anger of Ogoni people over the years of neglect and underdevelopment. Dr. Leton and Chief Kobani (president and vice president, respectively) were not satisfied with Mr. Saro-Wiwa's reason for Ogoni people to boycott it. The boycott, as canvassed by Saro-Wiwa, also compelled Ogoni people in government to resign their positions and stay away from public functions until the kingdom was developed. This meant that, as long as the Ogoni people were underdeveloped, the people should not participate in any public activities in the state and country. For him, staying out of government and public functions was the most effective way of driving home the Ogonis' demand to the government and international community. Going forward, whereas Dr. Leton and Chief Kobani faulted the boycott on the ground that it would be counterproductive, several Ogoni people, especially, the youths under the auspices of NYCOP, went ahead with Saro-Wiwa's propaganda for the boycott. As the disagreement degenerated and split the rank and file of MOSOP, Dr. Leton, Chief Kobani and their supporters were labeled as "vultures" (i.e., nickname for the pro-government officials) and pro–Ken Saro-Wiwa group as MOSOP.

After the said boycott, Saro-Wiwa expressed interest in representing the Ogoni people at the Constitutional Conference to be conducted by Sani Abacha to draw up a fresh constitution for the country. Dr. Leton and Chief Kobani then reminded him of his earlier position that Ogoni people should abstain from political activities in the state and country until the federal government has met all the terms and conditions embodied in the OBR. At that point, Ken Saro-Wiwa became apprehensive and used the NYCOP as his personal militia to ensure that he represented the Ogoni people. As the rivalry unfolded, NYCOP was allegedly mobilized by Saro-Wiwa to cause the death of four of his opponents—Albert Tombari Badey, former secretary to the state government; Chief Edward Kobani and Samuel

Ntete Orage, former commissioners; and Theophilus Nna Orage, secretary, Gokana Council of Chiefs at Giokoo on May 21, 1994.

Dumpe (1997) describes the youth actions as "misguided." According to the Rivers State Government publication titled *MOSOP: The True Story* (1996), "It was an ideological contradiction for him (Saro-Wiwa) to campaign to boycott all elections until the aims of OBR was realized, only to campaign to be elected into the Constitutional Conference." Unknown to the youths, rather than protect Ken Saro-Wiwa, their wanton display of extreme lawlessness was to form the basis for his arrest and trial. Eventually, ten officials of MOSOP and NYCOP were arrested and arraigned before Justice Auta's Panel. Apart from Barrister Ledum Mitee (vice-president of MOSOP), the other nine, including Saro-Wiwa, were convicted and executed by hanging on Friday, November 10, 1995. They (Ogoni 9) were

- Ken Saro-Wiwa (President, MOSOP)
- Felix Nuante
- Saturday Dobe
- Nordu Eawo
- David Kpokoo
- Paul Levura
- Dr. Barinem Kiobel (former commissioner)
- Baribo Bera
- John Kpuinem (vice-president, NYCOP)

The conviction and execution of the Ogoni 9 portrayed Nigeria in bad light to the extent that the country was expelled from the Commonwealth of Nations (Human Rights Watch 1995; Ihonvbere 2002). Thus, their death generated more problems for the Ogoni people and Nigeria as the country became a pariah state.

THE THEORETICAL AND METHODOLOGICAL CHALLENGES

It has been argued that because of the complex nature of social conflicts, no single theoretical framework can adequately provide a "holistic" explanation of the crisis in Ogoni Kingdom, in particular, and the Niger Delta, in general. Be that as it may, among the range of theories, the chapter believes the structural framework (Galtung 1990), complemented by the institutionally induced frustration-aggression framework (Dollard 1939; Lorenz 1966), is most suitable.

The main argument of structural conflict theoretical framework is that conflict is built into the particular ways societies in Nigeria, especially the Niger Delta, are structured and organized. The framework, therefore, looks at the social problems, such as political and economic exclusion, gross injustice, abject poverty, exploitation, and inequity facing the Ogonis and other oil-producing communities (OPCs) in the region as the main sources of conflicts.

The situation in the Niger Delta has been compounded by an emerging new type of "local bourgeoisie or leaders," being represented by the political class. They have consistently compromised, corrupted, and even led the people to criminality. They divert a lot of funds from public and private sources that have been invested in the region to their coffers. In an effort to perpetuate their domineering tendency, they promote violence and underdevelopment, which in turn benefits them. This was prominent in the Ogoni crises, especially the death of both the Ogoni 4 and Ogoni 9. The emerging local bourgeoisie have posed serious challenges in the region, and if they are not effectively checked, we will continue to have the umbilical link between the gross underdevelopment of the Niger Delta, the manner of control and management of its resources, the poor development of its human capacity, on the one hand, and the perennial crises in the region, on the other.

This is where the frustration-aggression theory propounded by John Dollard and his research associates in 1939 comes in. The theory, which has been expanded and modified by Leonard Berkowitz and Aubrey Yates, posits that when expectations are not met, people tend to confront those they hold responsible for the unmet expectations (Yates 1962). This is also the central point that Ted Robert Gurr's (1970: 74) "relative deprivation thesis" makes. The thesis states that "the greater the discrepancy, however marginal, between what is sought and what seem attainable, the greater will be the chances that anger and violence will result." The thesis is relevant here as the disparity between the amount of revenue generated from the OPCs, which, in case of Ogonis, was estimated at US $40 billion in 1990, and the expected value of benefits in form of infrastructural and human capital development is primarily responsible for the perennial conflicts in the region.

The disparity is in recent years no longer primarily induced by the Nigerian state and oil companies, but by a small group of "local bourgeoisie/leaders" earlier discussed. They manipulate the institutions and divert the funds meant to develop the communities to their private pockets. "The leaders," as Tedheke (2005: 427) puts it, "are similar to the organized piracy led to looting of Africa . . . piracy transplanted from seas to dry land, piracy reorganized, consolidated and adapted to the aim of plundering the material and human resources of our people." This means, the frustration-aggression theory in its present form, without the term "induced," is inadequate. Thus, it has been modified to that of "induced frustration-aggression" theoretical framework.

The method of data collection applied in this study to analyze these intricacies is the participant observation. This method is considered ideal for three reasons, namely, the author was involved in the six activity centers in the peace process at Figure 6.1, the observation took place in its natural environment and the study lasted for a relatively long time.

As Bailey (1982) noted, observation is very appropriate for detailed study of behavior or phenomenon in a particular setting. Kerr (1979) and Holdaway (1980), for example, applied observation method to study the use of space by "staff members within a hospital" and a "British Police station." Both studies found that "observational method allows in-depth study or analysis of the whole target group." It is for this reason Young (2000: 71) argues that sociologists are increasingly convinced that knowledge from participants observation "becomes valuable from both theoretical and practical standpoint, and enable us to predict the future as to possibly control it." Thus, "one frequent use of observation is for studying private behavior that individual and communities might not admit to on surveys" (Humphrey 1970).

The participant observation was, however, complemented by other methods, such as fact finding, interviews, focused group discussions, and document study, especially OBR and other relevant documents from WCC, MOSOP, state government, and Ogoni traditional rulers council.

Be that as it may, the author faced several methodological challenges, especially the difficulty of gaining entry at the initial stage, as the Ogoni people were suspicious of the peace process. They perceived it as a ploy for SPDC's re-entry to Ogoniland. As this was addressed, we faced the problem of control and quantitative measures often used in survey research and experiment. Nevertheless, we applied a variety of strategies to handle the challenges.

STRATEGIES OF THE PEACE PROCESS

The YGC was set up in 1992 as an NGO that is nonpartisan in politics and religion. The center aims to, among other things, promote the cause of Nigerian unity and peaceful co-existence, as well as undertake studies, research, and publications on issues of national integration and conflict resolution (Tyoden 1994: ix). It was in pursuance of these objectives that General Gowon—along with Sir John Kaputin, co-president of African Caribbean, Pacific, and European Union (ACP/EU) Joint Assembly, and Ambassador M. B. Ekpang, deputy chief-executive of the YGC—toured Ogoni land in April 1997. The team spoke to officials of the Rivers State government, the Internal Security Force, top management staff of SPDC, Ogoni leaders, and other stakeholders (Oyedel 1998: 21–32). The stakeholders and principal parties in conflict invited General Gowon/YGC to mediate (Godongs 2006: 135–143). Prior to it, the center, along with *Global 2000*, an international NGO promoted by the former president of the United States, Jimmy Carter, had campaigned for the eradication of "guinea worm" (NIGEP) in the endemic states of Plateau, Nassarawa, Benue, Enugu, Anambra, Ebony, Borno, Cross River, Oyo, Zamfara, Gombe, Ogun, Niger, and Kwara.

It should be emphasized that the acceptance of YGC to mediate is a reflection of the growing confidence communities repose in NGOs in resolving conflicts. This has stimulated NGOs to diversify their operations from predominately human rights and political activities at independence in 1960s to human capital development and capacity building for conflict resolution and peace-building.

Accordingly, the number of NGOs has risen from 61 in 1960 to about 6,000 in 2003. The most prominent ones in conflict resolution and peace building include

- Yakubu Gowon Centre (YGC), Abuja;
- African Leadership Forum (ALF), Ota;
- Niger Delta Forum Study Group (NDFSG), Port Harcourt;
- Nigerian Peace Centre (NPC), Kaduna;
- Arewa Consultative Forum (ACF), Kaduna;
- Corps of Mediators, Lagos;
- Human Rights Monitor (HRM), Lagos;
- Pan African Centre for Research in Peace (PACRP), Enugu; and
- Academic Associates Peace Works (AAPW).

Let's now discuss briefly their roles. The AAPW, PACRP, and NDSFG commonly apply case study, fact finding, and analysis meetings methods to provide the bases for various forms of interventions. Often, analysis workshops are used to validate research reports, decide whether or not there is need for intervention, and identify the appropriate entry points for intervention. The workshops are also used to assess potential risks and dangers and to simulate future attempts to transform conflicts (Otite and Albert 2002). While AAPW handled the Warri crisis, NDFSG has produced a compendium of political, economic, oil- and gas-related, land, and sociocultural conflicts in the Niger Delta (Etekpe et al. 2010).

The ACF and the Nigeria Peace Centre have, on the other hand, resolved several conflicts on settlers vs. indigenes, communal, and ethnic crises in the Middle Belt region of northern Nigeria (Yakubu et al. 2003). They are also into organizing short-term courses and trainings of traditional rulers, opinion leaders, and community-based organizations as peace advocates. The peace advocates play the role of independent mediators. "The mediators," as Godongs (2006: 135) puts it, "are experts in conflict resolution and therefore, are expected to bring to bear on a particular conflict the weight of their expertise and experience on the disputants to agree."

The ALF, founded by Chief Olusegun Obasanjo, former president of Nigeria, conducts trainings and other forms of interventions. It equally interfaces with federal agencies, such as the Institute of Peace Studies, to build capacity for conflict resolution and transformation, and applied the mediation strategies to resolve the recent Ife–Modakeke conflicts. The strategy has nine methods and eight interrelated and interdependent stages.

In the case of Ogoni peace process, we applied five of such methods and six stages interchangeably (Figure 6.1). Whereas the methods were communication, collaboration, negotiation, multi-track diplomacy, and reconciliation, the stages included initial meeting with signatories to OBR, assembling mediation team, organizing stakeholders' formal meetings, analysis conference, formation of all stakeholders' dialogue team, and consensus peace documentation. These methods (strategies) and stages involved different forms of intervention used to help the principal stakeholders reach a voluntary consensus settlement (Cooley 1992; Beer and Stief 1997: 3). As an independent mediator, General Gowon was saddled with the following five roles (Godongs 2006: 136–137):

1. *The Opener of Communication Channels* by facilitating a continuing discussion between disputants;
2. *The Legitimizer* by protecting the rights and interests of all the parties for purpose of facilitating negotiations;
3. *The Process Facilitator* by providing framework and procedure for discussion and negotiation;
4. *The Problem explorer* by assisting parties, especially, the Ogoni people in defining the basic issues and interest as well as identifying acceptable solutions; and
5. *The Process Planner* by providing a mediation plan. The plan specified the eight relevant stakeholders, the venue, procedures, and framework.

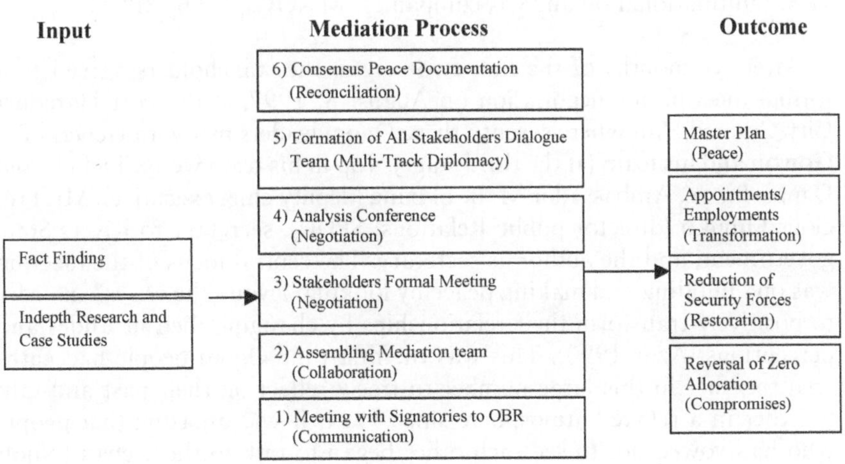

Figure 6.1 Components of Ogoni peace process. Yakubu Gowon Centre, Abuja, 1997–2002.

The peace process had three components: input, mediation, and outcome. It started with an analysis of the conflicts through case studies and fact findings. Here, we searched for and studied the OBR and other relevant documents from the WCC, Rivers State government, and so on, to establish the background, sources, and causes of the conflicts, whether or not there was need for intervention, identifying the appropriate entry points and strategies for intervention. The logic of case studies is that without a proper understanding and analysis of the conflict situation, the wrong intervention strategies might be employed, which would have been a fatal mistake (Otite and Albert 2002).

Having a proper grasp, we embarked on fact finding. This involved meeting with, first, the signatories to OBR that were still alive, and later the seven other categories of stakeholders to clarify doubt and help them gain confidence in the peace process. This progressed to the mediation process.

The first stage here was that of identification of those still alive among the thirty-six prominent sons that signed the OBR and to persuade them to join the peace process. This took three months, and majority of them, including, MOSOP agreed to participate. The scope was broadened at the second stage to include other stakeholders (i.e., 2–8). They are

1. all the signatories to the OBR;
2. chairmen of Khana, Gokana, Eleme, and Tai local government councils in Ogoni Kingdom in Rivers State;
3. officials of both Rivers State and federal governments;
4. MOSOP;
5. nongovernment and community-based organizations;
6. traditional rulers (i.e., all first class chiefs);
7. political class and opinion leaders; and
8. multinational oil and gas companies (MNOCs) led by SPDC.

After six months of the first two stages, the stakeholders agreed to a formal meeting for negotiation on August 8, 1997, at the Port Harcourt City Council Hall where seventy-three Ogoni leaders met with General Dr. Gowon and his team (at the third stage). Top in his team were Chief Harold Dappa-Biriye, Ambassador M. B. Ekpang (deputy chief executive), Mr. Precious Omuku (director public Relations, SPDC), secretary to Rivers State government, and the author as secretary. The central focus of the meeting was on "building and making peace by looking beyond the crises" in order to positively transform their relationships by changing their attitudes and perceptions (Azar 1990). This was the first time Ogoni people had gathered together in this large number to freely reflect on their past and talk together in a relaxed atmosphere since 1994. It was amazing that people who had vowed not to see each other began to talk to themselves (Nnoli 2003; Etekpe 2007b: 171).

When General Gowon noticed that MOSOP was no longer willing to participate for fear of being arrested by the security agents, he met the then head of state, General Sani Abacha, to solicit granting them amnesty. This was done, and Dr. Ben Naanen, secretary-general of MOSOP, led the group to the peace process. It added credibility and at the end of the meeting, it was resolved that four committees be formed as follows:

1. *Peace committee* to discuss with aggrieved persons, especially families of those who lost their loved ones during the crises, on how to embrace dialogue, instead of planning for revenge;
2. *Funeral committee* to arrange for proper burial of those who died in the crises, as well as work with the people for a "forgiveness session" among the families;
3. *A dialogue team* to talk with SPDC, state, and federal governments on how to redress the problems of Ogoni people to forestall a repetition; and
4. *A committee* to look into the sustainable development of Ogoni land.

It was also agreed that the venue for the peace process meetings be shifted from Port Harcourt to Bori, the traditional headquarters of Ogoni land, in order to carry along the local people.

The peace process moved to the fourth stage where the center organized an international conference on "Enduring Peace and Sustainable National Development" (Oyedele 1998: 15–50) on May 18–20, 1998 at Port Harcourt, Rivers State. The conference was well attended by the Ogoni people and it galvanized fresh ideas to continue negotiation. General Gowon used the period to meet with, first, elected national and state assembly members, and later with Ogoni leaders on May 22, 1998. At the meetings, the Ogoni people expressed satisfaction with the YGC's strategies and methodologies, and urged him not to abandon the peace initiative. We then constituted an Ogoni Development Committee (ODC) on August 11, 1998. The committee was to prepare a comprehensive development plan for addressing the deep-rooted immediate and long term nonpolitical aspirations of the Ogoni people. Best (2006: 68–69) emphasizes that the aspiration of the local communities is over the ownership of proceeds from sale of oil. The communities believe that the oil found in their land belongs to them, and as such they should own the proceeds and pay tax and royalties to the federal government. This is referred to as "resource control." While this may be seen as the position of the communities, the danger is that the local bourgeoisies may seize the opportunity to make huge income for themselves at the expense of the local communities.

The ODC, coordinated by the author, met several times and submitted the plan on April 18, 1999. The plan had two phases. Phase 1 was a request for electrification of the 126 towns and villages, while Phase 2 obliged the YGC to sponsor human capacity-building workshops on conflict resolution, as well as evolve a credible community-based master plan as a way forward in bringing about lasting peace in the kingdom and region.

The peace process progressed to the fifth stage: formation of an all-stakeholders dialogue team on June 9, 1999. It applied multi-track diplomacy by bringing together for mediation all the eight tracks, and fostered considerable cooperation between and among Ogoni people. The team critically examined the master plan, the impact of the Ogoni experience on the 3,000 communities in the Niger Delta region, and how such experience could be adapted for the benefit of the entire region so that similar trauma would be avoided in the region.

The all-stakeholders dialogue team, an innovation of the center, presented their report in another forum on January 20, 2000, where the issues raised were grouped and assigned to key stakeholders that had the wherewithal to discuss and address them (Table 6.1). The outcome of the discussions was subjected to a wider debate between April and June 2001, and the resolutions documented as a consensus position for the sixth stage. Table 6.1 is the classification of some of the key issues and players in the sixth and final stage.

Table 6.1 Issues, Players, and Stakeholders in the Niger Delta

S/No	*Description of Issues*	*Assigned Players/Stakeholders*
1	The Niger Delta Question:	State and federal governments
	-Resource ownership/control	Local, state, and federal governments
	-Power sharing	Political parties and traditional institutions
	-Boundary disputes	Federal, state, and local governments
2	Lack of development/ infrastructure	Federal, state, and local governments, MNOCs and NGOs
	-Unemployment	Investors and federal government.
	-Lack of human capacity building	NGOs, NDDC, federal, state, and local governments
	-Poverty	Federal and state governments, National Poverty Eradication Programme (NAPEP), and National Directorate of Employment.
3	Lawlessness in the Niger Delta	Police, Security Agents, Federal Government and MNOCs.
	-Vandalizing of pipelines and infrastructure	Traditional rulers and political class
	-Sabotage	Local and state governments.

While effective at the first five stages, the Ogoni peace process did not, however, successfully achieve the sixth stage, which was on signing a consensus peace pack at the presidency in Abuja. Two incidents accounted for it. The first was the federal government's interference through the National Reconciliation Committee (NARECOM), led by Chief Alex Akinyele (a one-time federal minister of information). The NARECOM was set up as a parallel organization to truncate the YGC's efforts. It inaugurated the Ogoni Negotiation Committee (ONC) headed by Dr. Mrs. Roseline Konya to pursue the cause of Ogoni people. This was similar to the Ogoni Development Committee (ODC) established by YGC. As a matter of fact, they both had similar objectives. We then approached His Royal Majesty Nzidee, the then president, Ogoni Council of Traditional Rulers (OCTR), and Hon. Emmanuel Deeyah, who was in the State House of Assembly to persuade the Ogoni people to discard NARECOM and ONC and fuse in to YGC's peace process. This was eventually achieved.

The other power block was the Ogoni People's Association (OPA), chaired by Hon. Barrister Magnus Abbey (then minority leader in the State House of Assembly and later, SSG, Rivers State). The OPA also kicked against the YGC's peace process and preferred to work with the ONC. We used Hon. D. K. Badom and Dr. Emmanuel Gwezia to persuade their brethren to disassociate themselves with OPA, a stooge of the federal government. We were equally successful. The third factor was that of dropping Eleme Clan from the track as the people (i.e., Eleme) were not enthusiastic about the peace process. This was fronted by Hon. Dr. Walter Ollor, and we delisted them from further participation. This did not adversely disorganize the program since they were not affected by the crises.

The fourth factor, which was most destructive, was SPDC's sponsorship of a parallel group in early 2002 when the process was at its final stage (i.e., Reconciliation Phase at Figure 6.1). The group was led by HRM G. N. K. Gininwa, *Menebua Tua Tua Tai*, who was by then a major contractor of SPDC. He was allegedly well funded and campaigned against the YGC as too slow. Several opportunists in our team joined him and so General Gowon and the YGC resolved to pull out in May 2002 after, submitting a comprehensive report to the federal government, Ogoni people, and SPDC. Thus, the process was not properly anchored.

Having achieved so much within the period, it was expected that SPDC's management would have re-evaluated the circumstance that led to the general's pullout and re-invite him to complete the process. This is where the Ogoni traditional institution, along with MOSOP that have earlier expressed their satisfaction with the YGC strategies should have mobilized the people against G. N. K. Gininwa the way they did during ONC. In addition, they were expected to make presentation to the federal government for YGC to properly anchor the peace process. The YGC also gave-up too quickly. Having generated so much goodwill from the stakeholders, General Gowon should have impressed on the federal government to complete the process, the way he did in securing amnesty for the MOSOP. The problem could have been avoided if at the negotiation (i.e., stakeholders' formal meeting) stage, sanctions were agreed upon against parties involved in double-stands, unethical practices, and acts considered inimical to the peace process.

The strategy employed had its own weakness, that is, mediation process is voluntary, as such the independent mediator has no control over the process. The Ogoni experience has, however, suggested the need to put in place relevant ground rules right from the initial stage to forestall "unwarranted" disruption of the peace process. Incidentally, the G. N. K. Gininwa's group did not introduce any fresh ideas. Instead, it was about to replay the "MOSOP-Vulture" ideological politics. SPDC, preempting the consequences, withdrew further sponsorship. And the situation literally returned to status quo until SPDC sponsored Rev. Father Matthew Kukah to "properly anchor the peace process from where YGC stopped," in 2006. Rev. Kukah did not succeed because the people suspected that SPDC is not "interested in genuine dialogue or reconciliation."

It should be emphasized that though the strategies employed were not totally successful, the peace process was not also a complete failure because before the pullout in 2002, the YGC had accomplished the following outcomes:

1. Securing the release of nineteen Ogoni youths arrested and detained since 1994 for celebrating the Ogoni Day;
2. Drastic reduction of the presence of internal security forces;
3. Appointment of Ogoni sons and daughters into positions of power and authority in the police, state, and federal government establishments, including ministries;
4. Reversal of the erstwhile Khana LGA zero allocation; and
5. Preparation of Ogoni master plan as platform for the development of Ogoni Kingdom.

THE LESSONS, IMPLICATIONS, AND SUGGESTIONS FOR THE FUTURE

The Ogoni peace process has brought to the fore several lessons with serious implications for the future. They include the following:

1. *The role of local bourgeoisie*: The activities of the emerging "local bourgeoisie/leaders" are very prominent in the Ogoni crises. Incidentally, such leaders are found in all the OPCs in the Niger Delta. As previously pointed out, they are easily compromised and corrupted. They also promote corruption and violence, as well as divert the huge amount of money invested in programs and projects to develop the region into their private coffers. The local bourgeoisies are easily

bought over to create anarchy, on the one hand, and then act as peace advocates, on the other. Chief Gininwa, Dr. Ollor, and officials of NYCOP fit into this category of persons. The MNOCs, led by SPDC, continue to use such leaders to pursue the concept of *divide-conquer-and-rule policies*. And as long as the structure is not changed, it would be difficult to build an enduring peace in the region. Rev. Father Matthew Kukah has fallen into this category of leaders. Unknown to him, he was to be used for the re-entry of SPDC to resume normal operations in Ogoni—an operation abandoned at the peak of the conflict in 1995. He did not make any headway for the re-entry programme and many Ogoni people have concluded that Fr. Kukah's assignment was a "failed mission" in the region. It is for this reason that MOSOP is never convinced of SPDC's commitment to genuine dialogue or peace in the region.

2. *Adoption of pan-Delta strategy*: The Ogoni crises have revealed an umbilical link between the gross underdevelopment of the Niger Delta, the manner of control and management of its resources, the poor development of its human capacity on the one hand, and the perennial crises in the region on the other. The lesson here is that there is need for a pan-Deltaic strategy (Rosel, 1995) where by the people would "apply coordinated measures" to impress on the federal government/SPDC to stop the exploitation of oil and gas in the region on their own terms instead of those of the people. To activate this lesson, the activities of the local bourgeoisies have to be checked through community action.
3. *Pursuance of constructive dialogue*: The final lesson is the need for the Ogoni people, in particular and the 3,000 communities in the region in general, to engage the federal government and MNOCs in constructive dialogue that would produce mutually beneficial results. The role of the federal government in this regard is very crucial. It has to demonstrate the political will to confront the MNOCs and get them to apply the same level of "corporate social responsibilities" in the Niger Delta as they would in Britain. "But what is happening in the Niger Delta" as Adejoh (2005: 353) puts it, "is the result of years of iniquity and high handedness. Pushed to the wall, the people of the region have realized that it is sometimes more honorable to die." The Nigerian state has to look beyond the concept of palliative measures (charity programs) to that of making the communities become partners. It is for this reason Harold Dappa-Biriye, patriarch of the Niger Delta, developed the doctrine of "from charity to partnership" and confronted General Abdulsalami Abubakar, former head of state and government in 1998 with it (Etekpe et al. 2003:130–3). Whereas General Abubakar neither appreciated nor operationalized the doctrine, President Yar'Adua's government came to terms with it and applied the doctrine as one of the cardinal post-amnesty programs. By it, the

federal government has conceded 5 percent equity shares of MNOCs to the OPCs. This is another landmark development that evolved from the peace process.

SUGGESTIONS

Based on the lessons learned from this project, the paper offers the following two suggestions for bringing lasting peace in the Niger Delta.

1. Involving the local people in oil ventures: It is natural that the OPCs should be incorporated into the oil business as shareholders. This would make them eager to protect oil installations and forestall restiveness. We foresee that as long as they are kept out of it, they will continue with the agitation at the detriment of the industry and society.
2. Resisting local bourgeoisie: The activities of the corrupt local bourgeoisies and leaders have to be checked through community action as well as strengthening the anticorruption agencies to arrest and prosecute them. The local communities should not merely watch these "dry land pirates" loot our collective resources. This is where the local and international NGOs become crucial in empowering the people through capacity building trainings/programs to frontally confront them. It is worth mentioning that the "process to change the structure" has started in some communities in Rivers and Bayelsa states, namely, Edegberi, Gbarain-Ekpetiama, Nembe, and Umuechem.

REFERENCES

Adejoh, P. E. (2005). "Armed resistance in the Niger Delta and the future of conflicts in Nigeria." In A. M. Yakubu (Ed.), *Crisis and conflict management in Nigeria since 1990*, Vol. 1, Kaduna: Nigerian Defence Academy:pp.337–53

Albert, I. O. (2004). *Introduction to third-party intervention in community conflicts*, Ibadan: Peace Transformation.

Azar, E. (1990). *The management of protracted social conflict: Theory and cases*, Worcester: Dartmouth.

Bailey, K. D. (1982). *Methods of social research* (2nd ed.), New York: Free Press.

Beer, J. E., and Stief, E. (1997). *The mediator's handbook*, Gabriola Island, BC, Canada: New Study Publishers.

Berkowitz, L. (1962). *Aggression: A sociological analysis*, New York: McGraw Hill.

Best, S. G. (Ed.). (2006). *Introduction to peace and conflict studies in West Africa*. Ibadan: Spectrum Books Ltd.

Boro, I. J. A. (1982). *The twelve-day revolution*, Benin City: Idodo Umeh Publishers.

Cooley, J. W. (1992). "Arbitration vs mediation: Explaining the differences." In J. J. Faleg and R. Armstrong (Eds.), *A peace reader: Essential readings on war, justice, non-violence and world order*, New York: Panelist Press: pp 60–2

Diamond, L. and McDonald, J. (1996). *Multi-track diplomacy: A system approach to peace*, West Hartford: Kumarian Press.

Dollard, J. (1939). "Hostility and fear in the social life," *Social Forces*, Vol. 17, No. 1, October:pp.25–7

Dumpe, B. B. (1997). "The military and state building in Nigeria: Federal–state relations in Nigeria's military federalism, 1966–1976." In A. B. Akinyemi et al. (Eds.), *Readings on Federalism*, Lagos: NIIA:pp.15–20.

Etekpe, A. (2007a). Minority politics in Nigeria: The case of south–south and Middle Belt regions, Lagos: Kemuela Publications.

Etekpe, A. (2007b). The politics and conflict over oil and gas in the Niger Delta Region: The Bayelsa State experience, Port Harcourt: TowerGate Resources.

Etekpe, A. (2010). *Conflict management and resolution in Nigeria: The Niger Delta perspective*, Port Harcourt: Pearl Publishers.

Galtung, J. (1990). "Cultural violence," *Journal of Peace Research*,27:p.3

Gurr, T. (1970). *Why men rebel*, Princeton, NJ: Princeton University Press.

Godongs, S. (2006). "Mediation and mediation process." In S. Best (Ed.), *Introduction to peace and conflict studies in West Africa*, Ibadan: Spectrum Books:pp.135–45

Holdaway, S. (1980). "The police station," *Urban Life: A Quarterly Journal of Ethnographic Research*, Vol. 9:pp.79–100

Human Rights Watch (HRW). (1995). *The price of oil: Corporate responsibility and human rights violations in Nigeria's oil producing communities*, New York: Author.

Humphrey, L. (1970). *Tearoom trade: Impersonal sex in public places*. Chicago: Aldine.

Ibaba, S. I. (2008). *Democracy and development in the Niger Delta*, Monograph Series No. 2, Department of Political Science, Niger Delta University, Bayelsa State.

Ibaenu, O. (2006). "Conceptualising peace." In S. Best (Ed.), *Introduction to peace and conflict studies in West Africa*, Ibadan: Spectrum Books Ltdpp.4–10

Ihejirika, S. (1998). "Workshop handbook on conflict management skills training for community leaders," *The Nigeria Peace Centre*, SEMA Ltd, Kaduna.

Ihonvbere, J. (2002). "A recipe for perpetual crisis: The Nigerian state and the Niger Delta question." In Raji, et al (eds), *Boiling Point: The Crisis in the Oil Producing Communities in Nigeria*, Lagos: CDHRpp.40–5.

Ikelegbe, A. (2006). "The perverse manifestation of civil society: Evidence from Nigeria," *Journal of Modern African Studies*, Vol. 39, No. 1:p25 Imobighe, T. A. (Ed.). (2003). *Civil societies and ethnic conflict management in Nigeria*, Ibadan: College Press.

Imobighe, T. A. et al. (2002). *Conflict and instability in the Niger Delta: The Warri case*, Ibadan: Spectrum Books Ltd.

Kerr, J. A. C. (1979). *Space use by medical surgical hospital ward staff.* Unpublished PhD dissertation, Los Angeles: University of California.

Kontech, R. (2006). "Responding to conflicts: The role of civil society in West Africa," *UNDP Programme Consultant*, ECOWAS Secretariat, Abuja, Nigeria, June 13.

Lorenz, K. (1966). *On aggression*. New York: Harcourt Brace.

Mattu, R. (2001). "Civil society in Argentina: What is civil society?" *Latitudes*, Vol. 4. pp.68–70. Nnoli, O. (2003). *Communal conflict and population displacement in Nigeria: A research Report*. Enugu: Pan African Centre for Research in Peace (PACRP).

Obasanjo, O. and Mabogunje, A. (Eds.). (1992). *Elements of democracy*, Abeokuta: African Leadership Forum.

Ochoche, S. (2006). "Non-governmental organizations and conflict management in Nigeria." In A. M. Yakubu (Ed.), *Crisis and conflict management in Nigeria since 1980*, Vol. 2, Kaduna: Nigerian Defence Academy:pp.792–6.

Opukri, C. O. and Etekpe, A. (2008). "The multi-track approach to peace-building in the Niger Delta," Niger Delta Digest Monograph Series, Centre for Niger Delta Studies, Niger Delta University, Bayelsa State.

Osaghae, E. (1994). "Inter-state relations in Nigeria," *Publius: The Journal of Federalism*, Vol. 24, No. 4:p.50

Osaghae, E. (2001). "From accommodation to self-determination: Minority nationalism and the restructuring of the Nigerian state," *Nationalism and Ethnic Politics*, Vol. 7, No. 1:pp. 40–6

Osaghae, E. (2009). "Ethnic nationalities and Nigerian federalism," Paper presentation at Ijaw National Congress(INC) Annual Lecture Series, Warri, Delta State, March 11.

Osiago, U. S. B. (2009). "Niger Delta Forum (NDF): The transition from a pressure group to NGO status: The challenges and the opportunities," Paper Presented on the *Occasion of NDF Interaction*, National Orientation Agency Conference Room, Port Harcourt, August 30.

Otite, O. and Albert, I. O. (2002). *Community conflict in Nigeria: Management, resolution and transformation*, Ibadan: Spectrum Books Ltd.

Oyedele, E. (Ed.). (1998). *African national unity, stability and development*, Ibadan: Spectrum Books Ltd.

Raji, M. and Sabine, S (Eds.). (2002). *Boiling point: The crisis in the oil producing communities in Nigeria*, Lagos: CDHR.

Rosel, J. (1995). *Ethnic nationalism and ethnic conflict in international politics and society*, Bonni: Friedrich Ebert Foundation.

Saro-Wiwa, K. (1985). *My story in Ogoni travails and trials*, Lagos: Civil Liberties Organizations.

Saro-Wiwa, K. (1989). *Genocide in Nigeria*, Port Harcourt: Saros International Publishers.

Tedheke, M. E. U. (2005). "The national question versus micro-national chauvinism: Issues in the dialectics of conflicts in Nigeria." In A. M. Yakubu et al. (Eds.), *Crisis and conflict management in Nigeria since 1980*, Vol. 2, Kaduna: Nigerian Defence Academy (NDA): p. 427.

Tyoden, S. G. (Ed.). (1994). *Nigeria: Youth agenda for the 21st century*, Ibadan: Sibon Books Ltd.

Wilmot, W. W. (1998). *Interpersonal conflict*, Boston: McGraw Hill.

Yakubu, A. M. (2005). *Crisis and conflict management in Nigeria since 1980*, Vol. 1. *Causes and dimensions of conflict*, Kaduna: Nigerian Defence Academy.

Yakubu, A. M. et al. (Eds.). (2003). *Management of social conflicts in a plural society*, Kaduna: Arewa Consultative Forum.

Yakubu, G. (1999). "Strategies for involving NGOs in successful implementation of poverty alleviation programme," Paper Presentation to the Presidential Panel on Streamlining and Rationalization of Poverty Alleviation Institutions/Agencies in Nigeria, Abuja: The Presidency, September 16.

Yates, A. (1962). *Frustration and conflict*. London: Methuen.

Young, P. V. (2000). *Scientific social surveys and research*. New Delhi: Prentice-Hall of India Ltd.

7 Land Reform, Land Rights, and Development Challenges in Nigeria

A Focus on the Niger Delta

Yinka Kehinde Binuomoyo, Johnson B. Ogbewo, Ephraim A. Okoro, and Okechukwu Ukaga

INTRODUCTION

Over the past five decades, Nigeria's economic pathway has been defined by oil. Most probably, all of the country's economic variables have the input of oil: budget, GDP, exchange rates, international trade, employment, and so on. The advent of oil has been helpful in ensuring that the country maintains its "giant of Africa" status in terms of politics and economics. But then, sadly, oil has also infected the country with the "Dutch disease,"[1] as all the other sectors including agriculture and manufacturing have been negatively affected, while corruption has become rife and alarmingly high throughout the country.

The preceding dilemma raises a question: Should government continue to rely on oil to finance its fiscal activities? This question may seem pointless as long as oil is not yet exhausted in the country. However, the question is important for at least one reason, which is that oil would definitely dry up one day and government would then be left without such a major source of funding (Humphrey 1986).[2] Even before Nigeria runs out of oil, new technologies such as electric cars and the discovery of other fuel alternatives may drastically reduce, if not eliminate, the economic benefit of oil. In any case, the Niger Delta which is the wellspring of the oil might be left to contend with poverty and devastated environment in the absence of the oil capital.

Another pertinent question arises: What is the government doing to invest part of the oil proceeds in sustainable development of the Niger Delta and the country as a whole? As Ibanga and Obi (2001) rightly noted, crude oil is an exhaustible resource but can have positive effects on both present and future generations "if the dictates of substitutability and sustainability are fully applied." Sustainability entails fairness regarding the treatment of present and future generations (Ibanga and Obi 2001; WCED[3]1987).

An analysis of the Nigeria's Land Use Act of 1978 would reveal an anti-citizenship structure that is not consistent with the growth and development goals the Brundtland Commission recommends that every country pursue.[4] It is, therefore, not surprising that a number of critics have called the existence of the act to question (Guardian 2008a; Guardian 2008c; Dafinone 2007; Michael 2009; Babatunde 2009). These critics argue that the Land Use Act has, among other things, hampered land ownership and transactions.

Against this backdrop, this chapter discusses the political and legal complexities of development and environmental sustainability in the Niger Delta. It takes into account the relationship between the political and legal structures and their effects on the social and economic frameworks of the region, by introducing a distinction between the macroeconomic interest of the country and that of the Niger Delta region.

For any policy reform to be declared successful, it should in the long-term result in conditions that are much better than the prevailing condition before the policy. Thus, by expansion, the Pareto analysis is applied to radical simplifications of the welfare theory in the light of legal, political, and economic transactions in respect of the Niger Delta. The chapter further examines the political and economic aspects of the Niger Delta condition and development strategy (Okaba 2008; Okonwa 2008; Nafziger 2008; Okereke 2008; Owugah 2008; Isa and Abang 2008; Olasupo and Erhum 2008; Nabhon and Perepreghabofa 2008).

There have been recurrent concerns about human rights problem in the Niger Delta region. What are the salient bones of contention within the Niger Delta? And what is the underlining reasoning behind these salient issues? Sustainable development—meeting current needs without compromising the ability of future generations to meet their own needs (WCED 1987)—involves appropriate use of natural and human resources to achieve economic growth, poverty alleviation, and environmental protection interrelated objectives (World Bank 1988). However, sustainable development does not appear to be the focus of government's agenda in the Niger Delta. The decay of social infrastructures, high unemployment, poverty, and contraction of the people's rights illustrates the above point. Thus, the violence in the Niger Delta is directly related to the prevailing social, economic and environmental condition in the region (Sam 2008; Ibeanu 2008). Indeed, a fundamental improvement of the physical and economic structures of the region similar to Lagos and the Federal Capital territory (FCT) would be helpful (Binuomoyo, n.d.).

According to the standard Paretian (Optimality) Criterion, welfare increases (or decreases) if at least one person is made better off (or worse off) with no change in the welfare of others (Jhigan 2004). From all indications, the overall welfare of the Niger Deltans has continued to decrease rather than increase, even as the oil companies, federal and state governments, and other powerful interests profit from their resources and degrade their social and economic environments. The constitutional provision of "overriding public interest" has been frequently utilized to serve the narrow interest of a few powerful or well-connected people and companies. The "public interest" rationality adopted by the government has resulted in an obvious imbalance in the Nigerian equation, attracting challenge by activists like of Ken Saro-Wiwa,[5] Owabukeruyele (2000), Okaba (2008), Okonwa (2007), and Otite (2008).

The current practice of deploying soldiers to the Niger Delta region to combat militants and protect oil pipelines rather than address the root causes of the problem—such as developmental inequalities, socioeconomic problems, and lack of faith or sense of belonging in Nigeria as a country—casts doubt on the promise and the responsibility of government. Indeed, it suggests that the government is more interested in the oil revenue than the welfare of the people (Binuomoyo 2009; Okonwa 2007; ThisDay 2009: 19). Nevertheless, the recent plan to give 10 percent of the oil revenue to the actual host oil communities in addition to the current allocation to the oil-producing states gives hope that an appropriate arrangement, like what they have in Alaska (United States) is possible in the Niger Delta.

NIGER DELTA, ITS OIL, AND THE DEVELOPMENT ISSUES

The place of the Niger Delta in Nigeria has often been debated. Being a region consisting of minorities, the Niger delta has experienced series of challenges including environmental, socioeconomic, and political problems—all having very serious negative impact on life. The issue of resource control has, in particular, been a recurrent bone of contention. Not only do the payments from the federal government to the oil-producing states often fall below the 13 percent derivation formula enshrined in the 1999 Constitution (FGN 1999), but the people would prefer to have outright control of the oil resource and pay revenues to the federal government. This has led to their call for the repeal of all land and mineral resources law which gave control of oil resources to the federal government (HRW 2002).

Within this debate, though, and over time, the political and economic responses of Nigeria to oil revenue have been mixed. And the place of the Niger Delta in charting its own course is relegated. As Okonwa (2008) noted, politics in Nigeria is neither a function of economic strength nor the desire for equal national development, but a self-serving system. This explains why the Niger Delta still feels relegated to the background with regard to the country's development and political setup despite contributing significantly to the development and growth of the Nigerian nation through oil. Even though the federal government established different commissions at different times to evaluate and address the Niger Delta development challenges, the region's claim to offshore oil revenue was nevertheless contested at the Supreme Court, thereby reducing its constituent states' revenue.

This and other actions by the Nigerian government that seem to disregard the region's interest are also perceived by most people as violation of their right to life, health, and good environment; to control their wealth and natural resources; and to be free of discrimination (HRW 2002). It is therefore not surprising that a Special Security Committee on Oil Producing Areas noted as follows:

1. The root causes of insecurity in the Niger Delta region has to do with the neglect, frustration, and the sense of abandonment shared by the people;
2. The meager derivation payments to the Niger Delta states is not enough for the massive developmental projects the area needs;
3. The Land Use Act, Petroleum Act, and other related laws have impacted the region and people negatively; and
4. The nonemployment of local people by the oil companies and government has contributed to great unemployment and vulnerability of the youths.[6]

Again, the lack of land and resource control rights is the principal issue the region is faced with. This has been aggravated by the large diseconomies following oil exploration and production. In all, the general level of poverty in the Niger Delta region has continued to rise, as people lose their means of livelihood due to pollution of the environment. Further, the absence of infrastructure has constrained sustainable development. To make the situation worse, oil workers tend to put upward pressure on price of goods and services with their relatively deep pockets thereby making things very expensive for the average Niger Delta resident.

THE LAND USE ACT, HUMAN RIGHTS, AND NIGERIA'S CONSTITUTIONAL PROVISION

Internal crises like the Niger Delta development problems are some of the reasons some observers doubt that Nigeria will exist much longer as a country. While this may be a very pessimistic view, more critical, however, is the fundamental problem of shying away from addressing the root causes of such crises, namely political and legal structures that do not respond positively to the needs of the people. In a "humane" society, laws are "constructed" to protect the people and to meet their development needs. In contrast, evidence has been provided on the anti-development orientation of certain Nigerian laws especially those dealing with resource-exploitation (Owabukeruyele 2000). For instance, the Land Use Act of 1978 along with the Petroleum Act of 1969 restrict local citizens' access to communal land while making it possible for the oil multinational companies to have unrestricted access to such lands. The Land Use Act 1978 (originally Decree No. 6 of 1978), provides that

> all land comprised in the territory of each state in the Federation are [sic] hereby vested in the Governor of that State and such land shall be held in trust and administered for the use and common benefit of all Nigerians.[7]

The Land Use Act of 1978 determines who has access to land, where, how, and for what purpose. It defines the systems of land ownership and in many cases suspends existing systems of land ownership. Though the former president, Umaru Yar'Adua, wanted to address the Niger Delta development situation with proposed amendment to Sections 5, 7, 15, 21, 22, 23, and 28 of the Land Use Act, he never achieved this goal.[8] While the president commissioned a task force to make this amendment successful, there was not a corresponding legislative appreciation of the need to reform the Land Use Act.[9]

The following are some of the notable problems with the Land Use Act in our opinion:

1. While the act intended to address the lack of security of title and the high cost and difficult process of accessing land, it generated more problems by creating more bureaucracy and opportunities for corrupt practices.
2. The act has resulted in government's confiscation of land from private hands without regard to the social and economic effect of such confiscation on the people.
3. The compensation provision stipulated by the act is arbitrary and not consistent with the prevailing economic and market realities.
4. The act gives absolute authority to the governors thereby turning them into dictators when dealing with land use.
5. The act does not protect or preserve the rights of all Nigerians to use and enjoy their land and the benefits thereof.

Tenure complexities, limited accessibility to land, nonimplementation of land ceiling, insecurity of certificates of occupancy, inhibiting consent provisions, high cost of land transactions, and nonenforcement of development provisions are some of the problems that the act has bred. The governors have also compounded the situations, brewing corruption with the dysfunctional law (ThisDay 2009: 19).

By the provisions of the 1979, 1989, and draft 1995 constitutions, as well as the Petroleum Act, the ownership and control of all petroleum resources within and under the Nigerian land (including its territorial waters) is vested in the government.[10] This represents the extension of government's land ownership and control by the Land Use Act. This law (Land Use Act of 1978) is arguably the law that has the most direct impact on the wellbeing of natural resource-dependent people like the Niger Deltans. It has strengthened other land and resource-related laws and policies, with attendant negative effects on the people.

The Land Use Act in the Context of Human Rights

The Land Use Act makes land expropriation possible for oil production and other purposes. Whereas the constitution provides that no right or interest in any property may be acquired compulsorily except as otherwise provided by law, in which case compensation should be paid as determined by a court of law or tribunal, this right has nevertheless been eroded by over-riding military decrees which in turn have been entrenched in succeeding constitutional amendments.[11]

Thus, the Land Use Act presents itself in a dictatorial manner. It not only empowers a state governor to revoke a land owner's right of occupancy for reasons of "overriding public interest" (e.g., mining or installing oil pipelines), but it also restricts court's jurisdiction over executive action in such matters. For instance, the act limits the courts' ability to freely determine whether the compensation paid (or to be paid) is adequate.[12] Notably, where land is acquired for mining purposes, the act provides that the occupier pays compensation as stipulated under the Petroleum Act (formerly Mineral Oil Act). Even though the Mineral Oil Act provides for compensation where a land is acquired, the Petroleum Act (Decree 51 of 1969) does not make such provision, although it requires the holders of oil exploration licenses, oil prospecting licenses or oil mining leases to pay "fair and adequate compensation for the disturbance of surface or other rights" to the owner. But the land owner is not entitled to royalties for oil extracted from the land.[13] The Oil Pipelines Act also provides for compensation with regards to surface rights and the loss of value of the pipelines-affected land, with compensation disputes to be decided by the court taking into consideration the economic value of the land.[14]

As rightly noted by Amnesty International, the exploration and production of oil continue to result in deprivation, injustice, and violence in the oil-producing Niger Delta region.[15] The land owners' rights to contest acquisition of their land and to obtain appropriate compensation are severely limited by legal restrictions imposed by the Nigerian government. The oil companies are intentionally given upper (free) hand to literarily operate as they please without regard to the people's needs and concerns. This promotes human rights abuses and environmental pollution as the oil companies have all the power and support while and the people have little or no protection. The continued flaring of natural gases for decades by the oil companies at great financial, environmental, and human costs to the country and the government's inability or unwillingness stop this deplorable activity despite the citizens desire to see flaring end, illustrates the preceding point. The occasional use of security forces to destroy communities and even kill people with apparent impunity just to protect the oil industry is also very instructive. Further, the production, use, trading, and disposals of toxic wastes and products in the region results in deaths, reduced life expectancy, life-threatening diseases, infant mortality, sterility, and other major handicaps all of which amount to abuse of the right to life. Beyond the right to life, other human rights at stake in the Niger Delta include: right to good standard of health, adequate food, remedy, gainful employment (work), and right to information and participation (Ibeanu 2008).

Revisiting the 2005 NPRC

Perhaps in an effort to avoid impending crisis, the Obasanjo administration partially conceded to a long-demanded organization for a sovereign national conference (SNC)[16] by organizing the National Political Reform Conference the (NPRC), which was supposed to address unfairness in the system, and recommend constitutional and policy amendments. The conference was designed to create a viable political renewal for the country. Some contentious issues were raised. The following are the fundamental ones that affect the Niger Delta (sometimes represented by the South-South):[17]

1. Oil revenue sharing formula
2. Resource control
3. Rotational presidency
4. Tenures of office for political electives
5. Abrogation or repeal of certain laws deemed obnoxious by the Niger Deltans (e.g., the Land Use Act 1978, the Exclusive Economic Zone Act Cap. 116, and the Petroleum Decree 1969)

Political reform to achieve these goals may increase tensions within the polity, at least in the short run. But if done fairly and effectively, reform might lead to stability, growth, security, and sustainable development in the long run. However, it is difficult to predict what the future holds for the Niger delta in particular and Nigeria in general.

Reconstructing the Legal Tablet

Appropriate legal framework is important for sustainable development (Sachs 1996). The former president Umaru Yar'Adua understood when in his 2007 campaign manifesto he listed land reform as key in his agenda. According to him, land reform would optimize Nigeria's growth through the release of lands for commercial farming and other large scale businesses. The idea is to facilitate easy but fair access to land, which in turn should boost output and improve capacity for wealth creation.[18] This would also preclude compulsory land acquisition, which does not guarantee fair access to land, but instead impedes the human rights of the original owners and occupants of the land.

A review of the country's constitution may help in solving the above problems (Belgore 2008: 52). The Constitution must address such grievances as the lack of equity in the allocation of resources. It can also serve as a moderator of social conflict around such issues as the lopsided distribution of power between the federal government and the supposedly federating units (Oyebode 2008: 9). Towards this end, Madunagu (2008) underscores the need to make other laws consistent with the basic laws of the constitution (which are Chapters 1–4). He also advised that the "national question" should not be confused with the "problem of federalism."

While the national question is essentially about the complex relationship between the various ethnic nationalities, the problem of federalism relates to allocation of power and resources between the center and the regions. Both need attention. The major challenge as is the case with the Niger Delta militants, the demand of the Igbos[19] for an additional state in the South-East geographical zone, and the campaign of the Movement for the Actualization of the Sovereign State of Biafra (MASSOB) against "marginalization" and "genocide," fall under the national question. Such problems can only be resolved through a true sovereign national conference. On the other hand, the campaign for a true federation as championed in the past by the Alliance for Democracy (AD) and Afenifere,[20] and the call for the shifting of the balance of power between the federal and state governments (more powers to the state) by the South-South Forum are problems of federalism. These can be resolved through constitutional amendments.[21] Obviously, only a people-driven constitutional reform could effectively address their basic needs.

THE LAND USE ACT, LAND RIGHTS AND THE PARETIAN CRITERION

Guaranteed land rights are key determinants of social and economic development. The lack of social and legal certainty around land policies, and the "locked" nature of land ownership, pose serious obstacles to economic development in Nigeria. These have constituted severe challenges to the poor. As de Soto (2000) noted, the lack of property rights impedes the transformation of assets and wealth of the poor into capital in view of the fact that land constitutes a major form of wealth and source of power for their livelihood. Land rights within the political and legal boundaries of Nigeria are somehow ambiguous. Land is a major source of income for the rural people and provides food security, cultural identity, and shelter, as well as a basic asset for empowering the poor and a safety net during hardships.[22] Hence, land (and related resource) rights of indigenous people are obviously critical for their well-being.

Challenges to developing new land policies and legislation, especially in Africa, include a conflicting heritage of statutory and customary systems, the pressures of economic growth, and disagreements among key stakeholders.[23] Further, land rights in particular and human rights in general are also about power. Notably, the Land Use Act takes away the peoples traditional power to control their resources and transfers it to government. And the government officials on whom the responsibility for land certification rests have often misused this power either for selfish gains or out of negligence and indifference.

As the World Bank (1996) explained, land reform deals with "changing the institutional structure governing man's relationship with the land, involving intervention in the prevailing pattern of land ownership, control and usage in order to change the structure of holdings, improve land productivity and broaden the distribution of benefits." This definition not only shows that power is the underlying factor in land ownership and distribution, but also highlights the following four important characteristics of land laws:

1. They give the direction of land ownership.
2. They specify the use of land.
3. They do not necessarily give absolute right of ownership to land owners.
4. They may alter prevailing ownership, distribution and usage, to align with evolving policies and land-related laws.

When the Land Use Act was promulgated in 1978, it was specifically intended to promote agricultural productivity. At the time, agriculture was not only Nigeria's largest employer of labor; it also contributed the most to the GDP. But, arguably, the country's agricultural prowess was being reduced by land tenure problems and the increasing conversion of agriculture-designated land for other uses. However, rather than solve the prevailing problems the Land Use Act seems to have mainly created new ones as discussed in this chapter. Hence, the call to reform the Land Use Act. Demands for greater social and infrastructural facilities, housing, and industrial structures have led to the need to relax the laws in order to ease transactions and enhance development. While equal access to land cannot be guaranteed, it is important to introduce a fair market mechanism that would ensure adequate reward system for the original land owners.

Land reform is imperative if the country is to avert future conflicts over land rights. This is possible either by agreeing mutually on a political structure that would assure the people's right to control their own resources, or enacting and enforcing laws that protect the human and constitutional rights of the people. Dale (2007) listed the goals of an ideal land reform as follows:

1. Transparent and secured land transactions
2. Reduction in the cost of land transactions
3. Access to other transactions and business deals like loans

4. Protection of not only minorities' rights but also those of every other person to ensure justice and equity for all
5. Promote the sustainability of the environment and inherent resources.

Toward this end, criteria and conditions for validating land transactions must go beyond recognition of rights of first occupants, to also take into account the principles of citizenship, democracy, and human rights (IIED 2002). In the case of the Niger Delta, people should be given legal security in respect of their rights and the arrangements they make with oil companies. This means backing them up with legislations that would favor their livelihood pre- and post-transactions.

Land rights as a tool for empowerment triangulates on three structures: legal, political, and economic. The political structure is essential for the proper functioning of the others as it lays the foundation for the effective operation of the legal framework. The legal framework is in turn responsible for distributing economic resources fairly among all actors in the polity (see Figure 7.1[24]).

Nigeria practiced true federation between 1953 and 1966 when each region had exclusive jurisdiction over its own natural resources, and this accounted for the competitive communalism and rapid development witnessed during that period. This, as Akiri (2008: 9) puts it, was the position

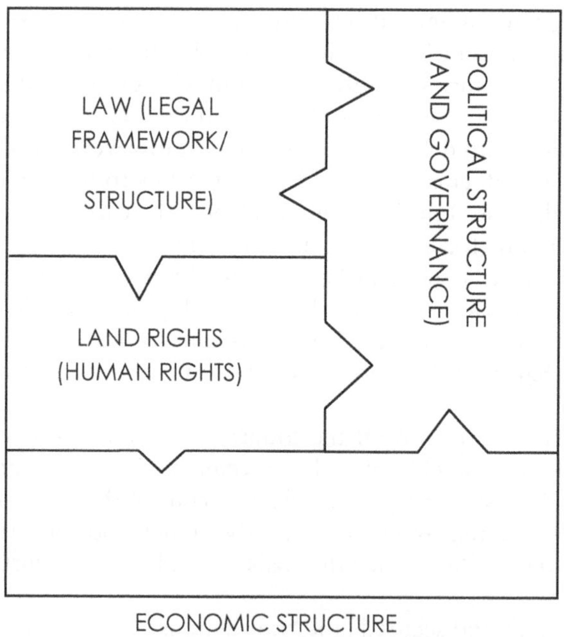

Figure 7.1 Gridlock of resource flow showing a polity's structural design.

of Chief Obafemi Awolowo in his book, *The Strategy and Tactics of the People's Republic of Nigeria*, as follows:

> In discussing the principle (i.e. of revenue allocation on the basis of derivation), I would like to make only six observations . . . In a capitalist society, whether it is a federation or not, it is untenable and dishonest in the extreme, to insist on sharing another person's or another state's wealth on the basis other than that which the rules of the capitalist game allow . . . every state is perfectly entitled to keep its wealth.

This strategy helped facilitate development in the whole country as each region strived to create wealth and did not depend on the centre for funding. When agriculture was the chief economic resource, the North, South-West, and South-East regions each enjoyed unlimited access to their land. However, with the discovery of oil the federal government enacted laws and decrees that effectively reduced citizen's access to their land. Now, they only have absolute ownership over their land, if it is not oil or mineral rich. Therefore, it can be stated that land right is determined by how valuable the resource in the land is. Further, priorities of the people are often not given preference except where the actions of the militant groups threaten oil production.

Niger Deltans (and indeed all Nigerians) should be granted full control of their own lands. This would not only enhance and support their livelihood by empowering them to utilize their land for any purpose they find appropriate. Obviously, land rights represents far more than land as it confers on the people a sense of control of their resources and destiny. But it also raises the challenge of optimizing (not maximizing) options to achieve welfare improvement for some people with no corresponding negativity on others.

It is assumed that land ownership is communal, and of course, not all communities in the Niger Delta have oil deposits. (And there are obviously other communities outside the Niger Delta that have oil deposits and/or other minerals). The Paretian criterion as choice of justice disposition makes a difference. Unlike A. C. Pigou's view of welfare economics, the Pareto optimality seeks a situation of welfare change for at least one person with no corresponding negativity on the other person (Jhingan 2004). It is on this basis that the Kaldor-Hicks Criterion is adopted in addressing series of externalities that might arise from one community to another. Kaldor-Hicks criterion is defined within the Niger Delta and the Nigerian economy as a whole, as follows:

1. As an ethical issue: Social welfare is increased in the case where some people are made better off and others not worse off, as the gainers from the change have compensated the losers (e.g. for negative externality due to pollution), without negatively affecting themselves as well by providing relieving social and infrastructural amenities.

2. As a political issue: The community that is better off pays taxes to the central government to be able to raise development structures in other parts of the country that can help even developmental gap.
3. As an economic externality effect: Because of the oil production and trade, there is created a high cost of living and a labor aristocracy of huge wages surrounded by a great mass of unemployment or underemployment; thus, there is a compensation payoff from the gainers through the taxes which help provide social and infrastructural facilities to reduce the cost of living.

The Pareto optimality thus enhances efficient allocation of resources so that within a political and resource-partial entity, there are no complaints and no developmental gaps; it distributes resources from the resource owners to non-resource owners on the basis of ethical, political, and economic externality effect criteria.

In the past few years, a number of strategies have been conceived in a bid to attain development sustainability in the Niger Delta region, including the recent call for the legal obligation of corporate social responsibility (CSR). Toward this end, a bill is currently making its way through the legislature, which if passed, would ensure that CSR goes beyond moral obligation to become legally binding on companies (Omamegbe 2009: 12).[25] Other strategies include the implementation of the Ledum Mitee-Led Presidential Technical Committee on the Niger Delta, which among other things, recommended an increase in oil derivation from the present 13 percent to 25 percent; establishment of empowerment scheme for the youths; free education up to the secondary school for the Niger Delta; establishment of a Community Trust Fund; oil companies' provision of insurance against pollution; initiation and completion of all social and infrastructural projects to open up the Deltas to other cities; establishment of a special Niger Delta Infrastructural and Intervention Fund; establishment of a Multi-Stakeholder Niger Delta Policy and Project Compliance Monitoring Committee; establishment of a Niger Delta Futures Trust Fund for Oil-Producing Communities; protection and advancement of the rights of minorities and micro-minorities; the repeal of all laws that regulate land and oil transactions, which have been having negative bearings on the region; and enforcement of laws to check and control environmental pollution in the region (Guardian 2008b; Akiri 2008; Guardian 2008c). The Ledum Mitee-Led Technical Report could possibly be regarded as a harmonization of recommendations from every other meetings and conferences, although it did not recommend the repeal of the so-called obnoxious laws like the Land Use Act of 1978, and Petroleum Act of 1999 (Guardian 2008a).

CONCLUSIONS

This chapter focused on Nigeria's Land Use Act and related laws affecting the Niger Deltans' land ownership. It also examined, among other things, the implications for sustainable development and human rights. Based on empirical evidence, review of relevant literature, and discussions with appropriate authorities, we found that intertwined with the oil resource control issue is the feeling of political and development inequity and injustice among citizens of Niger Delta. To successfully address this problem, the federal, state and local government should work effectively with local communities and the oil companies to assure appropriate infrastructural development and, more importantly empower the people to control their land, natural resources and destiny. Notably, there is an urgent need for political and legal frameworks for balancing the tension between land rights and expropriation with a market-based system in order to promote fair economic transactions.

NOTES

1. "Dutch disease" refers to an economic condition of negative consequences arising from large increases to a country's income, primarily associated with natural resource discovery, like oil. See Investopedia (2009).
2. The drying up of oil referred to here is not necessarily absolute, but to make the pint that oil is a finite resource.
3. The WCED, chaired by Gro Harlem Brundtland, worked examined policies and long-term strategies for achieving sustainable development.
4. For the Land Use Act, See Federal Government of Nigeria (FGN 1990a).
5. Ken Saro-Wiwa was a poet from the Ogoni village, an oil-producing community in the Niger Delta where environmental degradation is reportedly high. He was sentenced to death along with other eight colleagues of his by the military regime of Sani Abacha in 1995. See Etepke, in this volume, for some insights about this. See also http://www.umich.edu/ ~ snre492/cases_03_04/ogoni/ogoni_study.htm (accessed December 3, 2007).
6. See HRW (2002).
7. See the Land Use Act, Section 1, in FGN (1990a).
8. See FGN (2009) and FGN (1990a).
9. The yearning by Nigerians for the reform of the Land Use Act 1978 was positively responded to by the former president, Umar Yar'adua, with the set up of a Presidential Technical Committee on April 2, 2009 to undertake the reform of the land tenure situation in the country following the various problems emanating from the Act. The Committee is still in its test phase with the current president, Goodluck Jonathan pledging to pursue the land reform process started by his predecessor, Umar Yar'Adua. See Mabogunje (n.d.).
10. Several Decrees and Acts, including main constitutional provisions which have evolved thereafter upholds the Land Use Act, including the 1999 Constitution. See further, FGN (1990a, 1990b, 1990c, 1999) among others.
11. Most Nigerian laws are products of military decrees. The referenced can be sighted in the 1979 Constitution (Article 40); 1989 Constitution (Article 42 [3]); and the draft 1995 Constitution (Article 47 [1]). See also reference 23 above.
12. See Section 27, the Land Use Act, in FGN (1990a).
13. For the Petroleum Act, see FGN (1990b).
14. Oil Pipelines Act, Cap 338, Laws of the Federation of Nigeria, see FGN (1990c).

15. Amnesty International USA's 2006 Annual report for Nigeria covering events from January to December 2005.
16. SNC was actually the idea of pro-democracy activists in the country, but the Obasanjo administration shelved this for the NPRC, knowing that the outcome of a SNC would have a binding effect especially if backed by a referendum. The activists however went ahead with its own SNC, which did not really have any consequence.
17. The South-South is one of the six geo-political zones into which the country is ethnically divided and consists of the core Niger Delta states of Bayelsa, Delta, Edo, Rivers, Cross River and Akwa Ibom. Ondo state, though a South-West state, is also regarded as a Niger Delta state because of the presence of creeks and oil. The interest of the Niger Delta is often represented by the South–South.
18. Land reform as one of the cardinal focus of the late former president, Umaru Yar'Adua was part of the Seven Point Agenda, which he listed during his 2007 presidential campaign. And of course, before his death in 2010, he not only set up a high-powered committee but also submitted a bill to reform some critical provisions of the 1978 Land Use Act. See Yar'Adua's Seven Point + Two Special Interest Issues Agenda for Nigeria. Retrieved from http://www.cenbank.org/Out/EduSeries/Fiscal%20reforms.pdf (accessed February 7, 2011).
19. Nigeria officially has three largest tribal groups, one of which is the Igbos (to the South-East). Others are the Hausas (in the core North) and Yorubas (South-West). The emerging fourth dimensional ethnic group is the Ijaw in the South- South.
20. Afenifere is a pan-Yoruba sociocultural group which advances the cause of the Yorubas but well known for using aggressive and violent means in pursuit of their cause. The Alliance for Democracy is a major political party which evolved principally from the Southwest.
21. This whole paragraph is largely credited to Edwin Madunagu. See Madunagu (2008: 79).
22. See UN FAO factsheet on land tenure available at http://www.un.org/esa/sustdev/csd/csd16/documents/fao-factsheet/landtenure.pdf (accessed on December 9, 2009).
23. See http://www.iied.org/pubs/pdfs/7416IIED.pdf (accessed on December 9, 2009).
24. The arrow points in the direction of resource flow. Whenever and wherever the gridlocks are misaligned, there is resource wastage. Resource here refers to governance and policies, and their characteristics.
25. See FGN (2008), for the CSR Bill.

REFERENCES

Agiobenebo, T. J. and Aribaolanari, N (2001). "Rights, resource control and politico-economic equilibrium of the market for national union," Paper presented at the 2001 Annual Conference of the Nigerian Economic Society (NES) on August 28–31, 2001, in Port Harcourt, themed: Natural Resource Use, the Environment and Sustainable Development.

Akiri, C. (2008). "The Niger Delta and the conquistadors," *The Guardian*, September 30, 2008.

Amnesty International. (2006). *Annual report for Nigeria*, http://www.amnestyusa.org/annualreport.php?id=ar&yr=2006&c=NGA (accessed December 14, 2009)

Babatunde, L. (2009). "What to do with the Land Use Act," *The Guardian*, March 10.

Belgore, A. S. M. (2008). "Nigeria's underdevelopment: The problem of constitution or governance?" Being the text of an address at the Save Nigeria Movement Conference in Kaduna, *The Guardian*, November 5.

Binuomoyo, O. K. (2009). "Groaning and wearied: An assessment of the problems of a deregulated economy to Nigerians," *International Journal of Development Studies*, Vol. 4, No. 3, pp. 123–135.

Binuomoyo, Y. K. (n.d.). *Socio-political reform and entity identity: Nigeria's struggles towards stability*. Unpublished

Dafinone, D. (2007). "The Niger Delta crisis: Genesis, exodus and solution," *Vanguard*, November 16.

Dale, P. (2007). "Good land administration: Its role in the economic development," Keynote Speech delivered at the Land Administration in Transition International Workshop, Waanbaatar, Mongolia, June 27–29, 2007.

de Soto, H. (2000). *The mystery of capital: Why capitalism triumphs in the West and fails everywhere else*. New York: Basic Books.

Department for International Development) (DFID). (2002). "Focus on sustainability." *Developments*, Issue 18, Second Quarter, p. 3.

ENI S.P.A (n.d.). Energy and Economic Analysis Department (CD-Rom).

Federal Government of Nigeria (FGN). (1990a). *Land Use Act, Cap. 202*. Laws of the Federation of Nigeria, Abuja: The Federal Government Printer.

FGN. (1990b). *Petroleum Act, Cap. 350*. Laws of the Federation of Nigeria, Abuja: The Federal Government Printer.

FGN. (1990c). *Oil Pipelines Act, Cap. 338*. Laws of the Federation of Nigeria, Abuja: The Federal Government Printer.

FGN. (1999). *Constitution of the Federal Republic of Nigeria*, Abuja: The Federal Government Printer.

FGN. (2008). *Corporate Social Responsibility Commission (Establishment, etc.) Bill*, Abuja: The Federal Government Printer.

FGN. (2009). *Land Use Act (Amendment) Bill*, Abuja: The Federal Government Printer

Guardian. (2008a). "Conference of ethnic nationalities of the Niger Delta (CENND): The position of the CENND on the Nigerian Project," *The Guardian*, August 3.

Guardian. (2008b). "New hope for the Niger Delta?" *The Guardian*, December 17.

Guardian. (2008c). "Technical committee report on the Niger Delta," *The Guardian*, December 9, 2008.

Human Rights Watch (HRW). (2002). *The Niger Delta: No democratic dividend*. Vol. 14, No. 7 (A), October. New York: Author.

Humphrey, T. M. (1986). *Essays on inflation* (5th ed.). Richmond, VA: Federal Reserve Bank of Richmond.

Ibanga, I. and Obi, P. B. (2001). "Sustainability and depletibility of resource use in Nigeria: The case of crude oil," Paper presented at the 2001 Annual Conference of the Nigerian Economic Society (NES) on August 28–31, 2001, in Port Harcourt, themed: Natural Resource Use, the Environment and Sustainable Development.

Ibeanu, O. (2008). "Two rights make a wrong: Bringing human rights back into the Niger Delta discourse," Paper presented at the International Conference on the Nigerian State, Oil Industry and the Niger Delta held at Yenagoa on March 11–13, 2008. Yenagoa, Bayelsa State: Department of Political Science, Niger Delta University.

International Institute for Environment and Development (IIED). (2002). "Land tenure and resource access in Africa," CD-ROM of paper presented at

International Workshop for Researchers and Policymakers Held at Ouagadougou, March 19–21, 2002, London: Author.

Investopedia. (n.d.) "Dutch disease," http://www.investopedia.com/terms/d/dutch-disease.asp (accessed December 11, 2009)

Isa, M. K. and Abang, P. O. (2008). "The state, society and economy: The Niger Delta question," Paper presented at the International Conference on the Nigerian State, Oil Industry and the Niger Delta held at Yenagoa on March 11–13, 2008. Yenagoa, Bayelsa State: Department of Political Science, Niger Delta University.

Jhingan, M. L. (2004). *Advanced economic theory* (12th ed.). Delhi: Vrinda Publications Ltd.

Jhingan, M. L. (2005). *The economics of development and planning* (38th ed.). Delhi: Vrinda Publications Ltd.

Mabogunje, L. A. (n.d.). "Land reform in Nigeria: Progress, problems and prospects," http://siteresources.worldbank.org/EXTARD/Resources/336681-1236436879081/5893311-1271205116054/mabogunje.pdf

Madunagu, E. (2008). "In search of basic laws," *The Guardian*, December 11.

Meadows, D. (2006). "Limits to growth: The 30-year update," Presentation for SCORE at Wuppertal November 23.

Nabhon, T. A. and Perepreghabofa, F. D. (2008). "Development crisis in the Niger Delta: The resource control option," Paper presented at the International Conference on the Nigerian State, Oil Industry and the Niger Delta held at Yenagoa on March 11–13, 2008. Yenagoa, Bayelsa State: Department of Political Science, Niger Delta University.

Nafziger, W. (2008). "Nigeria's economic development and Niger Delta grievances," Paper presented at the International Conference on the Nigerian State, Oil Industry and the Niger Delta held at Yenagoa on March 11–13, 2008. Yenagoa, Bayelsa State: Department of Political Science, Niger Delta University.

Natufe, I. O. (2007). *Resource control and federalism: A reply to Mobolaji Aluko*, http://www.dawodu.com/natufe1.htm (accessed December 14, 2009)

National Bureau of Statistics (NBS). (2005). *Poverty profile for Nigeria*. Abuja: Author.

NBS. (2007). *Facts and figures 2007*, http://ww.nigerianstat.gov.ng/connections/fact2007.pdf (accessed July 5, 2009)

Njoku, C. (2002). "Burden of history," *The Guardian*, August 5.

Okaba, B. (2008). "Petrodollar, the Nigerian State and the crises of development in the Niger Delta region: Tends, challenges and the way forward," Paper presented at the International Conference on the Nigerian State, Oil Industry and the Niger Delta held at Yenagoa on March 11–13, 2008. Yenagoa, Bayelsa State: Department of Political Science, Niger Delta University.

Okereke, N. C. (2008). "Niger Delta crisis in political theory," Paper presented at the International Conference on the Nigerian State, Oil Industry and the Niger Delta held at Yenagoa on March 11–13, 2008. Yenagoa, Bayelsa State: Department of Political Science, Niger Delta University.

Okonwa, W. J. (2007). "Niger Delta in the economy and politics of Nigeria," Lecture delivered at the 1st Convocation Ceremony of the Niger Delta University, Bayelsa State, Nigeria.

Okonwa, W. J. (2008). "Oil, the Nigerian State and the development possibilities of the Niger Delta," Paper presented at the International Conference on the Nigerian State, Oil Industry and the Niger Delta held at Yenagoa on March 11–13, 2008. Yenagoa, Bayelsa State: Department of Political Science, Niger Delta University.

Olasupo, F. A. and Erhum, M. O. (2008). "Fiscal federation in Nigeria: Constitutional or Political question," Paper presented at the International Conference on the Nigerian State, Oil Industry and the Niger Delta held at Yenagoa on March

11–13, 2008. Yenagoa, Bayelsa State: Department of Political Science, Niger Delta University.

Omamegbe, I. (2009). "Co-regulation option in corporate social responsibility." *BusinessDay*, February 17.

Otite, A. (2008). "The Nigerian State and the Niger Delta crisis," Paper presented at the International Conference on the Nigerian State, Oil Industry and the Niger Delta held at Yenagoa on March 11–13, 2008. Yenagoa, Bayelsa State: Department of Political Science, Niger Delta University.

Owabukeruyele, W. S. (2000). *Hydrocarbon exploitation, environmental degradation and poverty in the Niger Delta Region of Nigeria*, http://www.waado.org/Environment/PetrolPolution/EnvEconomics.htm (accessed February 3, 2007)

Owugah, L. (2008). "The Niger Delta conflict: Resource control and revolutionary violence," Paper presented at the International Conference on the Nigerian State, Oil Industry and the Niger Delta held at Yenagoa on March 11–13, 2008. Yenagoa, Bayelsa State: Department of Political Science, Niger Delta University.

Oyebode, A. (2008). "Why we need a people's constitution," *The Guardian*, June 17.

Project Underground. (1997). *Ken Saro-Wiwa's closing statement to the military-appointed tribunal*, Port Harcourt: Project Underground, 1997

Sachs, J. (1996). "Globalization and employment," Public Lecture to the International Labour Organisation (ILO), www.ilo.org/public/English/bureau/inst/papers/publics/sachs/ch2.htm (accessed February 2, 2008)

Sam, V. (2008). "In search of elusive peace in Niger Delta," *The Punch*, October 2.

Sotade, A. and Ezea, S. (2008). "Politics, intrigues of constitutional review," *The Guardian*, November 5.

Sunnie, M. O. (2009). "Land Use Act: Impact of an act that tells the tasteless story of the housing sector," *BusinessDay*, February 26.

ThisDay. (2009). "Amending the Land Use Act," *ThisDay*, Tuesday, March 17.

Uga, E. O. (2001). "State creation, 'oil revenue' allocation and the political economy of resource control," Paper presented at the 2001 Annual Conference of the Nigerian Economic Society (NES) on August 28–31, 2001 in Port Harcourt, themed: Natural Resource Use, the Environment and Sustainable Development.

Vermeer, D. and Clement, R. (2009). "Why sustainability is still going strong," *BusinessDay*, May 12.

The World Commission on Environment and Development (WCED). (1987). *Our common future*, Oxford: Oxford University Press.

World Bank. (1988). *Environment and development: Implementing the World Bank's new policies*. Development Committee Pamphlet 17, Washington, DC: Author.

World Bank. (1996). *Land reform*. World Bank Paper, Rural Development Studies, Washington, DC: Author.

World Bank. (2003). *African development indicators*. Washington, DC: The IRBD/Author.

8 Challenges to Fundamental Rights of Women in the Niger Delta

Adaora Osondu

INTRODUCTION

The Niger Delta has attracted the attention of environmentalists, human rights activists, and fair trade advocates around the world (Shah 2004). Reports of environmental and human rights abuses by multinational oil companies operating in the Delta are common (Admin Report 2010). Studies have revealed that oil in Niger Delta has brought with it degradation, militancy, insecurity, and ultimately human rights violations. The Amnesty International Report (2009) titled *Nigeria: Petroleum, Pollution and Poverty in the Niger Delta* described the Niger Delta situation as "human rights tragedy." Notably, violations of the rights (e.g., to adequate standard of living, life, health, food, water, etc.) of people of Niger Delta have been going on for years. Amnesty International (2011) reported that people living in oil-producing areas of the Niger Delta have seen their human rights undermined by oil companies, and that the Nigerian government has failed to hold any to account. The discovery and exploitation of oil have undermined sustainable development and human rights of Niger Delta communities (Omorodion 2004). The hanging of the environmentalist Ken Saro-Wiwa and eight other members of the Ogoni ethnic minority was a major human rights violation that attracted worldwide attention in the 1990s. In assessing the situation in Niger Delta after the hanging of Saro Wiwa, Africa Focus Bulletin (2005) stated,

> Ten years after the execution of human rights campaigner Ken Saro-Wiwa and eight of his colleagues by the Nigerian government, the issues of human rights and environmental devastation in the oil-producing Niger Delta remain unresolved. Despite the return to civilian rule in 1999 and pledges by oil companies to implement voluntary corporate responsibility standards, new reports by Environmental Rights Action and Amnesty International document only limited action to correct abuses and deliver benefits to the residents of the oil producing areas.

Amakwe (n.d.) reiterated that the extreme sacrifice of Ken Saro Wiwa and eight others for the cause of their people was in vain as it did not halt the age long crisis in Niger Delta. Human Rights Watch (2002) reported that respect for human rights has hardly improved there (Niger Delta) since 1999, despite the change to a civilian government. Instead, "the transition from military to civilian rule in Nigeria has coincided with a marked increase in tension and insecurity in the Niger Delta" (Stakeholder Democracy Network 2008). Undermining of the peoples' fundamental human rights has been both an outcome and a driving factor of violent instability in the region (Stakeholder Democracy Network 2008). Widespread and unchecked human rights violations related to the oil industry have pushed many people deeper into poverty and deprivation, fueled conflict, and led to a pervasive sense of powerlessness and frustration (Amnesty International 2009). These are the critical situations that Niger Deltans have found themselves right from the military regime, down to present democratic dispensation. The sentiment expressed by the people of Niger Delta is that previous successive governments sold them away to be exploited by oil companies; and the hope that the democratically elected government would be different (Ekiyor, n.d.) was dashed. For example, the Nigerian government handling of Odi incident (the deployment of security troops in the community leading to the destruction of entire village) made old fears and suspicions re-surface (Ekiyor, n.d.). Given that Odi incident happened in a democratic dispensation, the people saw the face of Abacha (killing of Ken Saro Wiwa and eight others), in the government of Olusegun Obasanjo (razing down a whole community in Odi). It was the height of human rights or "lives" violations, as life became hellish for the communities. Human rights situation in Niger Delta was reported to be abysmal as the region became militarized. Chunakara (1994) explained militarization 'as the use of the threat of violence to settle political conflicts, the legitimization of state violence, the curtailment of freedom of opinion, the domination of military values over civilian life, the violation of human rights, extra judicial killings, and the gross repression of the people.'

The intense pollution of the Niger Delta, its consequence on the people, and their general poor standard of living has given birth to the phenomenon which is generally known as the Niger Delta crisis (Ajaero 2008). Poor environmental quality and inadequate compensation are causes of concern for the people in the region. The Niger Deltans grievances are born out of the fact that oil exploration in Niger Delta instead of bringing "benefits" brings "deficits" to the communities. To Ikelegbe (2005), the Niger Delta region has become one of growing immizeration. Okonta and Douglas (2001) made it clear that "oil companies in the Niger Delta have one of the worst environmental records in the world." The loss of Niger Delta communities' means of livelihood created tensions and resultant uprisings by the Niger Deltans. First, their uprising was targeted to oil companies by disrupting production, seizing of oil installations, among others, which made the companies less productive, thereby attracting government's attention. As Amnesty International (2009) report put it, armed groups explicitly sought resource control on behalf of oil producing areas, and have engaged in theft of oil and acts of violence that are sometimes claimed as retribution for the treatment of the people of Niger Delta by oil companies. Second, the Nigerian government move to quell any uprising by deploying military forces to the region exacerbated the issue as people of Niger Delta saw the government as "second enemy" ("the first enemy being oil multinationals") that they had to rival. The response by the government was seen to have intensified the crisis as "armed groups increasingly engaged the security forces, who in response had applied excessive use of force without regard to the impact on local population" (Amnesty International 2009).

With the upsurge of violence in the region, national and international attention has been focused on the level of human rights abuses as result of militant and military activities in the region (Eze et al. 2009). Abati (n.d.) asserted that there is a long list of instances of human rights violations by state security agencies and the oil multinationals in the Niger Delta. Nevertheless, the October 2009 Amnesty Program by the government has calmed both the militants and the military personnel considerably. With the new development, it seems the militants have been removed out of the picture when stakeholders in human rights violations are mentioned in Niger Delta, although other dimensions to human rights violations still abound. Amnesty International (2011) reported that even after the Amnesty Program by the Nigeria government, armed groups and gangs kidnapped dozens of oil workers and their relatives, including children, and attacked several oil installations. The security forces, including the military, continued to commit human rights violations in the Niger Delta, including extrajudicial executions, torture and other ill treatment, and destruction of homes (Amnesty International 2011). The Human Rights Watch (2010) made it clear that the government's amnesty for militants in the Niger Delta has failed to address the root causes of the violence, and that the Nigerian government has done little to improve Nigeria's poor human rights record.

Apparently, the report by Human Rights Watch bases its argument on lack of holistic approach to addressing the crisis in Niger Delta. For instance, while there has been an effort to calm the militants, other aspects of the crisis such as continuous environmental pollution and neglect of women's rights to adequate security have been ignored. Ikelegbe (2005) explained the situation of women in Niger Delta as follows:

> There is disproportionate representation of women in every strategic sector in Niger Delta region. Women are first victims of gender-based discriminatory practices. Second, women are victims of economic crisis- they are peasants and housewives who have been marginalised in the process of production and distribution. Women have benefitted least in employment from oil companies. Women have borne the brunt of adverse effects of the oil economy- soil degradation, water pollution,

social disruption, sexual harassment both from oil multinationals and security forces in the region, etc.

Amakwe (n.d.) noted that women of Niger Delta suffer great hardships during communities' conflicts with oil companies and government; women are subjected to all kinds of violence, sexual assault, physical violence such as beating, maiming, murder and destruction of properties. The soldiers sent to the region by the Nigerian government usually invade homes at nights, terrorizing residents with beating and raping women and girls (Mortished 1996). Amakwe (n.d) stated clearly that within the "unjustly Niger Delta milieu," the group of people who bear the brunt of this injustice the most is women. The differentiated socio-cultural construction of men and women's roles ("gender based") means that the linkages between people and the physical environment impact differently on both sexes (Organisation for Security and Co-operation in Europe 2009).

Notwithstanding the sufferings Niger Delta women undergo, the security discourse is yet to adequately include them. Given the different ways in which women's lives, livelihood, and rights are challenged in Niger Delta issues, it becomes necessary to examine in details gender-based security issues in Niger Delta with particular focus on women's security and why their rights to security matter. In other words, this chapter is premised upon the argument that there exists a dominant security approach to Niger Delta crisis that has excluded women, even though women have suffered most the adverse effects of Niger Delta crisis. Significantly, this work is necessary in a typical Nigerian setting like Niger Delta where tradition and societal norms subjugate and side-line women, and do not pay adequate attention to their needs and interests.

Thus, the succeeding sections proceed as follows. Section 2 gives conceptual clarifications of the concept of security and gender, as well as, security and women's rights. Section 3 examines security issues in Niger Delta crisis and the place of women? Section 4 analyzes why women's rights are important in Niger Delta security approaches. Section 5 draws its conclusion on women and security in Niger Delta and makes recommendation on what should be done to make women enjoy their human rights, right to security inclusive.

Overall, the submission of the chapter is that incorporating women's security in Niger Delta security issues is critical. And to do this, the Nigerian government has to meet its obligation to eliminate all forms of discrimination against women. Such discrimination as exclusion of women from decisions that affects them, not holding the oil companies accountable for pollution and under-compensation, and not bringing to book all those that cause sexual harm to women, among others, should be eliminated. Young women too have to rise up to the challenges of patriarchy in Nigeria by equipping themselves both academically and otherwise, as ways of addressing women marginalization. Ordinarily women cannot work alone in finding solutions, but their participation is vital to forging the consensus necessary for achieving comprehensive security in Niger Delta.

THE CONCEPT OF SECURITY AND GENDER

The understanding of the concepts (security and gender) is germane to grasping the full import of this work. Explication of the concept of security, as well as gender, will help reduce the ambiguities and inconsistencies of ordinary usage.

Security

The English word "security" originates from the Latin word "se-curus." "Se" means "without" and "curus" means "uneasiness." That is, "security" originally meant liberation from uneasiness, or a peaceful situation without any risks or threats. The English word "security" has a wide range of meaning including "to feel safe" and "to be protected," and is mainly used to describe a situation without any risks or worries.

The term security is subject to a myriad of definitions (Blanchard 2003). To some, security "conveys and demands public attention" (Paris 2003). There is no single precise definition of security. Originally, security was viewed mainly from the state-centered approach to security, otherwise known as national security. This conception envisions the state as guarantor of the security of its citizens from the threats of other states (Blanchard 2003). The school of thought associated with this thinking is the realists. Realists' notion of security is one that has to do with nation-states and territorial protection. For realists, sovereign, self-interested states are the primary actors in an anarchical international environment (Tickner 2001), and the security of the state is tied to its military capacity and its preparedness to fight wars (Tickner 1992). Toward the end of the twentieth century, emphasis shifted from an exclusive focus on state security to a broadening concept of security: human security. The term "human security" was first used by UNDP in its 1994 Human Development Report, where human development was defined as "the process of widening the range of people's choices," while human security was defined as the ability to pursue those choices in a safe environment, broadly encompassing seven dimensions of security: economic, food, health, environmental, personal, community, and political.

To Baldwin (1997), for the term security to be understood, it has to be mainly specified security for whom and security for which values. He went further to give other necessary specifications, such as security from what threats, how much security, by what means, at what cost, and in what time period. Of important note is Baldwin's clarification that all these specifications may not be used in definition of concept of security. As Baldwin

(1997) put it, "Not all the dimensions need to be specified all the time, the degree of specificity required will vary with the research task at hand." Baldwin's idea of specificity is important to help differentiate aspects of security, for as he questioned, are the proponents of economic or environmental security using a concept of security that is fundamentally different from that used by realists? Or are they simply emphasizing different aspects of a shared concept? What can be deduced is that whether state security or human security, they are all different aspects of a shared concept. The word security in all of them still points to the fact that the discussion has to do with protection and a situation without risks or worries; it is only what/who is to be secured that makes the difference. That is why the importance of specifying whose security is involved (security for whom) cannot be underestimated.

Apparently, the shift to human security has to do with the changing realities in international environment. The emphasis on security for human beings distinguishes human security from the objective of protecting state territories that dominated security policies in the nineteenth and twentieth centuries (Hoogensen and Rottem 2004). Human Security Centre (2005) report pointed that "the vast majority of wars are no longer inter-state but rather intra-state." For this reason, among others, realists' adherence to national security has come increasingly under attack by a diverse range of theorists (Hoogensen and Rottem 2004). One of such theories is the feminist theory. Hoogensen and Rottem (2004) have argued that "realists stance and its narrow conception of security as state-centric and militaristic emanates from a masculine bias inherent in the theory." For the feminist scholars, the gendered nature of the theory prevents it from viewing the whole picture with respect to security, seeing only "a partial view of reality" (Tickner 1992). Thus, they argued that this masculine bias is "projected (by realists) onto the behavior of states whose success as international actors is measured in terms of their power capabilities and capacity for self-help and autonomy" (Tickner 1992). The realists base their view of the state and behavior in the international system on "the behavior of men in positions of public power" (Tickner 1992).

Thus, by bringing in gender, feminists have exposed realists' conceptions of security as based on a hegemonic masculinity and are not reflective of the full reality of human experience (Blanchard 2003). The feminist scholars have increasingly promoted human security as a concept designed to "encourage policymakers and scholars to think about international security as something more than the military defense of state interests" (Paris 2003). While precisely what is encompassed by the concept of human security is subject to debate, there is general concurrence that this broader definition of security, while not exclusively moving away from the security interests of the state, places individual security interests more front and center (Hudson 2005). Tickner (2001) has argued that this broadening of the definition of security is "more compatible with most contemporary feminist scholarship" than the traditional definition espoused by realists. Even though the redefining of security has been more in line with the multidimensional, multilevel security advocated by feminist scholars, the human security approach often neglects gender and how it factors in to security issues (Hudson 2005).

The Concept of Gender

Gender is the state of being either male or female. Gender is not only about women as is sometimes wrongly assumed, but in fact denotes all qualities of what it is to be either a man or a woman (Pankhurst 2000). The term has increasingly acquired a social meaning where the word gender now defines how male and female gender relates in the society and how duties are allocated on the basis of one's sex. For example, the male gender is allocated nondomestic duties such as decision making, bread winning, and others that belong to the public sector (Clarion 2001). And this ordinarily means the reverse for female gender, which is allocated duties that belong to the private sector such as cooking, washing, and other domestic chores.

In differentiating between sex and gender, Hesse and Carger (2000) explained that sex is what one is born as, that is female or male and therefore is a biological concept, while gender is used to describe those characteristics of women and men, which are socially constructed (World Health Organization 2002). Borgotta and Montgomery (2000) noted that "through interaction with caretakers, socialization in childhood, peer pressure in adolescence, and gendered work and family roles, women and men are socially constructed to be different in behavior, attitudes, and emotions"—and that construction is what defines gender. According to FAO (1997), gender is a central organizing principle of societies, and often governs the processes of production and reproduction, consumption and distribution.

Reiman (2002) identifies three aspects of gender: individual gender identity, the symbolism of gender, and the structure of gender. Individual gender identity refers to the construction of meanings determining one's individual identity based on social norms. For example, masculinity is always equated with violence, and femininity entails the opposite quality of peacefulness. The second, symbolism of gender entails classification of men and women based on roles. Men and women are assigned different gender roles based on their gender identity. In line with this argument, Clarion (2001) posited that men are allocated public roles which are mainly political and women are allocated roles that are in the private sphere as mothers, carers, and nurturers, which are apolitical, and which ordinarily means exclusion of women from political sphere. The third aspect, the structure of gender, defines the organization and institutionalization of social action in the public and private spheres based on the above gender dualism (Reiman 2002). Reiman noted that not only individual identities are gendered, but also cultural norms and values, as well as social institutions and organizations.

One basic argument in all the definitions is that gender has been socially "constructed and classified." For instance, men are classified as those that could be "seen and heard" publicly and women to be "seen and heard" privately. No wonder Reiman (2002) stated that "in all societies the gender relations between women and men tend to be clearly to the disadvantage of women." Pankhurst (2002) argued that state bureaucracies, security services, and international bodies all tend to be structured and function according to norms of masculinity. And that is why it is important to look at the gender (women) dimension of security in Niger Delta, an aspect that has been "disadvantaged." Moreover, applying the gender lens to security is important because as Hoogensen (2005) pointed, it is subjective and does not assume that there is one view of the world. Gender perspective makes visible the power relations between dominant and non-dominant groups, and therefore exposes views of security from below (Hoogensen 2005).

With the explication of the concept of security and gender and the nexus between the two clearly shown, the definition of security is adopted as follows:

> Freedom of individuals (men and women) from any threats or unfavourable situations. Such threats or unfavourable situations could emanate from environment, human decisions/actions, among others. But for the purpose of this work, security is seen as the freedom of Niger Delta women from unfavourable situations in Niger Delta- oil pollutions, inhuman treatment meted to them by security forces, culture and tradition that excludes them from decisions that affects their lives, to say the least.

WOMEN'S RIGHTS AND SECURITY

As Shah (2010) rightly noted, women's rights is an important indicator of global well-being. Addressing women's rights is tantamount to addressing the whole nations' rights (Clinton 1995). The International Center for Research on Women (ICRW) has emphasized that the safety, security, and prosperity of people all over the world are intimately linked to the health, education, and well-being of women. What then constitutes women's rights? Simply put, women's rights are nothing but the human rights of women. In 1948, the United Nations adopted the Universal Declaration of Human Rights. For instance, Article 2 stated that everyone is entitled to human rights without distinction of any kind, such as race, color, religion, language, sex, political or other opinion, national or social origin, birth or other status.

The inclusion of sex as one of the prohibited cases of discrimination made it clear that internationally, human rights include women's rights (Lynn 2001). The notion of human rights embodied in the Universal Declaration of Human Rights affirms the principle of the inadmissibility of discrimination and proclaims that all human beings are born free, equal, in dignity, and with rights, and that everyone is entitled to all the rights and freedoms set forth therein, without distinction of any kind, including distinction based on sex (Lekha 2003).

In 1979, the United Nations reaffirmed the principle that women's rights are human rights by adopting the Convention on the Elimination of All Forms of Discrimination Against Women (CEDAW). The convention recognized that women were still not equal in practice, and that women confronted problems that were different enough from men's to require special attention (Lynn 2001). Thus, for the first time a pattern of legal machinery of the supra-national form has been provided by which fundamental rights of women could be treated no longer as mere empty formulas, but as genuine legal norms governing actual legal relationships (Lekha 2003). The large body of international covenants, agreements, and commitments about human rights give women political leverage and a tenable point of reference (Kramarae and Spender, n.d.).

The concept of women's human's rights functions as a kind of integrated structure to organize the analyses of women's experiences and plan action for change (Kramarae and Spender, n.d.). It is the "fundamental principles of human rights that accord to each and every person the entitlement to human dignity that give women a vocabulary for describing both violations and impediments to the exercise of their human rights" (Kramarae and Spender, n.d.). Bunch and Frost (2000) put it thus: "Women's rights are those rights that have evolved to give greater visibility both to the problems that women face every day and to the centrality of women's experiences in economic, social, political and environmental issues." For Bunch and Frost (2000), women's human rights success and proliferation owe it to the fact that it is both prosaic (it is simply the human rights of women that is unarguable) and revolutionary (its radical reclamation have profound transformative potential). Thus, Lekha (2003) stated that "it is crucial that women's rights attract special emphasis due to their unique social circumstances," which impinge on the 'social contract'—society protection.

Woman's human rights framework equips women with a way to define, analyze, and articulate their experiences of violence, degradation, and marginality (Bunch and Frost 2000). For instance, "CEDAW allows national and international commitments for action towards the empowerment and advancement of women" (Lekha 2003). CEDAW has been described as the Women's Bill of Rights because it contains comprehensive provisions on women's human rights including what actions should be taken to promote, fulfill, and protect women from the infringement of their rights. However, the concept of women's human rights opens up the exclusion of women as individuals and the exclusion of women's concerns and the specific rights abuses faced by women (Sunila and Marilee 2007). Whether this concept is used "in political lobbying, in legal cases, in grassroots mobilization, or in broad-based educational efforts, the idea of women's human rights has been a rallying point for women across many boundaries and has facilitated the creation of collaborative strategies for promoting and protecting the human rights of women" (Bunch and Frost 2000).

Thus with a clear idea of the concept of women's rights, it stands to say that human rights and security are intertwined. Human rights have always been concerned with the security of individuals (Gerb 2003). In Gerb's words, "security is a human right." Ramcharan (2004) noted that security requires the protection of human rights. Article 3 of the Universal Declaration of Human Rights ("Everyone has the right to life, liberty and security of the person") explicitly refers to security in the framework of human rights (Gerb 2003).

Given the author's adoption of the definition of security as freedom of individuals from any threat or unfavorable situations, it means that it is in consonance with the mission of UN human rights declaration to secure human beings in freedom. Ramcharan (2004) states that the Universal Declaration of Human Rights and the wider body of human rights instruments are all meant to make human beings secure in freedom, in dignity, with equality, through the protection of their basic human rights. And when human rights are secured, it means women rights too because they are human. According to Women International Peace Conference Report (1985) cited in Hoogensen (2005), security is nothing if it is built on the insecurity of others.

SECURITY ISSUES IN NIGER DELTA CRISIS AND THE PLACE OF WOMEN

Oil discovery in Niger Delta has been marked by protests by indigenous communities against the negative impact of oil on their land. Protests degenerated into crisis in the 1990s with the peak being the hanging of Ken Saro Wiwa and eight other Ogoni leaders. No wonder UNDP (2006) noted that "since the 1990s, the Niger Delta has assumed the character of a conflict ridden region and oil wealth coupled with extreme economic deprivations and neglects have combined to create a theatre of almost permanent violence." The multinational oil companies—mainly Shell, Chevron/Texaco, and Elf—have treated both the people and the environment with total disdain and hostility (Okonta and Douglas 2001). The region has suffered massive pollution of land, water, flora and fauna, which has decimated the resources on which the region depends (Ikelegbe 2005).

It is the consequence of the intense pollution of the Niger Delta on the people and their general poor standard of living that gave birth to the phenomenon that is generally known as the Niger Delta crisis (Ajaero 2008). The Niger Deltans grievances are born out of the fact that oil exploration in Niger Delta instead of bringing "benefits," brings "deficits to the communities." The sentiment expressed by the people of Niger Delta is that previous successive government sold them away to be exploited by oil companies, and the hope that the democratically elected government would be different (Ekiyor, n.d.) was dashed. Given that Odi incident happened in a democratic dispensation, the people saw the new face of Abacha (killing of Ken Saro Wiwa and eight others), in the government of Olusegun Obasanjo (razing down a whole community in Odi). Apparently, the Niger Deltans saw their dream of a new Niger Delta in 1999 civilian takeover shattered; their demands had been ignored by the oil multinational and from the part of government. Instead, they got suppression by security forces. Thus, they (especially the men) had to devise new means of making their demands heard: militancy. Niger Delta became militarized, with the militants and government forces in confrontation. Chunakara (1994) explained militarization as the use of the threat of violence to settle political conflicts, the legitimization of state violence, the curtailment of freedom of opinion, the domination of military values over civilian life, the violation of human rights, extra-judicial killings, and the gross repression of the people. UNDP (2006) reported that "the Niger Delta was virtually in a state of siege."

Activist Emem Okon, in an interview with the author on July 22, 2011, pointed that added to the environmental degradation and loss of means of livelihoods, life became hellish for the people especially the women due to the militarized state of the region. Emem went on to say that:

> security forces sent to the region began to harass women sexually, and some women that objected to their sexual demands were raped. Since the security forces had a government mandate to work in the region, their activities were even sometimes taking to the homes—women were raped in their houses and some young ones forcefully taken to their camps.

For instance, it is claimed that over 238 Ijaw women had been raped in four major crackdowns on Ijaw resistance in Kaiama, Yenagoa, Warri, and Odi (Onwuemeodo 1999).

In the reported cases of rape, Emem Okon stated that these security men were never brought to book, mainly because these women cannot afford the payment of a lawyer, and even when women NGOs like hers want to take up some cases that were reported to them they had always encountered some challenges—the women for fear of stigmatization hide from public view, and would not want to testify in court. The inhuman treatment meted to women by these security forces confirmed what Hoogensen (2005) said that "security could be a threat in itself." Emem also pointed that the militarized state of the region made some young women to engage in prostitution with the militants, who remits the proceeds from their activities (seizing oil installations, oil theft and bunkering) to them.

The issue of prostitution has also been reported more with oil companies' staff. In an interview with Esther Ogbara, a young lady from Famgbe community in Bayelsa State, she pointed that this group (oil workers) entice young women with money (that they could no longer make from their farming and fishing business due to degraded environment) and lured them for sex. According to Esther, prostitution has led to many young women becoming pregnant outside marriage; there is increase in single motherhood or what Emem called "childhood motherhood." Thomas (2003) contended that "women have been victims of the lustful oil men; they have been forced by poverty to respond to their lustful demands," which in most cases aggravates their problems. As Akoda (2008) asserted, these women who think they have found a solution to their problems realize later that they have made it worse. As they get pregnant, the oil workers/explorers abandon them because there was no solid relationship in the first place, Esther affirmed.

Apart from the sexual assault on women, militancy has placed more responsibilities on women. As these militants (who happen to be husbands to women) abandon home to stay in hideouts to engage in their acts of violence, women are then left to cater for their families. Most of men's roles have been left for women to perform, especially in families where men have been killed or have joined militants groups. Women have played significant roles in the Delta communities in the sense that they are the breadwinners in the real sense of the word, whilst the men are the breadwinners in the cultural and traditional sense (Brisibe 2001).

Ifie Lott (who was part of the team that produced the documentary *Poison Fire*, available on www.poisonfire.org) affirmed in an interview with the author that some of these men who engage in militancy die in the course of conflict, making women to bear emotional and financial burden. To Miss Lott, "men suffer death, arrest and torture if sometimes caught in the process of violence and these reverberates negatively on women, who these men are either their husbands or sons." Omoniye (2009), in her paper "Waging Peace in the Niger Delta," stated that war has terrible consequences, including female-headed households with limited social, economic, and educational resources.

Another dimension where women have been affected has to do with lack of compensation from oil companies; women hardly receive compensation from oil companies for pollution of their lands. Women have been excluded from the token compensation arising from acquisition, pollution, and devastation of farmlands and fishing waters by the oil multinationals (Ikelegbe 2005). In times of oil pollution, men are known to be the principal/only negotiators with oil companies because of the patriarchal nature of our society, and ordinarily any compensation goes to the negotiators. According to Amnesty International (2009), most negotiations are carried out by chiefs and youths, who are almost always men, even when women's activities in agriculture and fisheries are affected by oil industry damage. In reiteration of the above argument, Emem Okon in an interview with the author has this to say:

> When a community is affected by oil pollution, compensation is often negotiated with community representatives, who are mainly men; the oil companies never agreed to negotiate or pay compensation to women who are said to be neither household owners nor land owners. Also, Niger Delta women do not inherit land; the only way a woman could have a land in Niger Delta is except she buys, but that does not guarantee her access to compensation in oil spills because she would not been given the chance to negotiate with oil companies due to the gendered hierarchies in the society.

There is increasing awareness of the marginalization of women in the "trickle down" of benefits from the multinational oil companies (Ikelegbe 2005). The patriarchal nature of our society, and the use of culture as a cover, has encouraged exploitation by the oil companies and the government to disregard women in community decision making (Brisibe 2001). Indeed, cultural repression has mostly subjugated women. As Brisibe noted, it is important not to dismiss the role culture and cultural repression plays within a system that has been manipulated and exploited by the oil companies, the government and the men themselves within our communities. The marginality of Niger Delta women (especially by tradition that subjugates them as mere puppets in hands of men) is the result of emergence of women groups and activists in Niger Delta to speak out for the women, especially rural and illiterate ones. Emem Okon revealed in an interview that the neglect of Niger Delta women in issues that affects them due to tradition that discriminates against them spurred her to engage in activism and formation of her NGO, Kebetkache Women Development and Resource Centre in 2003. The formation of the NGO is to help equip and sensitize Niger Delta women on how to survive in an "unjust" and crisis laden environment, Emem pointed.

Therefore, as Omotayo (2005) stated, "what has become the incontestable character of contemporary intra-state violence is that women are the victims although not necessarily the targets of conflicts." Women and children are particularly vulnerable and, as has become well known, are frequently raped, humiliated, and deeply traumatized by their war experience. Cockburn (2001) noted that the brutality to the body in wars ("crises") is where the most marked sex difference occurs. And Niger Delta is no exception to the negative experiences of women in times of conflicts.

WHY WOMEN'S RIGHTS MATTER

Focusing on women's security does not mean in any way that men do not need security but "emphasis on insecurity of men may hide the fact that existing hierarchies predominantly threaten women's security" (Blanchard 2003), which is clearly seen in Niger Delta crisis and the dominant approach to security. In fact, Niger Delta men's engagement in militancy showed that they were insecure and needed freedom. Different protests by women in Niger Delta also revealed that they too were threatened, and need security. Gerb (2003) made it clear that "security is a human rights," and obviously everyone is entitled to human rights. To Ramcharan (2004), security requires the protection of human rights. Article 3 of the Universal Declaration of Human Rights ("everyone has the right to life, liberty and security of the person") explicitly refers to security in the framework of human rights (Gerb 2003). It is believed that the State would provide security by protection of rights but that has not always been so, as shown in the case of Niger Delta. Women's rights to security are frequently trampled upon. The following statement about state and security made by an India participant in a workshop organized by APRODEV illustrates this point:

> In the name of security, the State and militaries are creating insecurity. When military and arms are used without accountability, the result is rape and shooting of civilians. The State is supposed to deliver security but we are always faced with a sense of insecurity. The State says 'you need more security' and in that name, citizens are raped and put in jails. But unless you provide a sense of security, unless you are giving rights and entitlement, nothing is provided. (APRODEV Briefing Paper, 2005)

From previous discussion, it is shown that the case of Niger Delta is clearly reflected in the foregoing statement by the India participant. Until recently due to the Amnesty Program, the state's approach to security had been militaristic in nature, with women being victimized. It is women's experiences of victimization, exclusion, marginalization, among others in Niger Delta that draws attention to such question as; do women have rights? Do their rights matter?

The 1948 United Nations Universal Declaration of Human Rights stated categorically what constitutes human rights. For instance, Article 1 states that all human beings are born free and equal in dignity and rights, while Article 2 states that everyone is entitled to human rights without distinction of any kind, such as race, color, religion, language, sex, political or other opinion, national or social origin, birth or other status. In 1979, CEDAW reaffirmed the UN Declaration principles. The convention defines discrimination against women as

> Any distinction, exclusion or restriction made on the basis of sex which has the effect or purpose of impairing or nullifying the recognition, enjoyment or exercise by women, irrespective of their marital status, on a basis of equality of men and women, of human rights and fundamental freedoms in the political, economic, social, cultural, civil or any other field.

The convention is the only human rights treaty that affirms the reproductive rights of women and targets culture and tradition as influential forces shaping gender roles and family relations. Countries that have ratified or acceded to the convention are legally bound to put its provisions into practice. Nigeria signed CEDAW in 1984 and ratified it in 1985.

The foregoing shows that as human beings Niger Delta women have rights, and their rights matter due to the discrimination they face. Indeed, women in societies affected by conflicts are known to face systematic human rights violations, and that is why adequate attention should be paid to the rights of Niger Delta women. Specifically, as earlier explained, Niger Delta women have suffered from sexual assault, assuming the responsibilities as breadwinners, exclusion from compensation from oil multinationals, government, among others.

It is well known that Niger Delta women have protested on several occasions due to the violations of their rights—rights to adequate standard of living, right to work, right to remedy, right to health, and so on. It is, for instance, the neglect of women's basic human rights that caused women's disenchantment with oil multinationals and the state, leading to activism. For example, in January 1999, the Niger Delta Women for Justice (NDWJ), in conjunction with the Ijaw Youth Council, organized about 1,000 women in a protest march in Port Harcourt; there, they delivered a letter to the military administrator at the Rivers State Government House, protesting against the military occupation, human rights abuses, the rape and assault of women in Bayelsa State (Human Rights Watch 1999). Activist Caroline Omoniye in an interview with the author on July 23, 2011 asserted that the deprivations of women's human rights are visible in Niger Delta, and tradition is a major factor. Omoniye pointed again (just as Emem did) that it was the condition of women of Niger Delta (where their problems go unnoticed) that spurred her to form her organization, Niger Delta Women's Movement for Peace and Development, in 2005. Omoniye noted that her organization has been campaigning, among others for women's inclusion in decision making, and she has achieved great success in her community, Ozoro Kingdom in Delta State, where women now have say. Omoniye stated that because of the specific challenges women face in Niger Delta, campaigning for all stakeholders (government, oil multinationals, and Niger Delta men) involved in the violations to respect women became necessary.

According to Activist Emem Okon, it was not until the October 2009 Amnesty Program by the federal government to the militants that the Niger Delta has begun to enjoy relative peace; for women, there is not much fear of security officials harassing them, even though with the Joint Task Force present in the region, women may still experience sexual assaults. Omoniye confirmed this in an interview with the author. She categorically stated that "women rights to security are still ignored by the government, though this time not mainly by security officials." Citing the Amnesty Program, she pointed that women have not benefited from the program, for out of more than 20,000 militants, less than 100 women are being catered for in the program. Omoniye also explained that Amnesty Program has gone beyond "state pardon"; it is now a reintegration program that should benefit women too, but women are still the least benefited. Noting that the initial Amnesty Program never involved any woman, Emem Okon pointed that it took the efforts of the Technical Committee of the Niger Delta (set up in 2008 by Yaradua Administration to make recommendation on how to address Niger Delta Crisis) spurred by some women activists, herself inclusive, for women to be included in Amnesty Program, though their number is still insignificant. Emem Okon said that the knowledge that women played roles (there were certain cases where they were reported to have provided welfare services, sexual services to the militants) in militancy made them to join the campaign for government inclusion of women. Emem maintained that even though women were not combatants, they were women that lived with the militants in camps and those that were abandoned at home by their husband militants.

Therefore, recognizing and addressing women's rights in Niger Delta security issues is paramount because they share in the adverse effect of the Niger Delta degraded environment, and consequent crisis; they are also the group that has suffered more of victimization and exclusion in hitherto security approaches to Niger Delta.

What the author has been able to ascertain is that prior to the Amnesty Program, the dominant security approach to Niger Delta crisis was militaristic and made life hellish for the vulnerable group: women. In addition, due to the highly patriarchal nature of Nigerian society, Niger Delta women are hardly included in any decisions, program and packages meant for the affected communities/individuals. But what this work is yet to ascertain is whether the oil companies, government and Niger Delta men know that women's rights are violated by their actions, and if yes, what steps have been taken by them. This is an area for further research.

CONCLUSIONS

Applying the gender lens to security issues in Niger Delta crisis has unveiled biased tactics by oil multinationals and Nigerian government in security approaches to Niger Delta. It also uncovered the dominant approach employed in Niger Delta security issues as not reflective of the full reality of women's experiences in Niger Delta. The loss of Niger Deltans' means of livelihood as a result of oil degraded environment impacted not just on men but on women too who also make their living from the environment. Unfortunately, the interests of women are hardly considered in addressing the Niger Delta issues. The major challenge Niger Delta women face has to do with tradition and cultural norms—only men are allowed to partake in public decisions. This cultural bias has impeded women's right and freedom to negotiate and receive compensation from oil multinationals in times of spills.

In addition, during the Niger Delta militants confrontations with the government (i.e., government-deployed security forces), the vulnerable groups—women, and of course their children (not the focus of the chapter)—were trapped in the middle. Women were dehumanized through involuntary sexual relationships with the security forces and militants. Both young and old women were violated, and used as weapons of war, especially by the security forces deployed to the region. Their experiences went unnoticed as no provisions were made by government to safeguard the rights of women during the crisis. Furthermore, in the present Nigerian government Amnesty and Re-integration Program for the militants, women are scarcely included. Clearly, the dominant security approaches to Niger Delta issues have been militaristic, discriminatory, and ultimately gender biased.

The chapter recommends among others that Nigeria government should abide by its obligation to eliminate all forms of discrimination against women as ratified in CEDAW, as this would be a major step in fighting victimization of Niger Delta women. Niger Delta women NGOs and activists should intensify their campaign against women marginalization and exclusion by organizing forum where the government and oil multinationals would be represented; where they would be educated on the need to respect and accord women their human rights such as give women voice in decision making, any negotiations (whether from oil multinationals and government), and offer them compensation as they too are affected by insecure environment emanating from "oil business." Also women activists should also encourage or even "incite" women that have been "violated" to speak up in order to help bring the perpetrators to book. That way, such reprehensible acts would be reduced, if not totally phased out.

Finally, women NGOs should enlighten young women in Niger Delta on the importance of acquiring education (attending school) as a means of survival in a male dominated society. Generally, an educated woman is an independent woman, who could challenge those subjugating and cultural norms that impede women's enjoyment of their human rights.

REFERENCES

Abati, Reuben. (n.d.) "Still on the Niger Delta question," The Adaka Boro Centre, http://www.adakaboro.org (accessed July 1, 2011)

Abdulla, H. (2000). "Economic, social and cultural rights in Nigeria", A Study Prepared for the Swedish NGO Foundation for Human Rights, Social and Economic Rights Action Center, http://www.serac.org (accessed 5April, 2009)

Admin Report. (2010). "Environmental pollution in Niger Delta," Hope for Niger Delta Campaign, http://www.nigerdeltacampaign.com (accessed July 1, 2011)

Africa Focus Bulletin. (2005). "Nigeria: Delta oil and human rights," November 13, http://www.africafocus.org (accessed July 5, 2011)

African Commission on Human and Peoples' Rights Decision. (2002). Being decision made at the 30th Ordinary Session of the African Commission on Human and Peoples' Rights as filed by the Centre for Economic and Social Rights on Behalf of Ogoniland, Banjul, October 13–27, http://www1.umn.edu/humanrts/Africa (accessed October 18, 2010)

Ajaero, C (2008). "The Men behind the Trigger in Niger Delta," *Newswatch*, Vol. 48, No. 10, September, pp. 12–19.

Akoda, W (2008). "Youth, rule of law, order and national security in the Niger Delta Region since 1966," Paper presented at the Historical Society of Nigeria, October, Gombe, p.14

Amakwe, Mary John Bosco E (n.d) "The Niger Delta Oil Crisis and the Victimization of Women: A Socio-ethnographic Analysis" Theology in Africa, http://theologyinafrica.com (accessed 17 April, 2011)

Amnesty International (2011) "Annual Report 2011: State of the World's Human Rights" Human Rights by Region, Africa: Nigeria, http://www.amnesty.org/en/region/nigeria/report-2011 (accessed 5 August, 2011)

Amnesty International (2011). "Clean up oil pollution in the Niger Delta", Amnesty International Report, http://www.amnesty.org (accessed July 1, 2011)

Amnesty International(2009). "Petroleum, pollution and poverty in Niger Delta", Amnesty International Publication, http://www.amnesty.org (accessed January 15, 2010)

APRODE Briefing Paper. (2005). Statement by an Indian Participant at a workshop titled, "Whose Security? Human Rights seen from a Gender and Southern perspective."

Baldwin, D. A. (1997). "The concept of security," *Review of International Studies*, Vol. 23, pp. 5–26.

Blanchard, E M (2003) "Gender, International Relations and the Development of Feminist Security Theory", Signs: Journal of Women in Culture and Society, Vol. 28, Issue 4, pp 1289–1312

Borgatta, E. F. and Montgomery, R. J. V. (Eds.) (2000). "Encyclopedia of Sociology" (2nd ed.), Vol. 2, New York: Macmillan Reference.

Brisibe, A. (2001). "In the face of oil hostility and the Niger Delta women," Nigeria World, http://www.nigeriaworld.com (accessed July 10, 2011)

Bunch, C. and Frost, S. (2000). "Women's human rights: An introduction." In *Routledge International Encyclopaedia of Women: Global Women Issues and Knowledge*, London: Routledge, http://www.cwgl.rutgers.edu (accessed July 8, 2011)

Chunakara, M. G. (1994). "The militarisation of politics and Society: Southern Asia experience", Hong Kong: Daga Press.

Clarion. (2001). "An introduction to gender, law and society," Constitutional Debate, No.11, Published by ClariPress Nairobi.

Clinton, H (2005) "Women's Rights are Human Rights" Famous Speech by Hillary Clinton Beijing, China: 5 September 1995, Famous Speeches Index, http://www.famousquotes.me.uk/speeches/Hillary-Clinton (accessed 10 May, 2011)

Cockburn, C. (2001). "The gendered dynamics of armed conflict and political violence." In C. O. N. Moser and F. C. Clark (Eds.), *Victims, perpetrators or actors? Gender, armed conflict and political violence*, London: Zed Books, p. 22.

Ekiyor, T. (n.d.). "Women in peace building: An account of the Niger Delta women," WANEP Brief, http://www.wanep.org (accessed June 30, 2011)

Eze, C., Osakwe, B., Akosile, B., and Mere, E. (2009). "Ending the Niger Delta crises: Exploring women's participation in peace processes," WANEP, http://www.wanepnigeria.org (accessed June 28, 2011)

FAO. (1997). "What is gender?" *FAO Corporate Document Repository*, http://www.fao.org (accessed July 7, 2011)

Gerb, O. (2003). "Human rights and security: The two towers," Centre for the Study of Human Rights, Discussion Group, February 11, http://www2.lse.ac.uk (accessed July 12, 2011)

Hesse-Biber, S. and Carger, G. L. (2000). "Working women in America: Split dreams" New York: Oxford University Press.

Hoogensen, G (2005) "Gender and Human Security for Kvinneforskermaraton 2005" University of Tromso, Norway, http://www2.uit.no/ikbViewer/Content/185373/Gunhild%20Hoogensen.pdf (accessed 20 June, 2011)

Hoogensen, G and Rottem, S V (2004): "Gender, Identity and the Subject of Security" Security Dialogue, Vol.35, No. 2, pp 155–171

Hudson H (2005) "Doing Security as though Humans Matter: A Feminist Perspective on Gender and Politics of Human Security" Security Dialogue, Vol.36, No.2, pp 155–174

Human Rights Watch (2002) "The Niger Delta: No Democratic Dividend" Report on Nigeria, Vol 14, No.7 (A)- October 2002, http://www.hrw.org/reports/2002/nigeria3 (accessed 20 December, 2010)

Human Rights Watch. (1999). "New crackdown in Yenagoa and Kaiama," Human Rights Watch, http://www.hrw.org/nigeria (accessed September 9, 2010)

Human Security Centre. (2005) "Human security report: War and peace in the 21st century", The University of British Columbia, http://www.humansecurityreport.info (accessed July 2, 2011)

Ibeanu, O. (2008). "Two rights make a wrong: Bringing human rights back into the Niger Delta discourse," Conference Proceeding of the International Conference on the Nigerian state, Oil Industry and the Nigeria Delta, Organised by Niger Delta University, Department of Political Science, Wilberforce Island, Yenagoa.

Ikelegbe, A. (2005). "Engendering civil society: Oil, women groups and resource conflicts in the Niger Delta Region of Nigeria," *Journal of Modern African Studies*, Vol. 43, Nol. 2, pp. 241–270.

Jegede, A. (2008). "Human rights crisis in Niger Delta," http://www.pambuza.org (accessed January 5, 2010)

Kramarae, C. and Spender, D. (n.d.). "Women, education, health to hypertension." In *Routledge International Encyclopaedia*, http://books.google.com.ng (accessed July 7, 2011)

Lekha, K. P. L. (2003). "The concepts of rights, its impact and importance on women in contemporary societies: A legal overview," *Jurnal Kemanusiaan*, Vol. 16, No. 1, pp. 1–7

Lynn, W (2001) "Women's Rights: A Global View" Greenwood Publishing Group, Inc. Westport, USA http://books.google.com.ng (accessed 3 July, 2011)

Mortished, C. (1996). "No Longer in Glorious Isolation: Shell petroleum development," *The Times* (London), July 8, pp. 1–4.

Okonta, I. and Douglas, O. (2001) "Where Vultures Feast: Shell, Human Rights, and Oil in the Niger Delta" San Francisco: Sierra Club Books

Omoniye, C. (2009). "Women waging peace in the Niger Delta," Presentation to UPF, Women for Peace Seminar on MDGs and the Role of Women, United Nations Plaza, New York.

Omorodion, I. F (2004) "The Impact of Petroleum Refinery On The Economic Livelihoods Of Women In The Niger Delta Region Of Nigeria" JENDA: A Journal of Culture and African Women Studies, Vol. 6, 1SSN 1530–5686

Omotayo, B. O. (2005). "Women and conflicts in new information age: Virtual libraries to the rescue," World Library and Information Congress, 71st IFLA General Conference and Council, http://www.ifla.org (accessed July 1, 2011)

Onwuemeodo, S. (1999). "2,626 Ijaws killed since 1997," *Vanguard*, December 10, 1999, p.15.

Organisation for Security and Co-operation in Europe (2009) "Gender and Environment: A Guide to the Integration of Gender Aspects in the OSCE's Environmental Projects" Published by OSCE, Office of the Secretary-General, Gender Section, Wallnerstrasse, Vienna. http://www.osce.org/gender (accessed 15 February, 2011)

Pankhurst, D. (2000). "Women, Gender and Peacebuilding". Working Paper No. 5, University of Bradford.

Paris, R. (2003). "Human security: Paradigm shift or hot air?" In R. W. Mansbach and E. Rhodes (Eds.), *Global politics in a changing world: A reader* (2nd ed.), Boston: Houghton Mifflin Company, pp. 253–260.

Ramcharan, B. (2004). "Human rights and human security," http://www.unidir.org (accessed June 28, 2011)

Reiman, C. (2002). "Opening up spaces: Engendering protracted social conflict and conflict transformation", PhD Thesis, University of Bradford.

Shah, A. (2010). "Women's rights," Global Issues, http://www.globalissues.org (accessed July 7, 2011)

Shah, A. (2004). "Nigeria and oil," Global Issues, http://www.globalissues.org (accessed June 8, 2011)

Stakeholder Democracy Network. (2008). "Groundwork: A human rights platform for the Niger Delta," *Human Rights Draft*, SDN, http://www.stakeholder-democracy.org (accessed January 5, 2010)

Sunila, A. and Marilee, K. (2007). "Gender mainstreaming: An obsolete concept?" *Isis International*, http://www.isiswomen.org (accessed June 28, 2011)

Thomas, J. (2003). "Women and the challenges of the Niger Delta", Port Harcourt: Centre for Advance Social Sciences.

Tickner, J. A. (1992). "Gender in International Relations: Feminist perspectives on Achieving Global Security." New York: Columbia University Press

Tickner, J. A. (2001). "Gendering World Politics: Issues and approaches in the post–Cold War Era". New York: Columbia University Press.

UNDP (2006) "Niger Delta Human Development Report", Published by United Nations Development Programme, UN House, Garki, Abuja, Nigeria

United Nations Development Programme (UNDP). (1994). "Human Development Report, 1994", New York: Oxford University Press.

World Health Organization. (2002). "Integrating Gender Perspectives into the work of WHO," http://www.who.org (accessed July 1, 2011)

9 Conclusion

Reclaiming Politics and Reforming Governance: Options for Sustainable Peace and Development in the Niger Delta

Ukoha O. Ukiwo, Okechukwu Ukaga, and Ibaba Samuel Ibaba

INTRODUCTION

The nexus between natural resources, violent conflict, and sustainable development in the Niger Delta, which is the theme of the book, has gained currency in academic and policy circles in the past two decades. Scholars and practitioners have focused their searchlights on the impact of natural resources on human security and development. Elementary international politics conceptions of natural resource endowments as one of the sources of national power and effective instrument of foreign policy has been overtaken by perspectives with less sanguine views of the potential and actual contributions of natural resources to state building and human development. This demonization of natural resources is evidenced by the proliferation of epithets for resources both in the generic and specific senses. Wittingly or unwittingly, the social science and related policy lexicon is now awash with terms such as "resource wars," "resource curse," "blood oil," "conflict diamonds," ad nauseam. There is a strong suggestion in an influential strand of the literature on the political economy of contemporary conflicts that resources necessarily beget violent conflicts. The chapters in this book transcend this simplistic, deterministic, and ahistorical narrative. The underpinning argument of all the chapters is that Niger Delta conflicts derive from mal-exploitation and mismanagement of natural and human resource endowments rather than the resources qua resources. In fact, Obi (Chapter 2) poignantly captures the meat of our argument as follows:

> It should be emphasized that the issue of whether oil becomes a curse or blessing depends on the activities of several actors: local, national and transnational, including the people, who ultimately determine what oil will represent for better or for worse. We cannot conceive of oil as a curse or a blessing outside of those forces that control it, and thereby shape the structure of global economic and political power.

The chapters have therefore been devoted to identifying actors and processes that have contributed to misuse and abuse of natural resources and exploring how such abuses have manifested in social tensions and conflicts that have undermined sustainable development. In addition, the policy focus of the chapters underscores the centrality of human agency in our perspective. It indicates an appreciation of the need to identify options that the people of the region can take to escape the paradox of poverty in the midst of plenty and attendant conflict trap. This edited volume seeks to consolidate these options into a broader perspective of reclaiming politics and reforming governance.

It derives from a paradigm shift in political economy toward the rediscovery of the political variable in development discourses. After decades of fascination with the economic factor (sub-structure), Ake (1996) made a detour by arguing that it is politics that underdevelops Africa. He argued that African development was contingent on addressing the political question. This is the question of who wields power, why, and how. Ake argued that development has eluded Africa because the people who fought for independence and in whose name independence was secured had been marginalized from the political sphere that had been captured by an ever-narrowing circle of political elite. He cautioned that early twenty-first-century democratization processes, which he called "democratization of disempowerment," risked strengthening and legitimizing the status quo of politics without people because the electorate was absent in elections. The rationale for reclaiming politics therefore stems from the centrality of political marginalization and emasculation to the story of the Niger Delta. Reclaiming politics is fundamental because resource allocation is the reason of politics. Eastonian conceptualization of politics as the authoritative allocation of values suggests that in operational terms politics is using public authority to allocate public resources for the public good. It simply follows therefore that when the people (public) are essentially not the source of authority—a travesty of public authority—resources would seldom be allocated for the public good.

The case for reforming governance derives from the perverse effects of weak governance structures and distorted governance logics on development in the Niger Delta. Since the increase of the proportion of the Federation Account allocated on the basis of derivation to 13 percent, oil-producing Niger Delta states have attracted more revenue than other states. The region has also been recipient of transfers through the Niger Delta Development Commission (NDDC) and the Niger Delta Ministry as well as social responsibility budgets of oil-producing companies. Even while taking the social and physical environmental challenges into consideration, development outcomes are grossly incommensurate with such inflows of resources, suggesting a basket case syndrome in the region.

By proposing both political and governance measures to addressing challenges in the region, we intend to go beyond current unidirectional approaches. As Ukiwo (2011) has shown, there is a tendency for actors within the Delta to emphasize political solutions while actors outside the region emphasize governance measures. Moreover, we transcend the tendency to restrict political solutions to enhanced resource allocation to states and local councils to devolution of resources to local communities. The next section revisits the arguments and evidence linking natural resources to conflict and underdevelopment. This is followed by an examination of recent policy responses to the negative impact of unsustainable use of resources at the global level. We then proceed to examine political and governance responses in Nigeria and the Niger Delta and underscore how the political question and poor governance regimes are undermining reform initiatives.

RESOURCES, CONFLICTS, AND UNDERDEVELOPMENT: A RECAP OF THEORETICAL FRAMEWORK

The untoward effects of natural resources to the development of countries was first noticed in the Netherlands in the early 1960s as the country increasingly began to depend on revenues from export of natural gas. Economists easily noticed that growth in the hydro-carbon sector paradoxically generated negative growth rates in the real sectors of the economy. This development was subsequently referred to as the "Dutch disease," especially as it became more prominent with the oil booms of the 1970s (Sachs and Warner 1995). During the 1970s boom also, political scientists developed the concept of rentier state to describe the emergence of a new kind of state (Karl 1997). The rentier state is one that derives most of its revenue from rents from the exploitation of natural resources especially extractive industries.

The rentier state had certain unique features. Flow of petrodollars into the public treasury raised the stakes for political power and therefore political contestations. This manifested as political instability in several countries, making the oil boom years to become contemporaneous with military coups in oil-producing developing countries. The impacts of resource rents on political stability derived from several interrelated mechanisms. First, the revenue windfall reduces to a ridiculous level the rate of public finance that accrues from taxation. This leads to a situation where the state becomes more autonomous from civil society and therefore more insulated from the demands of democratic accountability. Under the liberal state framework, the political obligation of taxation imposes responsibility on the state. Second, rents from resources make the state "the means of production," triggering an endless struggle to control the state. This struggle is destabilizing to the extent that politics is framed in a zero-sum context. Institutional regulations for political behavior are jettisoned due to the emerging logic of politics where the end of winning the state justifies any means. Third, the strategic importance of the resource on which the state depends attracts several external actors (powerful foreign governments, multinational corporations, and international criminal networks) whose predatory activities contribute to political instability. The cumulative effect of these dynamics is the emergence of an environment that is inhospitable to democracy (Ross 2001).

To be sure, these processes are not inexorable. Comparative experiences of resource-rich countries reveal that the trajectory depends on the level of development of civil society and the private sector as well as the character of social classes, especially the dominant social classes. The investment interest of the dominant ruling class of Botswana in the agriculture sector was significant in mitigating the effects of the discovery of alluvial diamonds in the country (Poteete and Gramajo 2005). Time is also an important factor. The stage in a country's history when the resource is discovered influences the capacity for developed institutions to mitigate the effects of sudden deluge of revenues. This explains why developing countries appear to produce more empirical evidence of the resource curse. For instance, Norway had a developed economy and strong industrial base before the advent of oil. Even in the case of the Netherlands, the "disease" was short-lived, as growth resumed in the real sectors of the economy and did not distort the economy in the long-term. As Corden (1984: 359) has rightly argued,

> The true Dutch Disease in the Netherlands was not the adverse effects on manufacturing of real appreciation but rather the use of Booming Sector revenues for social service levels which are not sustainable, but which has been politically difficult to reduce.

It is apposite therefore to surmise that the phenomena of Dutch disease and rentier state linked to the advent of natural resource revenues is associated with the tenuous link of dominant social classes to production. It is not surprising that Nigeria became a classic representation of both phenomena given the historical role of the emerging indigenous bourgeoisie as middlemen, commission agents, manufacturers' representatives, and so on. Added to this is the extent of state involvement in natural-resource exploitation and the property rights regime. In contexts where state is both regulator as well as entrepreneur and where property rights regimes are weak or non-existent, rent seeking becomes rife and distorts the potential contributions of natural resources to economic growth and sustainable development. As Binuomoyo, Ogbewo, Okoro, and Ukaga show in their contribution (Chapter 7), the abrogation of property rights through the Land Use Act negates efficient resource management and sustainable development in Nigeria.

It is under these circumstances that natural resource–rich countries become prone to violent conflicts. More pointedly, it is possible to isolate five modalities through which conflicts tend to result from dependence on natural resources (Humphreys 2005). These are the pernicious effects of pervasive rent seeking on the polity; rising grievances over inequitable distribution of natural resource wealth among individuals and groups; and economic instability due to high dependence on commodities with fluctuating prices. Furthermore, availability of natural resources increases the feasibility of conflicts by providing resource for financing conflicts and removes incentives for peaceful behaviour as economic interests become driving forces of conflict (see also Collier 2000).

POLICY RESPONSES TO NATURAL RESOURCES AND VIOLENT CONFLICTS

The end of the Cold War, where conflicts in the developing world were often attributed to superpower rivalry, has drawn the attention of scholars and policy makers to internal dimensions of violent conflict. This is particularly the case since the end of the Cold War witnessed an increase rather than the anticipated diminution in incidence of conflict across the world (Gray 1997; Holsti 1996; Kaldor 1999). The gory humanitarian emergencies, the spectre of collapsed and failed states, and the proliferation of criminal and terrorist groups and networks associated with conflicts have made conflict prevention and resolution top priorities of global governance institutions.

Conflict resolution initiatives have been directed at the multidimensional aspects of conflict. However, given the seeming intractable character of conflicts linked to natural resources and their sheer number, a lot of the initiatives appear to be customised to addressing the resource dimensions of conflicts. Policies have been devised to address the "greed" and "grievance" factors underpinning and perpetuating the conflicts. These have involved a number of political and governance-related factors.

To start with the political issues, the international community has encouraged a number of initiatives to address conflicts. These include amnesty and disarmament and demobilization and reintegration (DDR) programs, truth and reconciliation commissions (TRC), constitutional reforms for power sharing, introduction of multi-party elections and term limits for incumbents, federalism and decentralization schemes, and affirmative action programs. In some post-conflict settings, fundamental changes such as land reforms and privatization are implemented. These initiatives are aimed at addressing the underlying causes of the conflict especially grievances associated with horizontal inequalities and social exclusion. DDR and TRC initiatives, which essentially seek to promote reunion among protagonists and antagonists in conflict situations, stem from some recognition of the political underpinnings of the conflicts. Similarly, the *raison d'être* of constitutional reform is to effect a reconfiguration of the power matrix from one of power concentration to that of power dispersal. The modalities for power dispersal find expression in the introduction of prime ministerial positions in executive presidential systems, introduction of term limits to preclude life presidency, and replacement of simple plurality majoritarian electoral systems with proportional representation. In addition, countries with unitary systems of government are encouraged to federalize or at the minimum promote decentralization. The rationale for the power-dispersing political institution is the expectation that the shared power would facilitate more equitable distribution of resources. This redistributive rationale is most evident in affirmative action programs, land reform, and privatization where there are conscious efforts to transfer or return resources to marginalized and dispossessed groups. The key challenge of implementing such programs intended to address the political question remains how to ensure that the power gets to the people for whom it is intended. Experiences show that the aforementioned initiatives create benefit captors and new inequalities. Notable examples in the Africa region include the Broad Based Black Economic Empowerment program in South Africa and the decentralization program in Sierra Leone that have only transformed the fortunes of some elites (Chabedi 2001; Fanthorpe 2006).

In the area of governance, global governance structures, and influential nongovernmental organizations have introduced several initiatives to tackle both the "greed" and "grievance" motivations for violent conflicts in natural resource–dependent countries. Some of the initiatives seek to remove or minimize opportunities for profiting in warfare and consequently discourage violent group behaviour. Examples include the numerous initiatives aimed at curtailing conflict trade and finance. There are mobilizations, for instance, toward extension of global norms and regulatory regimes for money laundering, drug trafficking and illegal trading in weapons to the exploitation of natural resources in countries experiencing violent conflicts or recovering from conflict. The advocacy is for prohibition of trade and investment in conflict commodities.

"Conflict commodities" have been defined as commodities that are sold by any participant in a conflict to generate resources that can be used for political or military purposes in connection with the conflict and on which taxes have not been paid (Balentine 2005: 452). One prominent example is the Kimberly Process that provides a regime for controlling trade in conflict diamonds. Obviously, such prohibitions have limitations in that they target supply effectively without correspondingly looking at the demand side. The consequence is that unmet demands trigger processes that ultimately increase the worth of the prohibited goods and *ipso facto* the level of risks that violators may want to take to procure the commodity. Moreover, prohibition is usually tied to specific commodities. Thus, it is possible for groups in conflict to switch to exploitation of other natural resources. Charles Taylor's switch from export diamonds to export of timber is an excellent case in point. Moreover, embargoes have grave implications for civilian population. It is worth noting, however, that there have been great improvements in trade and finance controls. The Libyan example shows the progress that has been made in using trade, aid, and finance embargoes to end conflict. The United Nations authorized timeous freezing of Libyan assets to prevent Col. Muammar Ghaddafi from using it against the popular revolution and has quickly authorized release of the funds to the Transitional National Council (TNC) to prevent escalation of humanitarian disasters. It is, however, pertinent to note that while it is yet early to assess the TNC, the deplorable treatment (including alleged extrajudicial killing) of Black people (Libyans as well as foreign nationals) in areas under TNC control is very troubling.

There have also been international initiatives for promoting responsible natural resource management for both conflict prevention and post-conflict reconstruction. As Ballentine (2005: 459) argues, the objectives of the policy regimes are twofold, namely, (1) creating accountable and transparent methods of resource management and distribution and (2) installing measures to ensure that resource exploitation is sustainable and conflict sensitive. The first set of objectives has led to the evolution of publish what you pay (PWYP) campaign and the extractive industries transparency initiatives (EITI). The aim is to promote transparency and accountability through publication of rents paid by extractive industries to governments and disclosures by government on what they have received from extractive industries. The second set of objectives has influenced the emergence of future generations or sovereign wealth funds, community trust funds, and proactive social performance programs by extractive industries. One of the initiatives is the Voluntary Principles on Human Rights and Security, which was introduced and adopted by some governments, extractive industries and nongovernmental organizations in 2000. The signatory governments and extractive industries agree to ensure that exploitation of natural resources is done in such a way that recognizes and guarantees the rights and security of host communities and employees of extractive industries. Although these initiatives are voluntary and not universal, they increasingly foreshadow global best practices in natural resource management.

NATURAL RESOURCES, CONFLICT, AND SUSTAINABLE DEVELOPMENT IN THE NIGER DELTA

A cursory examination of the foregoing discussions shows some replication in the Niger Delta experience. This should not be surprising as one of the points made in this book is that the Niger Delta has been part of globalization for the past two centuries. Indeed, it is plausible to suggest that some of the developments briefly discussed in this chapter are partly responses to the Niger Delta crisis that has since the mid-1990s attracted more attention in the international community. This section of the chapter therefore examines the record of both political and governance responses to the Niger Delta conflicts.

Political Responses

Since the 1990s, when longstanding frustrations in the Niger Delta began to increasingly result in conflicts, the key political responses include creation of states and local government areas, establishment of development commissions and ministry, upping of derivation revenues, and the Amnesty Program.

Creation of States and Local Government Councils

As part of efforts to address minority fears, successive governments have created states in response to demands of aggrieved groups. The Niger Delta peoples were historically at the forefront of the demand for states. The historic mobilizations by the Mid-West State Movement and the COR State Movement yielded the Mid-West Region in 1963 and Cross River State and Rivers State in 1967. Apart from boundary adjustment and change of names, the region was not affected by the 1976 state creation exercise that saw the creation of six more states. One state each was added to the region in the state creation exercises of 1987, 1991, and 1996. Although new states and local councils have created more opportunities for employment and infrastructural development, but it remains a subject of debate whether they have contributed to improvements in the living standards of the people. Rather, if social indicators are anything to go by, it is evident that levels of poverty and inequality have risen with the creation of new states. Moreover, creation of states and LGAs has contributed to the fission of groups and exacerbation of inter-group conflicts. Clearly, the elites seem to have conspired to ensure that the benefits of states creation do not trickle down to the people as Akinola and Etekpe show in their contributions to this volume (Chapters 3 and 6, respectively).

Development Commissions and Ministry

Another political response to conflicts in the Niger Delta is the creation of development commissions with special funds for development in the region. These include OMPADEC and the NDDC. However, these special bodies have not fared better than the states but have actually been undermined by the same class of benefit captors. The commissions have failed to use oil revenues to create the basis to transform the economy of the region but have rather reinforced the orientation toward dependence on rents that, as Bubou and Egai in this volume have shown (Chapter 5), discourages development of entrepreneurship. The failure of development commissions to make the desired impact obviously catalysed demands for the creation of the Ministry of Niger Delta Affairs. It is yet early days to assess the Niger Delta ministry, but complaints over the shoddy work on the East West Road administered by the ministry suggests that it might just be business as usual.

Increase of Derivation Revenues

A major political initiative was the increase of derivation revenues from between 1.5 and 3 percent to 13 percent in 1999. Although, this falls short of the minimum of 25 percent the Niger Delta delegates demanded at the botched 2005 National Political Reform Conference, it represents a considerable among of extra funds for development in the region. Concerns that the derivation revenues have not made significant impact on the average person in the region are obvious in demands for more revenues and the replication of derivation principle at the state and local council areas. Some state governments in the region have established special commissions to manage the 13 percent derivation funds without any significant impact on the peoples' standard of living. Perhaps, the only notable impact of the 13 percent derivation revenue is that the Niger Delta region boasts of producing the only two governors of the Fourth Republic that have so far been convicted and jailed for stealing and laundering public funds.

The Amnesty Program

In 2009, the federal government under the leadership of President Umar Musa Yar Adua granted amnesty to Niger Delta youths that had taken up arms against the state. The militant activities of the youth represented the most violent manifestation of the longstanding conflicts in the region. In exchange for immunity from prosecution and financial rewards, the militant youths agreed to a disarmament and demobilization and reintegration (DDR) program. So far about 22,000 youths have been demobilized, cantoned, and undergone a reorientation program that entails pledging allegiance to the Nigerian state and denouncing violence. The Amnesty Program has recorded great short-term successes as it has led to a significant reduction in attacks on the Nigerian oil industry. Nigeria's oil export has also picked up after losses of about 25 percent of production levels recorded at the height of militant attacks. Moreover, the program seems to have a longer term outlook as many of the demobilized youths are undergoing training to prepare them for life after militancy. The challenge of the future is how to guarantee job and investment opportunities for the youths after training. Furthermore, one of the key objectives of the Amnesty Program, which is to promote an orientation of nonviolence among youths in the region, would only be achieved if youths that did not participate in militancy are not abandoned to their fate.

Governance Responses

Increasing realization that some of the political responses discussed so far have not had the desired impact have led to the introduction of governance reforms. In order to ensure that proceeds from the exploitation of oil and gas in the region are better managed for the wellbeing of the people there has been efforts to mainstream emerging international norms on transparency and accountability in the operations of government and oil companies. We discuss progress on some of these initiatives in the following section.

Extractive Industries Transparency Initiative (EITI)

Since November 2003 when President Olusegun Obasanjo expressed the commitment towards EITI, Nigeria has made some impressive progress in implementing the EITI. In 2004, the federal government started making public the amount shared from the Federation Account on a monthly basis among the federal, states, and local governments. The passage of the Nigeria Extractive Industries Transparency Initiative (NEITI) bill in 2007 made Nigeria the first member country to give a legal backing to EITI. Taking cognizance of these commitments, which include establishment of a national stakeholder group and secretariat for NEITI, publication of audit reports on government receipts and commitment to implement recommendations of audit report, Nigeria was certified as an EITI compliant country in March 2011. One of the achievements of NEITI is that between 2004 and 2006 government recovered the sum of N130 billion from oil companies (Idemudia 2009: 12). However, there are a number of hiccups in the implementation of EITI. The audit reviews are not conducted in a timely manner. The last review conducted so far is that of 2005. It is clear that NEITI has no powers to prosecute offenders. Consequently, for all the malfeasance uncovered by the 1999–2005 audit reports, no one has been prosecuted. Moreover, resistance to publication of revenue allocation remains very strong. The Federal Ministry of Finance suddenly stopped monthly publication of federal allocation. Above, NEITI remains a federal law and is yet to be domesticated at state and local council levels. Consequently, most Nigerians are unaware about its existence and operations.

The only attempt to domesticate the initiative at state level has not generated any success story. Almost four years since it was introduced the Bayelsa Expenditure and Income Transparency Initiative (BEITI) has not been backed by law. Proactive efforts by the BEITI secretariat to publish revenues and budget of the state government were apparently stalled by political interest groups as the publications uploaded on the BEITI website were withdrawn without notice. Budgets in most the Niger Delta states are not yet public documents. Analysis by civil society groups suggested that state governments are not being transparent about budgets. For instance, the Niger Delta Citizens and Budget Platform comparative analysis of state budgets reveal that budgets do not specify projects and that projects executed in previous budgets are retained in budgets of the following years (Niger Delta Citizens and Budget Platform 2011).

Due Process Initiatives

Both the federal government and several Niger Delta state governments have initiated a cocktail of transparency programs that are increasingly referred to as due process initiatives. These include the establishment of a Due Process Office and passage of laws on public procurement and fiscal responsibility. The initiatives are responses to criticisms of corruption in government which is implicated for service delivery failures and the lack of competitiveness of the Nigerian (and Niger Delta) economy. The laws and bureaus established are yet to make any meaningful impact on the way in which government business is done. The public procurement and fiscal responsibility laws have not been invoked to prosecute any offender. The laws are often undermined by ouster clauses that allow chief executives a lot of flexibility on public expenditure. For instance, Section 21(4) of the Rivers State Public Procurement Law (RSPPL) states,

> Notwithstanding, the provisions of this law, with respect to the award of contract, the governor shall have power to award for the execution of projects and other jobs which total value shall not exceed 30 percent of the total annual budget approved for the execution of projects and other jobs in the state: PROVIDED ALWAYS that the bureau shall exercise supervisory powers in the execution of such projects.

The act also provides that the law would not apply for procurements on security and in situations of emergency. Interestingly, most of these obnoxious clauses were passed even though most of the civil society groups that attended the public hearing organized by the State House of Assembly had asked for the removal of the clauses as they constituted a travesty of transparency.

Due Process offices are marginal players in most states and lack the capacity to checkmate the governor and his lieutenants. There is more concentration on chasing and giving completion deadlines to contractors rather than focusing on how contracts are awarded and whether there is value for money. It would seem that the real reason for the Due Process initiatives is to whitewash the image of the governments.

Improvement of Constituency Relations

Another important governance initiative that has become fashionable in the Niger Delta states is the movement toward institutionalizing periodic meetings between elected officers of state and their constituents. The objective of such forums is to allow government officers give account of their stewardship and for the public to make inputs into how government should be run. Assessments of such forums however reveal that they are gradually becoming public relation stunts for the governors. Rather than serving as platforms for account for public revenues and expenditures, the town hall meetings have only provided opportunities for communities and groups to make sundry requests from the governors. More worrisome is the fact that legislators who are mandated to have constituency offices and have periodic consultations with constituents seldom establish functional offices. The local government chairpersons and councilors are also inaccessible to the people. The result is that the people at the grassroots are not being reached though these media.

Sovereign Wealth Fund (SWF)

On May 27, 2011, two days before the expiration of his first tenure, President Goodluck Jonathan signed the Nigerian Sovereign Investment Authority Act 2011 into law. The act, which was swiftly passed by both chambers of the federal legislature, was expected to put to rest the controversies surrounding the constitutionality and operations of the Excess Crude Account (ECA). The ECA was supposed to pool revenues in excess of projected revenue based on benchmark price for crude oil for future use. Its popularity among Nigerians encouraged Rotimi Amaechi, the populist governor of Rivers State to initiate a legislation which would compel the state government to save a fixed sum of N1 billion of its monthly allocation.

However, perennial disagreements between the federal government and state governments undermined its smooth operations. The state governors' ostensible reasons for opposing the ECA were its unconstitutionality and violation of the principles of fiscal federalism. However, there was no doubt that many governors who faced increasing public demands to deliver democracy dividends had become cynical about a project on saving for the future. It was therefore hoped that the passage of the sovereign wealth fund bill with the support of the state governors would make Nigeria to conform to best practices. Incidentally, before the passage of the act, Nigeria is the only member of the Organization of Petroleum Exporting Countries (OPEC) without a futures fund.

The objective of the SWF is threefold. First, it seeks to tackle the Dutch disease phenomenon by pooling excess revenues from hydrocarbons into investments in tradable sectors. This ensures that exploitation of hydrocarbons is no longer detrimental for economic growth. Second, SWFs insulate oil rich countries from shocks arising from cyclical fluctuations in demand and supply of oil in the global market. It therefore mitigates the impact of periodic booms and bursts. Third, SWF contributes to sustainability. It guarantees that future generations would benefit from the oil wealth when there would be no more oil to exploit. The Nigerian version of the SWF seeks to achieve the three objectives by establishing three funds. These are the Future Generation Fund, the Infrastructure Fund and the Stabilization Fund.

However, progress on implementation of the NSIA Act may be slowed by renewed opposition by the state governments. The State Governors Forum in August 2011 called on the federal government to suspend implementation of the act pending resolution of some undisclosed issues. The sudden volte face of the governors on the SWF might not be unconnected with the pressures for the implementation of the National Minimum Wage and the recognition that governors do not have any effective influence on the management of the SWF (Rasheed 2011).

New Corporate Social Responsibility Practices

Constant attacks on oil installations and oil company personnel have forced oil companies operating in the Niger Delta region to recognize their status as actors in the perennial conflicts in the region. As a response, most of the companies have redesigned their corporate social responsibility programs to be conflict sensitive and more transparent. Based on the modest success of community development foundations (Idemudia 2007) most of the companies have adopted the global memorandum of understanding (GMOU) model of engagement with host communities. The memorandum commits the companies to providing funds for community development initiatives provided that communities are able to guarantee security for their operations. Unlike previous practices where companies were directly involved in service delivery, the GMOU framework allows communities to undertake project implementation. The different structures created by the GMOU also allows for more possibility for checks and balances. These include processes that allow communities to generate their development plans, prioritize projects and select contractors as well as monitor project implementation.

The following assessments suggest that some progress has been made through the GMOU in the direction of transparency:

> Many of those who were interviewed acknowledge that the GMOU model has clearly shifted Chevron's engagement focus towards projects instead of the previous practices of selective patronage that had created upheavals in several communities across the Niger Delta. However, many people in communities that signed the GMOU continue to expect and express preference for cash payments and contract awards. Many of them also regretted that as soon as their communities signed the GMOU, they lost access to several benefits that they previously enjoyed by virtue of their status as host communities (unemployment allowances, payment for "ghost workers", compensation for environmental disruption, Christmas and New Years gifts, land rent and/or compensation for landlords, security contracts, etc) or as officials (homage to elders, contracts and payments to community executives and youth groups). Many perceive the discontinuance of these payments as a demonstration of a lack of respect for community leaders and members. (Faleti 2009: 23)

However, the challenge remains that of ensuring that the development councils are democratically selected and do not flout laid down rules.

CONCLUDING REMARKS

Natural resources have generated conflicts in the Niger Delta because its management in general and production and distribution processes in particular have not been directed at meeting the interests of the peoples of the region. As chapters in this book have tried to show, several initiatives have been attempted to effect some changes from the longstanding pauperization of the ordinary people of the region despite its great resource endowments. However, the efforts have failed to deliver the intended benefits to the majority of the people. One of the realities of the Niger Delta is that oil has been exploited without regard to environmental sustainability (UNEP 2011). This is primarily because the dominant classes that depend on rents are not involved in agricultural activities. The people who subsist on the environment, especially the womenfolk are marginalized in decision making processes (see Osondu in this volume).

The political and governance initiatives whose advertised objective is to turn oil from a curse to blessing would only make the desired impact when the ordinary people begin to matter. The people need to reclaim politics which has presently been captured by a class of politicians. Reclaiming politics would at the barest minimum require the conduct of free and fair elections both at party primaries and general elections. Most of the political and governance initiatives labor under the politics of patronage. For instance, a major challenge facing development agencies is that key management staff and board members are representatives of political godfathers whose interests are at variance with the good of the people.

It would also entail greater support for civil society at levels of the Nigerian society. The present configuration of the Nigerian political economy which concentrates power and resources on the state is inimical to the growth of civil society and sustainable development. The Petroleum Industry Bill (PIB) holds some promise in this direction. The possibility of reviewing the joint venture structure, promoting local content, and engendering direct transfers to oil bearing communities is likely to reduce state monopoly. Niger Delta civil society need to intensify advocacy and pressures to ensure that only the most popular version of the PIB becomes law.

REFERENCES

Ake, C. (1996). "The political question." In O. Oyediran (Ed.), *Governance and development in Nigeria: Essays in honour of Professor Billy J. Dudley*, Ibadan: Oyediran Consults, pp. 22–32.

Ballentine, K. (2005). "Peace before profit: The challenges of governance." In K. Ballentine and H. Nitzschke (Eds.), *Profiting from peace: Managing the resource dimensions of civil war*, Boulder, CO: Lynne Rienner, pp. 447–484.

Chabedi, M. (2001). "Whither the rainbow nation? The ANC, the Black middle class and changing perceptions of 'Blackness' in the post-apartheid South Africa," Johannesburg: University of the Witwatersrand, History Workshop 1.

Collier, P. (2000). "Doing well out of war: An economic perspective." In M. Berdel and D. Malone (Eds.), *Greed and grievance: Economic agendas in civil war*, Boulder CO: Lynne Rienner, pp. 91–111.

Corden, W. M. (1984). "Booming sectors and Dutch disease economics: Survey and consolidation," *Oxford Economic Papers*, Vol. 36, pp. 359–380.

Faleti, S. (2009) 'Challenges of Chevron's GMOU implementation in Itsekiri communities of the Western Niger Delta' in C. Boutillier (ed.) *Proceedings of the IFRA Conference on Conflict and Violence in Nigeria*, Ibadan: IFRA (available at http://www.ifra-nigeria.org/spip.php?article156, accessed on 27 August 2011).

Fanthorpe, R. (2006). "The limits of liberal peace: chiefs and democratic decentralization in Sierra Leone," *African Affairs*, Vol. 105, No. 1, pp. 27–49.

Gray, C. H. (1997). *Post-modern war: The new politics of conflicts*, London: Routledge.

Holsti, K. J. (1996). *The state, war, and the state of war*, Cambridge: Cambridge University Press.

Humphreys, M. (2005). "Natural resources and armed conflicts: Issues and options." In K. Ballentine and H. Nitzschke (Eds.), *Profiting from peace: Managing the resource dimensions of civil war*, Boulder, CO: Lynne Rienner, pp. 25–46.

Idemudia, U. (2007). *Corporate partnerships and community development in Nigeria's oil industry: Strengths and limitations*, Markets, Business and Regulation Working Paper No. 2, Geneva: UNRISD.

Idemudia, U. (2009). "The quest for the effective use of natural resources revenue in Africa: Beyond transparency and the need for compatible cultural democracy in Nigeria," *Africa Today*, Vol. 56, No. 2, pp. 3–24.

Kaldor, M. (1999). *New and old wars: Organized violence in a global era*, Stanford, CA: Stanford University Press.

Karl, T. L. (1997). *The paradox of plenty: Oil booms and petro-states*, Berkeley: University of California Press.

Niger Delta Citizens Budget Platform. (2011). *Spend and borrow: Citizens report on state and local government budgets in the Niger Delta 2010*, Port Harcourt: Social Integrated Development Centre.

Poteete, A. and Gramajo, A. M. (2005). *Overlapping sectors: Botswana's inoculation against the Dutch disease*, Working Paper, No. 60, Braddock, VA: Mercatus Centre, George Mason University.

Rasheed, O. (2011). "Sovereign Wealth Fund: Of governors' grouse and Jonathan's lecture," *Punch* (Lagos), August 30.

Ross, M. L. (1999). "The political economy of the resource curse," *World Politics*, Vol. 51, No. 2, pp. 297–322.

Ross, M. L. (2001). "Does oil hinder democracy?" *World Politics*, Vol. 53, No. 3, pp. 325–361.

Sachs, J. D. and Warner, A. M. (1995). *Natural resource abundance and economic growth*, Development Discussion Paper No. 517a, Cambridge, MA: Harvard Institute for International Development.

Ukiwo, U. (2011). "The Nigerian state and the Niger Delta crisis." In C. Obi and S. Rustad (Eds.), *Oil and insurgency in the Niger Delta*, London: Zed Books, pp. 17–27.

United Nations Environment Programme (UNEP). (2011). *Environmental assessment of Ogoniland*, Nairobi: Author.

Contributors

SAMSON RANTI AKINOLA

Affiliation: Covenant University, Nigeria

Dr. **Samson Ranti Akinola** lectures at Covenant University, Nigeria. His research interest focuses on policy and institutional analysis, polycentric development planning, community governance, the environment, and poverty reduction in Africa.

GORDON M. BUBOU

Affiliation: Federal Ministry of Science and Technology, Nigeria

Mr. **Gordon M. Bubou** currently works with the South-South Office of the National Centre for Technology Management (an agency of the Federal Ministry of Science and Technology, Nigeria) as a senior scientific officer. He is also the coordinator of the Postgraduate Diploma in Technology Management Programme, Yenagoa Study Centre. He is currently a doctoral candidate in technology management at the University of Port Harcourt, Nigeria.

YINKA KEHINDE BINUOMOYO

Affiliation: Forum for Development Strategy, Ilorin

Mr. Yinka Kehinde Binuomoyo earned his BSc (Hons) in economics from the University of Ilorin, Nigeria. In 2006, he was admitted as an associate member of the Institute of Chartered Economists of Nigeria. He is currently a research affiliate with the Forum for Development Strategy, Ilorin. His research interests are in pensions, development, and environment economics.

AUGUSTINE OKHOBO DOKPESI

Affiliation: University of Benin, Nigeria

Dr. **Augustine Okhobo Dokpesi** earned his PhD in sociology from the University of Ibadan, Nigeria. He is currently a lecturer at the Department of Sociology and Anthropology, University of Benin, Nigeria. His major research interests include development studies, environmental sociology, political sociology, and industrial sociology.

NIMIYE A. EGAI

Affiliation: Niger Delta University, Bayelsa State, Nigeria

Dr. **Nimiye A. Egai** is a lecturer and consultant in the Department of Economics, Niger Delta University, Wilberforce Island, Nigeria. He is a chartered economist and a fellow of the Institute of Chartered Economics of Nigeria. He is also a fellow of the Nigerian Institute of Corporate Administration and president of the Institute of Finance and Control of Nigeria. He is a scholar at the International School of Management, Paris, and a resource person with the National Centre of Technology Management, Nigeria.

AMBILY ETEKPE

Affiliation: Delta University, Bayelsa State, Nigeria

Dr. **Ambily Etekpe** is a former senior research fellow at the Yakubu Gowon Centre; aide to Chief Harold Dappa-Biriya, Patriarch of the Niger Delta; and special adviser to the government of Bayelsa State on civil society and nongovernmental organizations. His focus is in Ijo (Ijaw) and African political thought and administration, Niger Delta, Middle Belt, and peace and security studies. He is currently the chairman of Niger Delta Forum Study Group and lecturer in the Department of Political Science, Niger Delta University, Bayelsa State.

IBABA SAMUEL IBABA

Affiliation: Niger Delta University, Bayelsa State, Nigeria

Dr. **Ibaba Samuel Ibaba** is affiliated to the Department of Political Science, Niger Delta University, Nigeria, where he lectures political science and engages in research focused on conflict analysis and resolution, peace building, and development. He is currently the acting head of the university's political science department.

MICHAEL IRABOR IBIEZUGBE

Affiliation: University of Benin, Benin City, Nigeria

Mr. Michael Irabor Ibiezugbe is a senior lecturer in the Department of Sociology and Anthropology, University of Benin, Benin City. He earned his BA (Hons) in political science and MA in social work from the University of Delhi, India. He also earned MSc in social work from Obafemi Awolowo University, Nigeria. His current research and professional interest is in the social welfare of children and families.

CYRIL OBI

Affiliation: Nordic Africa Institute, Uppsala, Sweden

Dr. **Cyril Obi** is currently senior researcher and leader of the Research Cluster on Conflict, Displacement and Transformation at the Nordic Africa Institute, Uppsala, Sweden. He is also associate research professor, on leave, from the Nigerian Institute of International Affairs. His scholarship focus areas include globalization, African politics, development, peace and security, and international relations. He has also written widely on oil politics in the Niger Delta.

JOHNSON B. OGBEWO

Affiliation: Niger Delta University, Wilberforce Island, Nigeria

Dr. **Johnson Bright Ogbewo** earned his doctorate degree from the University of Calabar, Nigeria. He currently lectures in the Department of Economics, Niger Delta University, Nigeria. His research emphasis includes energy and oil economics, as well as development economics.

EPHRAIM A. OKORO

Affiliation: Howard University, Washington, DC, United States

Dr. **Ephraim Okoro** is an assistant professor in the School of Business, Howard University. He teaches business communication, marketing communication, management communication, and principles of marketing. His primary research interests probe the interface between intercultural communication and workforce diversity.

ADAORA OSONDU

Affiliation: Obafemi Awolowo University, Ile-Ife, Nigeria

Ms. Adaora Osondu is currently pursuing her PhD in the Department of International Relations, Obafemi Awolowo University, Ile-Ife, Nigeria. Her areas of research interests include China's international relations, China's African policy, and human/women's rights.

OKECHUKWU UKAGA

University of Minnesota, St. Paul, MN, United States

Dr. **Okechukwu Ukaga** is a program director and professor at the University of Minnesota where he provides leadership for integrated education, research, and outreach projects/programs that promote sustainable development and community vitality. Before coming to Minnesota, he served as the managing director of the International Institute for Sustainable Development at Colorado State University. In that capacity, he worked with organizations and people from countries in Africa, South America, Asia, and the Middle East to plan and implement a variety of projects. He has also previously worked/taught at Penn State University and Florida A&M University. He earned his PhD from Penn State University, University Park, PA, United States.

UKOHA O. UKIWO

Affiliation: University of Port Harcourt, Nigeria

Dr. **Ukoha O. Ukiwo** is a senior lecturer at the Department of Political and Administrative Studies, University of Port Harcourt. He earned his doctorate degree from University of Oxford, United Kingdom, and was visiting research fellow at Institute of International Studies, University of California, Berkeley, and research fellow at Centre for Advanced Social Science, Port Harcourt. His areas of scholarship include democracy, governance, conflict and security in Nigeria and the Niger Delta in particular.

Index

For Product Safety Concerns and Information please contact our EU representative GPSR@taylorandfrancis.com Taylor & Francis Verlag GmbH, Kaufingerstraße 24, 80331 München, Germany